SHRI KRISHNA: YESTERDAY, TODAY & TOMORROW

"KRISHNA ELEVATING BHARAT (INDIA) TO EXCELLENCE"

GOKUL UPADHYAY

Copyright © Gokul Upadhyay, 2024

All rights reserved.

For reproduction or other matters of the book please contact the author or the Soul and Society, Inc. USA at

gokulup@gmail.com

First edition: May 2024

Printed in U.S.A.

ISBN-13: 979-8-9902558-0-7

Pictures: Shri Devendra Sharma, Indore India

Cover design: Shri Satheesh Chandra, Udupi India

*****

The Non-profit Organization (NPO/NGO) 'Soul and Society, Inc.' (www.soulandsociety.org) has supported publication of

"Shri Krishna: Yesterday, Today & Tomorrow"

["Krishna Elevating Bharat (India) to Excellence"]

The proceeds from this book will help fulfill the mission of "Soul and Society Inc." to benefit 'children in need' for their education, health, and overall development.

*****

DEDICATION

Dedicated to
Shri Krishna
the Creator of the Universe,
the Eternal Supreme Being,
the Omniscient, Omnipotent, and Omnipresent
Universal Conscience,
and an Avatar in human form.

Though nameless, formless, and beyond time,
we humans perceive Him in different forms such as
Creator, Sustainer, Destroyer
(Brahma, Vishnu, Mahesh),
always integral with
His eternal energy
Adhya Shakti.

Shri Krishna
always exists
within our Innermost-Self, energizing us
to accomplish our destined duties
and witnessing
all what we do!

CONTENTS

Acknowledgment xiii
About the Author xiv
Preface xvi

PART 1 – YESTERDAY
Krishna the Creator and the Avatar

CHAPTER 1
KRISHNA: THE CREATOR
(Yesterday).............................. 2

1. THE ORIGINAL SUPREME CREATOR

Creation: The Big Bang Theory
The Supreme Existence
Creation And Radha-Krishna
Purusha (Soul) And Prakriti (Nature)
The Cosmic Memory
We are all integral components of Krishna's grand design
Krishna's initial 'Will' emerging as 'desire'
Infallible (Achyut) and Undiminished (Akshar)
The Consort
The Life Journey (The Journey of Existence)
The Two Energies
The Concept of Ego
Krishna: The Ultimate Truth

2. THE AVATAR

The concept of Avatar
Different Avatars of the Creator
Shri Krishna Avatar

CHAPTER 2
INFINITE UNIVERSES AND WE
(Yesterday)........................ 31

We all are expansions of Krishna
Our Nucleus and the Universe
Illusive worldly love v/s Radha-Krishna's Divine Love

We all are moving towards perfection

CHAPTER 3
THE CREATOR MAINTAINS EQUALIBRIUM
(Yesterday)…... 43

The equilibrium of the three Gunas (qualities)
The Three Gunas (Qualities)
Ego and divinity
Relation between three qualities and ego
Equilibrium of two tendencies (Swabhav)

CHAPTER 4
KRISHNA: AN AVATAR
(Yesterday)…………………………… 52

Krishna: as the formless "Supreme Creator"
Krishna as an "Avatar" in human or worldly form
The magnificent Krishna Avatar
Krishna-consciousness
Floating in Krishna's divine love

CHAPTER 5
KRISHNA: HIS CHARM, LOVE & SMILE
(Yesterday)……….. 66

Krishna's love and divine bliss
Krishna's smile
The Truth, Soul, and Presence of Krishna
Most valuables: Only within
Shunya (void) and Anant (infinity): In Krishna's Love

CHAPTER 6
THE COSMIC BODY OF KRISHNA & HIS MAYA
(Yesterday)……….. 75

The Cosmic Time Waves
Krishna and his Maya
Krishna and the concept of time

CHAPTER 7
SIGNIFICANCE OF SHRI KRISHNA AVATAR
(Yesterday)…… 85

Characteristics of Krishna
Krishna, Bharat, and human dignity
Krishna supports Bharat's Unity and Integrity
After the disappearance of Krishna
Recent 1000 years in Bharat

PART 2 - TODAY
KRISHNA NOW FOR BHARAT & THE WORLD

CHAPTER 8
KRISHNA's PARTIAL AVATAR IN BHARAT (Today).......... 112

A few words about TODAY
Bharat Varsh also referred as India

Krishna and Bharat
The New Krishna partial-Avatar
Circumstances leading to the Krishna Avatar
Dharma and Adharma
Today's Krishna Avatar
New Krishna Avatar growing, getting stronger
Krishna Avatar energizing Bharat
Krishna's Avatar: As per Vedic scriptures

CHAPTER 9
KRISHNA's MISSION FOR BHARAT (Today)..................... 138

Indigenous Bharatiya Rishis are scientists
Bharat spreads positive energy of the Vedas' worldwide
Global Excellence of Bharatiya intellectuals and Diaspora

CHAPTER 10
KRISHNA FOR SPIRITUAL BHARAT, NOT FOR SECULAR INDIA
(Today).. 149

Bharatiya Culture and Vedic Philosophy (Wisdom)
Killing the Soul of Bharat through pseudo-Secularism
Secularity abuse vs Oriental and Occidental philosophies
Krishna transforming the alien, foreign mindset
Krishna-consciousness and Nature for Sanatani Excellence
Protection of Indigenous Bharatiyas, true Hindus (Sanatanis)

Byproducts of 1000 years' slavery of Indigenous Bharatiyas
Shri Ram's Pran-Pratishtha and the Foundation of Ram-Rajya
Ram-Rajya
Ram-Rajya flourishment with Krishna-consciousness

CHAPTER 11
KRISHNA REMOVING DEMOGRAPHIC IMBALANCE OF BHARAT (Today) 175

Demographic imbalance dangerous for Bharat's integrity
It is a matter of real concern
Krishna inspires for true love, eliminates trap of pseudo love
Krishna Inspires for Protecting Indigenous Sanatan Dharma
Democracy, demography, and numbers game

CHAPTER 12
KRISHNA'S PRUDENT GOVERNANCE (Today).................. 188

Krishna's patience and tolerance for the Shishupals of today
Tolerance of Krishna
Krishna differentiates between "Genuine and Fake Tolerance"
Who are Krishna-conscious Sanatani people?
Krishna's Eternal Energy: Hanuman Ji
Krishna, the icon of Fearlessness and Dharma
Krishna inspires for prudent "Truth and Non-violence"
No Raas-Leela for Krishna when there is Maha-Bharat
Krishna enlightening the new generation of Bharat
Krishna's effective and glorious governance
Krishna inspires equality: No castes (Varnas) - Only Sanatanis

CHAPTER 13
KRISHNA WELCOMES ALL TO SANATANA DHARMA (Today)................................ 215

Home-coming and New-entries
Welcome global Home-coming!
Invasions, conversions, and now reversion/re-conversion
Revolutionary transformation: Era of Shift in Consciousness

CHAPTER 14
ANTICIPATED CHANGES IN BHARAT IN 21ST CENTURY (Today).............................. 227

Bharatiya Constitutional amendments or a New Constitution
Likely developments in Bharat in a few decades

CHAPTER 15
KRISHNA FOR THE WORLD
(Today).............................. 247

Krishna inspires for stronger East
Krishna inspires for Grand Alliance of Friendly Nations
Krishna inspires for War against Terrorist-mindset
Transformation of madness (insanity) into rationality
Krishna's love for pious and punishment for wicked
Krishna is always for Development, Progress & Liberation

PART 3 - TOMORROW
KRISHNA FOR FUTURE BHARAT & FUTURE WORLD

CHAPTER 16
KRISHNA FOR FUTURE BHARAT
(Tomorrow)................. 262

Krishna and Bharat tomorrow
Only the truth prevails
Lead me from untruth to the Truth (Asato ma sadgamaya.)
Bharat: The Future World-Superpower
The Hindu Nation "Bharat"
Optimal population management
Improved Governance and Well-rounded Advancement
Overall growth of Bharat
Superior Military and Defense Capabilities of Bharat
Merger, Union, and Alliance of Many Nations with Bharat
New Bharatiya Media Power in The World
Neutralizing Anti-Hindus & Anti-Bharatiya Intellectuals
Managing the Film industry

CHAPTER 17
RESTORATION OF ANCIENT VEDIC GLORIES & ADVANCING BEYOND
(Tomorrow)... 286

Vedas, Bharat, glorious past and advanced future
Expansion of Sanskrit language across Bharat and the world
Research on Vedic scriptures in Bharatiya languages
Bharatiya village scholars, philosophers: Defenders of Dharma
Satyam – Shivam – Sundaram
Satyameva Jayate
Vasudhaiva Kutumbakam

CHAPTER 18
KRISHNA FOR THE FUTURE WORLD
(Tomorrow).............. 300

Cosmic Time Waves
Krishna Inspired Wisdom Globally
Global spread of Vedic Wisdom
Human upliftment in Veda-based research & advancements
Global Advancement of All Sciences Tomorrow
Global research on Yoga basics and practices tomorrow
More explorations in planetary and interstellar systems
Krishna Will Inspire Bharat's Global Dominance
Bharat's Ascendency in Asia, Global South & Worldwide
Bharat's Eastern & Western Alliances Based on Vedic Wisdom
Krishna inspired Asian Cultural Alliance
Krishna for protection of Nature and Environment
Krishna inspiring Bharat for key role in world peace
Comprehensive Restructuring of the United Nations
The mischief and stupidity in the name of religion will end
Krishna's Divine Universal Love
Krishna's love for the devoted wise ones

PICTURES INDEX

1: The Big Bang (Kalpa-Aadi) starting at absolute zero time ... 5
2: Explosion at singularity - The Start of time ... 6
3: Energies - Purush and Prakriti - Krishna & Radha ... 9
4: Lesser the ego, more devotional & elevated is brain ... 11
5: Different names of the Creator Lord Krishna ... 29
6: The Big Crunch (Kalpa-Ant), condensing Universe ... 32
7: Cycles of infinite Big Bangs triggered by Creator/Krishna .. 33
8 - Nucleus of a being and the Universe   ... 36
9: Beyond Maya (Kamini, Kanchan, Kirti) is Krishna / Moksha. 42
10: Krishna maintains equilibrium of 3 qualities Sat, Raj, Tam...44
11: Satva, Rajas, Tamas transformation 47
12: Krishna's Positive Energy keeps flowing to devotees ... 55
13: Creator's Krishna Avatar in Dwapar Yug... 56
14: Krishna gives feeling of protection, fearlessness divinity .. 61
15: Krishna's Beauty, Brain, Bravery & Love rejoices all ... 69
16: Krishna's shelter gives success to both (extrovert & introvert) .. 73
17: Sinusoidal waves (f~1000-2000 yrs) with Ripple waves .. 77
18 - Outside is Maya, inside is feeling of divinity, Krishna ... 80
19: Shri Krishna - A Purna Avatar   ... 87

20: Krishna's miraculous activities. Childhood till old age ... 106
21: Sanatan Dharma is the Dharma since ever, forever ... 115
22: Creator: Soul of Universe, Avatar Krishna: Soul of Bharat .. 120
23: Bharat's leader - Vairagi, Sanyasi, Aapt Purush, Gyani, Mukt ..129
24: Today's Krishna Avatar - Created by "the Power of votes"... 131
25: Krishna's vision for Bharat and Bharatiyas ... 141
26: Global excellence of Bharatiya brains due to Vedas ... 145
27: Krishna – Core of Sanatan Dharm & Bhagavat Gita 151
28: No Secularism in Bharat, Only Sanatan Spirituality ... 153
29: The constitution of Bharat will follow Gita/Sanatan 155
30: The New Ram-Mandir in Ayodhya, at Ramlala Birthplace... 167
31: Shri Ramlala Pran-Pratishtha in Ram Mandir Ayodhya ,,, 168
32: Historic Auspicious & Gracious Moments after 500 years .. 170
33: Ram and Krishna are inseparable forms of the Creator ... 172
34: Krishna's energy protecting all from criminals, anti-Sanatanis..177
35: Avatar Krishna protecting Sanatani women from love jihad... 180
36: Krishna doesn't tolerate invaders, criminals & anti-Sanatanis .. 193
37: Hanuman ji defends pious devotees, destroys demonic people.. 197
38: Krishna's attraction encouraging Homecoming to Sanatana ... 220
39: Krishna welcomes home-comers, punishes anti-Sanatanis ... 225
40: Bharatiya Constitution should confirm to the soul of Gita ... 230
41: Happy Homecoming to Sanatana due to Avatar -Krishna ... 232
42: Krishna-empowered soul Nurturing the excellence of Bharat .. 240
43: Krishna elevating Sanatani Bharat to top of the world ...245
44: Avatar Krishna supporting sane-forces, punishing insane ones..251
45: "Whole of the Earth is a family" - Sanatan philosophy ...270
46: Vedic scriptures: Roots of vibrant-glorious Sanatan Dharma...289
47: Vasudhaiva Kutumbakam - "Whole of the Earth is a family".. 297
48 - Sinusoidal waves 1000-2000 yrs, Ripple waves 50-100 yrs...302
49: Creator maintains equilibrium of Positive & Neg. Forces ... 304
50: Krishna-empowered Peace-loving alliance punishing rogues... 317
51: Person without desire, envy, anger, ego .. are dear to Krishna .. 330

BIBLIOGRAPHY... **333**

OTHER BOOKS BY SHRI GOKUL UPADHYAY....... 334

ACKNOWLEDGEMENT

I am deeply grateful to my parents and Paramatma for their continuous blessings bestowed upon me.

I wish to convey my sincere appreciation to the talented cartoonist, Shri Devendra Sharma, for his insightful interpretation of the book's themes and for his creation of numerous illustrations that convey profound messages.

I extend special acknowledgment to the cover designer, Shri Satheesh Chandra, for skillfully crafting the captivating front and back covers.

Furthermore, I would like to express my heartfelt gratitude to my friends and devotees at the Hindu Society (Temple) of Minnesota (HSMN) in Maple Grove, MN, as well as devotees and friends from USA, Bharat and all-around for their steadfast support of the noble mission for Sanatan Dharma and humanity.

Last but not least, I am appreciative of all my family members for their consistent love and support. The most generous and talented among them helped me in various stages of formatting and bringing out this book.

ABOUT THE AUTHOR

Gokul Upadhyay is a humble devotee of Paramatma. He holds a degree in engineering from SGSITS, Indore Univ. India, and an MBA from Indiana Univ. of PA, USA. Along with India, he has worked in Kenya, Uganda & Saudi Arab, finally settled in the USA. Gokul served as a priest in his family's Hanumanji temple during his student years in Indore. Following retirement, he resumed his role as a priest and also took on responsibilities as a Temple Manager at various Hindu Temples across states incl. NY, PA, VA, WA, SC, & MN in the USA.

Gokul authored "Gita for Business Management, Leadership, and Performance," as well as several others referenced on the final page of this book. His presentations on the Gita have been well-received at various institutions and forums in both the USA and India, including at:

- Maharishi University of Management, Iowa USA
- Indiana University of Pennsylvania, Indiana PA USA
- S. V. Temple, Edina MN USA
- Synergy Institute of Management, Pune MR INDIA
- Guru Nanak Inst. of Techno., Hyderabad, AP INDIA
- Saanvi PG College, Hyderabad AP INDIA
- Vivekananda Inst. Of Tech./Sci., Karim Ngr AP INDIA
- Indian Inst. of Plann./Mangt (IIPM), Indore MP INDIA
- Krishi Vigyan Kendra, Shajapur MP INDIA
- Many Social and Spiritual Groups in USA & INDIA

As the Founder and President of Soul and Society, Inc. USA (www.soulandsociety.org), a Non-profit Charity Organization, he is pursuing a mission to help 'children and families in need' for their education, nutrition, and overall development.

Email: gokulup@gmail.com

In this around 14 billion years old cosmos (of this Kalpa)

considered

"Yesterday"

as the past, spanning before a few centuries,

going back till the start of Creation at

the Big Bang, around 14 billion years ago (Kalp-Aadi).

"Today"

as the present,

spanning just a few centuries; and

"Tomorrow"

as the future, extending for indefinite years,

after a few more centuries

until the end of the creation (Kalp-Ant).

*As the Supreme Creator, I know everything that has happened in the past, all that is happening at present, and all things that are yet to happen in future. I also know all living entities; but Me no one knows. - **Krishna*** *(Gita Ch. 7:26 - vedaham.....kashchan)*

PREFACE

Inspired by Shri Krishna, I started authoring this book in late 2017 and had completed nearly 95% of it by early 2019. Around that time, I took on the role of Temple Manager at the Hindu Society of Minnesota (HSMN) in Maple Grove, USA. Initially, I had planned to finish the remaining portion of the book within a few months and have it published by early 2020. However, the demanding workload of managing various activities at the grand temple made it challenging for me to delve deep into my soul, gather inspiration, and elevate my thoughts to the level required for the book. This continued until mid-2023 when, once again inspired by Shri Krishna, I made the decision to resign from the temple and move to Seattle, WA.

In late 2023, I restarted work on the book. During this time, there were significant changes in Bharat (India) and the world, which led me to revise and rewrite several chapters. Now, with innovative ideas and chapters incorporated, the book is finally set to be published in early 2024, almost four years later than originally planned.

Now, returning to the book, scholars and devotees have been expressing their reverence for Shri Krishna for millennia through writing, singing, praying, and lecturing. Countless pages have been devoted to depicting various aspects of His life, teachings, and activities in different languages. Attempting to add more on Krishna may seem insignificant compared to the wealth of existing literature.

So, why did I feel compelled to write about Him, the Supreme Being beyond description and understanding? Honestly, I am not entirely sure. All I can do is follow the inspiration provided by Shri Krishna within and contribute my thoughts modestly. The true reason behind this calling remains known only to Him.

The Creator is the-only-One nameless, formless, infinite Eternal Consciousness, perceived in various parts of the world in different names and forms. In this book, the Creator with the name Krishna represents ॐ 'Om,' the Paramatma (including Brahma, Vishnu, Mahesh, Venkatesh, Rama, Aadi-Shakti Durga-Lakshmi-Saraswati, Rudra, Hanuman, along with their different names and forms), as perceived in the Vedic Bharat-Varsha (India). Devoted Hindus/Sanatanis are not much bothered with names. For them, all names are of the same Paramatma. **'Krishna' includes all these names.**

Spirituality is the heartbeat, the lifeline of Bharat. Even the illiterate villagers and forest-tribes talk and live spiritually. *No real and long-lasting reform, revolution or development in Bharat is possible unless it is associated with spirituality, with the Paramatma.* Paramatma (Krishna) is not only for Pooja in homes or temples, or for discourses and Satsang. Krishna (also as Rama, Shiva, Adhya-Shakti) is active and living with us each moment, in each of our routine activities. It is the Sanatani spirituality.

Paramatma, as Krishna, is eternal and is ever present as Krishna-consciousness or Sanatana-energy universally. Yesterday, today, and tomorrow are only in our fragmented perception. We live with this perception till we transcend worldly perceptions, transcend time and merge with

Preface

eternity, eternal consciousness. For Krishna it is a unified, singular eternal existence.

Part 1 "Yesterday" is devoted to creation, expansion, Nature, and Avatars, specifically the Krishna-Avatar.

Part 2 "Today" has been devoted to the present (a few hundred years') conditions in Bharat (India) and the world, and Krishna's role at present, and

Part 3 "Tomorrow," has been devoted to future conditions (after a few centuries till Kalp-Ant) in Bharat (India) and the world, and Krishna's role to save Dharma, human dignity, human values, and humanity, considering whole of the earth as a family (Vasudhaiv Kutumbakam).

In this world we live in the ocean of Krishna-consciousness or Sanatan-energy, spread universally like intense electronic signals. Like calling on a specific cell phone number and connecting with it, when we live and perform in this Krishna-conscious-world, we are tuned with the Krishna-energy. **Partial accumulation of this energy incarnates 'partial-Avatars' (mini-Avatars), and intense accumulation of this energy incarnates 'Major Avatars.'** There are always many known or unknown 'partial-Avatars' and only a few 'Major Avatars' globally.

Bharat is the land of Krishna-Avatar, the major Avatar, the perfect Avatar, and His Leela (pastimes), activities. In Bharat, there have been hundreds of partial and major Avatars, only a few are known or realized or believed by most devotees. A lot has been written about past Avatars. It fills the hearts and minds of all humans with great hope that *at present also there are many unknown Krishna-conscious or Sanatana Partial-Avatars in India and around the globe.* We cannot always clearly claim and name them, but we realize their presence, their existence, their energy, and their influence.

These partial-Avatars, charged with Krishna-consciousness, Krishna-energy or Sanatan-energy are holistic, mysterious, beneficial, and super-active. Only a few of them are supercharged and come in partial limelight. All these keep on performing their holistic roles and disappear, as planned by the Creator. Empowered by the Creator, these partial-Avatars effectively perform their roles of maintaining the balance in Nature, saving Nature, and saving decent people and virtuousness (Dharma). They neutralize or eliminate the miscreants or evils, and establish the rule of law, social-order and justice, the Dharma globally. This role of Krishna has been continuing, in Bharat and around the globe, and will keep on continuing in all ages till the end of this creation.

In this book, we are visualizing Krishna as the Original Creator and an Avatar as well, based on combination of scriptures, scientific theories, philosophy, natural and holistic principles, related stories, and common beliefs as well. We blissfully feel connected with Krishna in all situations in life and get inspiration and strength from Him to come out of any situation, trouble, or odds in life, and find solution of any problem. Along with working hard with full focus, with wisdom and determination, we still need divine help of partial Avatars. We feel that currently we have been getting that.

In fact, when we unwaveringly and humbly introspect deeply within ourselves, without ego, we find Him residing in the Innermost-self of each of us, energizing

Preface

and elevating us. This ultimately leads us to unity (Yoga) with Him, our original form, Perfection, the Absolute Truth, the Moksha, Eternity, the ultimate goal of life. For us humans, the Avatar Krishna means Perfection personified, the embodiment of Perfection. Krishna represents the infinite potential existing in everyone, in each being. Krishna represents the ultimate possibilities in a person in all the fields of human evolutions, existence, consciousness, and performance.

In His current partial Avatar (mentioned in the relevant chapters), Krishna is associated with restoration of moral and ethical Sanatani values, defending virtuous people, annihilation of wicked ones and establishing Dharma. **For sure, the existence of Krishna even as a partial Avatar today means peace, bliss and prosperity among its citizens and elevation of Bharat to excellence.** Even the poorest of poor and the richest of riches in Bharat believes it. It is the Sanatani belief-system. Based on His Gita-teachings, Krishna Avatar is ensuring:

- **Moral and ethical leadership and governance:** Lord Krishna is emphasizing the importance of righteous conduct and moral values. The leaders of Bharat are inspired by His teachings, and are governing with integrity, fairness, and a strong ethical foundation. This has been contributing to a more just and equitable society in which excellence and progress flourish.
- **Socio-economic development:** Lord Krishna is also emphasizing the importance of performing one's duties without attachment to the results. This philosophy has been leading to a more focused and dedicated approach to work, education, and societal

contributions. This mindset, combined with the principles of equality and social welfare, has been contributing to the overall development of the country and its people.

- **Preservation of cultural heritage:** Lord Krishna is an integral part of Bharat's cultural tapestry and the Hindu faith. By honoring and preserving this cultural heritage, there is a deeper understanding and appreciation for the traditions and values that have shaped the nation. This cultural resurgence has also been attracting global attention and contributing to Bharat's standing as a top nation in the world.
- **Unity and Self-defense capabilities:** For the excellence of Bharat, it is most important that all Bharatiyas remain united and have self-defense capabilities against the ill-intended enemies, neighbors, rogue elements all around and also rogue nations. Krishna has been empowering Bharat with these capabilities and unity.
- **Societal compassion and empathy:** Lord Krishna is full of love and compassion for all beings. With Vasudhaiva Kutumbakam theme, He has been motivating individuals from different occupations and inspiring people to develop a more compassionate and empathetic attitude towards others. This has been contributing to the well-being and upliftment of society, with people supporting and uplifting each other to elevate Bharat to excellence and help in elevating whole of the world.
- **Self-control, self-sustenance, and destruction of internal enemies:** The Gita principles of self-control, self-sustenance, and destruction of internal

Preface

enemies for an individual are also being applied to the nation Bharat for its excellence. Sanyam, Vivek, Sadaachar, Anaasakt-Nishkam Karmyoga are being used as the main tools to achieve these.

- **Spiritual enlightenment and self-realization:** Lord Krishna's Avatar, as per His message in the Bhagavad Gita, has been emphasizing the importance of self-realization and spiritual enlightenment. As the people of Bharat have been practicing these teachings, it has been leading people to personal transformation and a deeper understanding of one's true nature. This spiritual awakening in turn has been fostering a sense of unity, compassion, and universal brotherhood, which has been leading Bharat to excel.

Probably, this is what Krishna inspired me to partly reveal through this book. *Hopefully, it inspires and helps the humanity, through the intellectuals, committed selfless spirituals, devotees, nationalistic leaders & professionals, and all patriots by transforming this spiritual message into the grass-root level revolution in the masses, motivating them for good Karma, determination to defeat and destroy the evils; and to boost up dignity, prosperity, and enlightenment of all decent people aka Sanatanis.* I feel that through this book, Krishna inspired me to put the refined seeds for the germination and growth of the new generations of the Krishna-conscious (Ram-Bhakt, Shiv-Bhakt, Devi-Bhakt) Sanatani patriotic Hindus and the advanced Bharat, the likely most powerful nation on the earth very soon.

🪷 🪷 🪷

PART-1:

YESTERDAY

***

KRISHNA THE CREATOR AND THE AVATAR

All yesterdays –

as the past, spanning before a few centuries,

going back till the start of the Creation at

the Big Bang, around fourteen billion years ago

(Kalp-Aadi).

Chapters: 1 to 7

CHAPTER 1

KRISHNA: THE CREATOR

(Yesterday)

Know that these two (My higher and lower Natures) are the womb of all beings. So, I am the source and dissolution of the whole universe.
(Krishna - Gita Ch. 7:6 – etadyo ini Bhutani .... pralayastatha).

From the unmanifested all the manifested (worlds) proceed at the coming of the "day;" at the coming of the "night" they dissolve truly into that alone which is called the unmanifested.
(Krishna - Gita Ch 8:18 – avyaktad vyaktayah.... ...Avayakt sangyake).

The nameless and formless Absolute Truth, possessing omniscience, omnipresence, and omnipotence, is the Original Creator, recognized as the Supreme with limitless knowledge, boundless energy, endless possibilities, unparalleled beauty, immaculate purity, boundless peace, infinite bliss, unconditional love, and infinite kindness.

Our perception of this Supreme entity is manifested through the revered appellation "Shri Krishna" or simply "Krishna" mentioned in ancient texts like the Bhagwat

Geeta (Gita) and the Vedas. Krishna is comprehended in two distinct forms:

1. THE ORIGINAL SUPREME CREATOR
2. THE AVATAR

1. THE ORIGINAL SUPREME CREATOR

The original form of the Creator is transcendent, mysterious, unified, Avyakta, and devoid of any specific name or form. But we know Him as Krishna, the Original Creator. In the Shrimad Bhagavatam Canto 2 (Dwitiya Skandha), Ch. 9 through the Chatuh Shloki Bhagavatam - verses 33, 34, 35 & 36, Krishna reveals Himself as follows: *Aham evāsam evāgre .... yat syāt sarvatra sarvadā.* - *Catuh-Shloki (SB 2.9 - 33/34/35/36).*

The Creator Krishna tells His creation, His son Brahma –

It is I, who existed before the creation, when there was nothing but Myself. Nor was there material nature, the cause of this creation. That which you see now is also I, and after annihilation what remains will also be I only. (33)

Whatever appears to be of any value, if it is without relation to Me, has no reality. Know it as My illusory energy, that reflection which appears to be in darkness. (34)

The universal elements enter the cosmos and at the same time do not enter the cosmos; similarly, I Myself also exist within everything created, and at the same time I am outside of everything. (35)

A person who is searching for the Supreme Absolute Truth, most certainly search for it up to this, in all circumstances, in all space and time, and both directly and indirectly. (36)

Thus, Krishna is not of this material world. He is the creator of it. Krishna's body, Krishna's activities, everything about Krishna are transcendental. They are not of this material world. They are divine, Divyam. He is eternal, existing ever, forever. Anything, any existence without Him is an illusion. He is light, and His absence reflects darkness.

So, before the creation, Krishna existed. When we speak of Krishna, it does not mean Krishna was alone. Krishna means with His form, with His pastimes, His glories, with His accessories, with His entourage, everything.

When we speak of a king, it does not mean king is alone. As soon as we speak of a king, we must mean the king, king's kingdom, king's secretaries, king's ministers, king's queen, king's palace, so many things attached with king.

Similarly, when we say Krishna was alone before creation means He was with all His excellence, grandeur, infinite potencies. He still is and will remain so eternally.

Also, Lord Shri Krishna (as the Creator) has said in: Gita (Ch 4: 6 – Ajo api san avyayatma……..atm mayaya.) - *"Although I am unborn and immortal, and although I am the Lord of all beings and material things, I manifest Myself through My own Yogamaya, keeping my Prakriti (Nature) under control."*

He further said in: Gita (Ch 10: 3 – yo mam ajam anadim……..pramuchyate.) – *"He who knows Me as the unborn, as the beginningless, as the Supreme Lord of the Universe, he undeluded among humans, is freed from all sins."*

Creation: The Big Bang Theory

According to scientists, the Big Bang Theory posits that approximately fourteen billion years ago, all matter and energy in the Universe were concentrated into an infinitesimally small and dense point of zero area. Subsequently, a sudden and intense explosion, known as the Big Bang, occurred. This event marked the dawn of Creation (Kalp-Aadi), the emergence of Time (Kaal), and the birth of Nature (Prakriti).

The initial point rapidly expanded and continues to expand, giving rise to billions of galaxies, each containing countless stars. Our own galaxy, the Milky Way, housing our solar system including Earth, is just one of these myriad galaxies (see Pics. 1 and 2). In the Pic. 1: The Big Bang (Kalpa-Aadi) can be considered starting at absolute zero time at the bottom (Bottom to top). While acknowledging the scientific validity of this theory, it is worth noting that

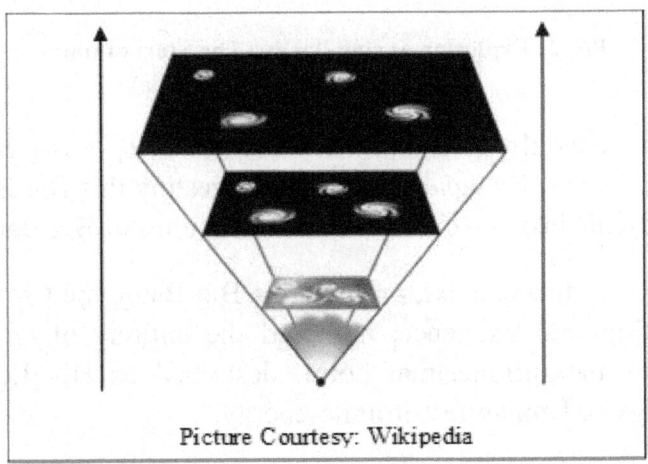

Picture Courtesy: Wikipedia

Pic. 1: The Big Bang (Kalpa-Aadi) - can be considered starting at absolute zero time at the bottom (Bottom to top).

Part-1, Chapter 1: Krishna the Creator

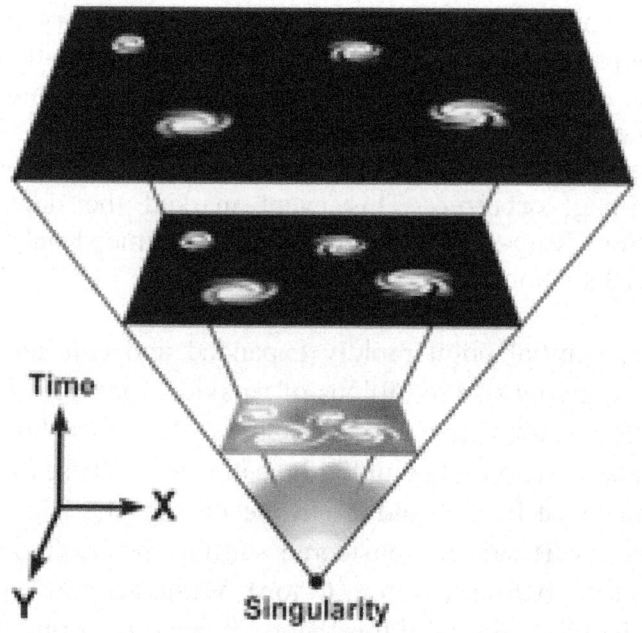

Pic. 2: Explosion at singularity -The Start of time
(Picture Courtesy: Wikipedia)

Vedic texts also posit the existence of *multiple Big Bang occurrences throughout eternity,* suggesting this Big Bang represents just one event in an infinite series of Big Bangs.

In this context, prior to this Big Bang, the Creator, the Supreme Existence, harbored the entirety of energy within the infinitesimal point, described as His Latent Energy or Unmanifest-infinite-energy.

This signifies the Absolute Oneness at Absolute Zero time.

The Supreme Existence

The Supreme Existence (the Absolute Truth), which is beyond names and forms, is a singular and perfect entity with infinite memory.

According to Vedic wisdom, this Supreme Existence willed to manifest and multiply itself. It willed *"I am alone, will become many"* (Sankalp: eko aham, bahu syam). As It "willed," It's Latent Energy got triggered and there was Big Bang! Creation instantly started at this *Absolute Zero Time*. It was the creation of the concept of Time too. Pic. 2.

Creation And Radha-Krishna

Referring to this nameless entity as Krishna (although diverse cultures use different names), as per the Gita, we acknowledge that Krishna represents the Creator. Additionally, Krishna's latent energy, which embodies infinite and cohesive love, is personified as Radha. Radha, also known as AadiShakti, MahaLakshmi, JagatJanani, Maa, Jagadamba, ParaShakti, among other names, represents this unseen female manifestation of energy. Krishna and Radha are inseparable and integral to one another.

The creation process is a result of the interplay between two complementary forces that either support or balance each other. Sometimes referred to as positive and negative forces, male and female energies, or Krishna and Radha, they effectively complete or complement each other.

The formless manifestation of Krishna becomes tangible through the divine union of Krishna and Radha, or Radha-Krishna.

Part-1, Chapter 1: Krishna the Creator

Purusha (Soul) And Prakriti (Nature)

My primitive nature, known as the great Brahma, is the womb of all creatures; in that womb I place the seed of all life. The creation of all beings follows from that union of Matter and Spirit. (Krishna - Gita Ch.14:3 -mam yonihi mahad brahm.......bhavati Bharat).
For all species of life Prakriti or Nature is the conceiving mother, and I am the seed-giving father. (Krishna - Gita Ch. 14:4- sarv yonishu......pita).
Prakriti or Nature consists of the three Gunas (modes) - Sat, Raj, and Tam (goodness, passion, and ignorance). When the living entity comes in contact with Nature, he or she becomes conditioned by these Gunas. (Krishna - Gita Ch. 14:5 - satvam rajah......avyayam).

At the moment of the Big Bang, the Creator's "Will" was dispersed as "desire" and marked the beginning of time. During the process of creation and expansion, the Creator's potential energy transformed into two interconnected components: Spiritual Energy, which reflects His all-encompassing love, the Soul, and Material Energy, which embodies desire, Maya (Nature), and its twin Time. With these elements, the Creator manifested Himself in countless forms and permeated all of space as an omnipresent force.

The Creator continues to connect with and sustain the entire universe by infusing it with Spiritual Energy, which emanates from His intense cohesive love at the core of each individual existence. Meanwhile, the Material Energy surrounding each form receives this energy and is invigorated by it. Material Energy further expands into various levels of existence, encompassing eight elements - earth, water, fire, air, space, mind, intellect, and ego. These facets serve as building blocks for both inanimate (material) and living creations as they progress and evolve.

The essence of the Spiritual Energy can be referred to as the Purusha, a primal male energy symbolizing the Father and the extension of the Soul or Spirit. Surrounding this core, we have the eightfold Material Energy known as Prakriti, representing Mother Nature or Maya, serving as a complement to the Purusha and reflecting latent energy.

As previously mentioned, the dispersion of the "Divine Will" takes the form of desire, which manifests as the eightfold Material Energy (Prakriti, Nature, Maya) permeating all creations. This energy is witnessed or energized by the Spiritual Energy at the core (Purusha, Soul, Spirit). In the life cycle of a being, when desire is eliminated, the influence of Prakriti diminishes, and the individual becomes united with the Purusha at the core,

Pic 3: Energies - Purush and Prakriti - Krishna & Radha

which is essentially an expansion of Krishna (Supreme Existence) Himself. This state of oneness with the core represents Yoga (union) with Krishna and is often referred to as Liberation or Salvation (Moksh, Mukti, Perfection, Nirvaan). It is the goal for all beings and can occur at any time and in any virtuous individual, continuously transpiring at various stages of life. It is always an ongoing process.

The Cosmic Memory

That (Creator) is Whole. This (creation) is Whole. When the Whole (creation) comes out of the Whole (Creator), what remains is still the Whole (Creator). ["Om Purnam adah purnam idam purnat purnam udachyate, purnasya purnam aaday purnam ev avashishyate. (Brihadaranyaka Upanishad - 5.1.1)."]

Prior to the Big Bang, the entirety of the Universal memory existed in an unmanifested form within Krishna. His original infinite memory, represented as a singular seed or point, was subsequently distributed among all particles and beings, with His empowering energy at the core of each existence.

It is important to note that Krishna has not experienced any loss of His original Infinite Memory, which remains intact with Him. Even after the Big Bang and subsequent expansion, He continues to maintain His Supreme Existence.

Divine memory and closeness with Krishna

The concept of memory is intricately intertwined with the functioning and maturation of the brain. Memories form a complex network within the brain, playing a crucial role in facilitating various bodily processes and activities. This

Pic 4: Lesser the ego, more devotional & elevated is the brain

network of memories is akin to the storage and retrieval of information in a seed or DNA. Like how a seed contains the blueprint for the growth of a plant or tree and DNA carries the genetic instructions for all living organisms, the memory embedded within these structures serves as a fundamental cause that ultimately manifests in the physical form and functioning of a plant or organism.

The level of development or evolution of a being is contingent upon the awakening and quality of the memories within. Memories, both worldly and divine, form the basis of the brain's composition. Various brains are structured with different networks of these memories. It is important to recognize that brain function is dependent on memory. The brain is the processing plant of memories.

As desires diminish and ego diminishes with it, there is a reduction in worldly memory and a corresponding increase in the retrieval of the original divine memory. A lesser ego allows for a diminished attachment to materialistic memories, facilitating the awakening of divine memory and consequently cultivating a closer connection with Krishna, the Creator.

The deeper we dive within our Innermost self, the fresher, clearer, and divine becomes our memory, the closer we are to ourselves and our infinite energy, the closer we are to the realization and functioning of an Avatar (Krishna). This diving deeper within our Innermost self happens through deep meditation, and much deeper, intense meditation called Samadhi.

The Samadhi happens through egoless or selfless devotion, and through performing prescribed duties (karma) with detached and selfless mindset. For Samadhi, a person does not necessarily sit still in a posture. While performing Karma without attachment, without any desire or without expecting results, or surrendering to Krishna in full devotion, a person may be in Samadhi.

This should be understood that to delve deeper into our true selves and tap into the infinite energy within, we must engage in profound meditation and reach a state of egoless devotion or detachment while performing our prescribed duties.

This process allows us to access our innermost self and awaken purer and clearer memories. It is through this connection to our innermost self that an Avatar, such as Shri Krishna, can perform supernatural feats that transcend the laws of nature.

Among the many miracles attributed to Shri Krishna, one notable instance involved the elongation of the Saree (garment) worn by Queen Draupadi. When the malicious Kauravas attempted to shame Draupadi and Pandavas by forcibly removing her garment, renouncing ego she dived deepest into her innermost self, in Samadhi and prayed to Krishna.

Krishna immediately helped her and extended Saree's length greatly, miraculously and saved her honor. This act played a significant role in the downfall of the evil Kauravas and the subsequent destruction of the wicked Kauravas dynasty.

We are integral components of Krishna's grand design

The Supreme Intelligence, Krishna, orchestrated the creation of the Universe according to His divine Will to manifest in multiple forms. This Will encompasses precise expansion designs, principles, and rules that govern every aspect of existence. It can be likened to the "Software" of His creation.

Krishna has tailored plans for each living and non-living entity. These plans are intricately woven into the fabric of their existence, as complex natural, scientific, moral, and ethical codes. They function seamlessly through automated systems such as DNA and the laws governing physics, chemistry, and society. In modern technological parlance, we can perceive it as an imperceptible, fully programmed microchip embedded within the consciousness of every being. Accordingly, throughout life, all actions are guided by this program which concludes upon the fulfillment of its intended purpose. When the program for this life has ended, the current life ends and the program for the next life starts.

Krishna's initial 'Will' emerging as 'desire'

The fundamental 'Will' that initially emerges as 'desire' encompasses all individuals, leading us through an array of transient emotions and experiences, including pleasure and pain, success and failure, and various opposites prevailing in our material world.

These occurrences are all part of a predetermined plan, governed by established rules already ingrained in our collective memory. However, only a small fraction of this memory is consciously activated within each being, as the majority remains concealed by the influence of desire, Vasana, or Maya.

When desire is eradicated, the influence of Prakriti (nature) dissipates, giving way to the awakening of pure, untainted, divine memory. Instantaneously, we connect with our essence, our true Innermost-self, the Purusha, which is always in union with the divine entity, Krishna, the Creator, the Supreme Existence.

Infallible (Achyut) and Undiminished (Akshar)

In the context of the Supreme Existence, it is notable that even after the phenomenon of the Big Bang, the infallible (Achyut) and undiminished (Akshar) nature of the

Supreme Being (Krishna) remains unchanged. Thus, the infallible and undiminished nature of the Supreme Being is evident through His ability to sustain His existence despite the occurrence of the Big Bang. While the Universe continues to expand, His latent energy remains intact because of His will.

This signifies that when the Whole emerges from the Whole, the Whole still remains. This concept can also be described as the manifestation of the Perfect from the Perfect, leaving the Perfect behind. (As expressed in the mantra: *Om purnamadah purnamidam purnat purnam udachyate purnasya purnamaday purnamev avashishyate*). Thus, even with the distribution of memory among countless particles and beings, the Supreme Being retains His infinite memory.

The Consort

Turning our attention to the relationship between Krishna and Radha, it is important to recognize that when Krishna is remembered, Radha is already intimately connected to Him with boundless love. Similarly, when Radha is recalled, Krishna exists harmoniously with her, also enveloped in profound love. They are true consorts, perpetually intertwined and unified. Radha represents the energy of Krishna, while Krishna serves as Radha's energizer. They are never separate entities.

Thus, the relationship between Krishna and Radha is that of eternal consort. They exist together with infinite love, inseparable and unified. Radha is the embodiment of Krishna's energy, while Krishna serves as the source of Radha's vitality. They are in constant union, representing non-duality (Adwait), singularity, and perfect equilibrium. This state signifies Absolute Truth, Knowledge, Energy, Love, Existence, Freedom, Peace, Purity, Bliss, Beauty, and Perfection. It is the infallible and undiminished state of Radha-Krishna's existence. The laws of physics, chemistry, and other sciences do not apply to Radha-Krishna as they are the creators, not the creations. These laws pertain to creations. In this context, Radha-Krishna in union symbolizes the entirety and perfection of existence. Radha represents latent energy, while Krishna represents the Supreme Existence and Consciousness. Thus:

Creator = Energizer = Supreme Existence = Supreme Consciousness = Absolute Truth = **Krishna**

The Consort = Latent Energy = Aadi Shakti = **Radha**

The union of Radha-Krishna is ingrained in the collective memory of all elements and beings.

The Life Journey (The Journey of Existence)

The Universe is Dwait (duality, plurality) born from Adwait (singularity). In the state of absolute unity, before the Big Bang, Radha and Krishna exist as one entity, symbolized by the silent ॐ OM. However, with the advent of duality after the Big Bang, the silent ॐ OM transformed into a vibrant ॐ OM, which expanded and continues to expand.

Thus, the Universe we know, which has been expanding for approximately fourteen billion years, was brought into existence through the vibrant ॐ OM. However, the Creator remains unchanged and unaffected by the creation process.

This expansion gave rise to the concepts of nature with time (Prakriti) and the soul (Purush). The separation between Prakriti and Purush resulted in the countless divisions and manifestations we see today, such as particles, atoms, planets, celestial bodies, dark matter, galaxies etc. Despite the creation of the universe, Radha and Krishna still remain in their original state as the silent ॐ OM, unaffected by the expansion.

The vibrant ॐ OM continues to expand while the creator Radha-Krishna, unchanged, encompasses infinite universes within themselves. This current universe is just one among an endless series of creations that have existed since time immemorial. Universes are continuously created, expanded, contracted, and then recreated through the cycle of Big Bangs. This cycle, and thus the journey of life, the journey of existence, continues indefinitely.

The Two Energies

Following the phenomenon of the Big Bang (around fourteen billion years ago), the concepts of Prakriti (nature, time) and Purusha (soul, spirit) emerged as complementing energies within the material elements and all creations. Accompanied by the presence of 'desire' and the 'attraction-repulsion' phenomenon, these energies originated from the original 'Will' or 'Sankalp' of the Divine.

Krishna's 'Will' became fragmented in the form of various desires. Similarly, the original force of cohesion became fragmented into the attraction and repulsion phenomenon observed in the natural or material world. It is through this desire and attraction-repulsion phenomenon that ego (including mind and intelligence) arise, eventually leading to the creation of material bodies and living beings.

Life on Earth has evolved in the relatively recent past, spanning billions of years, with Homo sapiens (humans) appearing only a few hundred thousand years ago. Throughout this process of life's evolution, Prakriti and Purusha appear clouded by the presence of ego, represented by the mind and intelligence.

In practical terms, desire, mind, intelligence, and ego are closely intertwined, dependent on each other and mutually reinforcing concepts. When there is desire, there is an active mind, and the related ego. When there is an active mind, there is ego, and desire. When there is an ego, there is the desire, and an active mind.

The Concept of Ego

The concept of 'ego' pertains to the perception of a distinct separation between Prakriti-Purush (the two components that reflect Radha-Krishna individually). However, true self-realization involves the dissolution of ego, where Prakriti merges with Purusha at its core, resulting in a sense of unity.

In other words, through the attainment of self-realization in a state devoid of ego, Prakriti merges harmoniously with Purusha at the fundamental level, resulting in oneness of silent ॐ OM.

By delving deeply into this sense of unity, one can reach the ultimate essence of 'Oneness' (similar to the moment of the Big Bang at its initial state). At the core of this ultimate essence resides Krishna, with His latent energy

Radha merged as a singular existence (Adwait). Therefore, the initial step towards comprehending the unity of Radha-Krishna lies in the abandonment of ego; a state achieved by being devoid of desires (Vaasana), with a well-controlled or eliminated mind, and residing within a state of transcendent or divine consciousness.

The absence of ego allows one to connect with their innermost self, aligning with Radha-Krishna or simply Krishna, who remains intrinsically connected to Radha. Thus, egolessness serves as both a crucial initial step and a guarantee towards achieving unity with Krishna or attaining the state of perfection. If there is no desire, there is no ego. No desire is achievable through total surrender to Krishna.

Krishna: The Ultimate Truth

Krishna embodies the Absolute Truth, the Ultimate Truth representing perfection in its purest form. To attain this state of perfection, one must align themselves with the path of truth, honesty, and sincerity every moment in life.

The pursuit of truth is intrinsic to attaining peace and happiness. Achieving perfection necessitates the consistent adherence to truthfulness in all aspects of life, thoughts, and actions. Achieving Krishna (perfection) through truth:

- Perfection is exclusively achieved through the earnest pursuit of truthfulness in all aspects of life. By consistently adhering to principles of truthfulness, individuals are poised to attain perfection.
- Time itself, arising from the Absolute Truth, favors and supports those who embody truthfulness in their thoughts, actions, and daily interactions. This

- genuine adherence to truth ultimately leads to a harmonious existence.
- Falsehood may have momentary illusive victories, luring many with its multiple disguises. However, these temporary wins inevitably crumble in the face of truth, as the singular, unwavering nature of the truth prevails over falsehood in the end. Satyameva Jayate (only the truth wins).
- Truth remains constant and consistent throughout time, illuminating its path from beginning to end. By embracing and embodying the truth, individuals are guided towards Krishna, who represents the Ultimate Truth and serves as the pinnacle of perfection. The radiance of truth is eternal.
- The Truth is Krishna. Krishna is the Truth. Absolute Truth is Perfection. The path to perfection is through the truth.
- Peace and bliss are essential ingredients of the truth. Only the truth prevails (Satyam ev jayate). Falsehood never wins.
- The Truth is only one. It is as it is. The truth keeps on shining from the beginning to the end, and ultimately leads to Krishna, the perfect, the Ultimate Truth.

2. THE AVATAR

The concept of Avatar

Reincarnation of the Creator on the earth in any form is known as an Avatar. The Creator keeps on appearing on the earth like Avatars during different millenniums, even multiple times during the same millennium. The Avatar is Creator's physical form (animal-like or human-like, or of mixed appearance), known as the worldly manifestation.

The Avatar exists simultaneously within both the transcendental and worldly realms, engaging in actions that align with the predetermined purpose or cause. This concept is also hinted at in the Bhagwat Geeta (Gita).

Whenever there is a decline in religious practice, and a predominant rise of irreligion—at that time I descend or incarnate Myself.
(Krishna - Gita Ch.4: 7- yada yada hi......aham).
To protect the pious and to annihilate the miscreants, as well as to reestablish the principles of religion, I advent Myself millennium after millennium. *(Krishna - Gita Ch.4: 8- paritranay........yuge yuge).*

As per Vedic scriptures Avatars serve multiple purposes. The primary purpose of avatars is to restore cosmic balance or Dharma whenever it becomes disrupted. Some key purposes of Avatars are:

- Avatars happen to protect and uphold Dharma (righteousness) during times of chaos and moral decline. They combat evil forces and restore order in the world.
- Avatars impart spiritual wisdom and teachings to guide human beings and show them the path towards self-realization and liberation. They set an example through their own actions and narratives.
- Avatars also happen to rescue and liberate human beings from suffering and ignorance. They offer salvation and provide the means for individuals to attain moksha (liberation from the cycle of birth and death).
- Avatars inspire devotion and worship among their followers. Devotees express their love, respect, and faith through various forms of rituals, Poojas, prayers, and acts of services.
- Avatars often transcend social, cultural, and religious boundaries. They aim to bring people

together from diverse backgrounds, fostering unity and shared values among all humans. Avatars can be seen as unifying figures that bridge the gap between human beings and the divine.
- Avatars also happen to protect the universe and its inhabitants from powerful demons or negative forces that threaten the balance of creation.
- Avatars engage in divine plays and perform various miraculous acts (Leelas) to entertain, dazzle, and captivate their devotees. These Leelas are symbolic and hold deeper spiritual meanings.
- Avatars provide moral and ethical guidelines for human conduct through their actions and teachings. They demonstrate virtuous behavior and inspire people to lead righteous lives.
- The presence of Avatars inspires deep devotion and Bhakti (devotional love) among their followers. Devotees develop a personal and emotional connection with Avatar, which strengthens their spiritual journey.

Overall, Avatars play a pivotal role in maintaining cosmic order, imparting spiritual knowledge, inspiring devotion, and leading humanity towards enlightenment and liberation.

Different Avatars of the Creator

As per the Gita and other Vedic scriptures, Lord Shri Krishna is revered as the Original Creator. He is omnipotent, omniscient, and all-pervading. Lord Krishna, as Maha-Vishnu, manifested Himself in three forms known as Trimurti – Brahma, Vishnu, and Mahesh. According to the Vedic scriptures, Brahma represents the power of creation, Vishnu represents the power of preservation (sustenance), and Mahesh (Shiva) represents the power of destruction. These three deities are considered various aspects of the Supreme Creator Krishna.

In addition to being the Creator, Shri Krishna is also regarded as the source of all other Avatars through His Vishnu form. Thus, all Avatars of Vishnu emanate from Lord Krishna. He periodically incarnates on Earth to restore Dharma (righteousness) and maintain cosmic balance. These incarnations are known as His Avatars.

As mentioned earlier, Maha-Vishnu is considered the Supreme Creator (Krishna) and also one of the three main forms of Vishnu, alongside Brahma and Shiva. Maha-Vishnu is believed to be lying in a divine ocean of milk (Kshir-Sagar) and is responsible for the creation, maintenance, and destruction of the cosmos.

Maha-Vishnu is also depicted with multiple heads and arms, holding various symbolic objects (Virat-Swaroop). This Virat form He showed to his devotee and friend in Kurukshetra battlefield also while preaching the Gita, as mentioned in the chapter 11 of the Gita.

There are ten Avatars of the Creator Krishna, through Shri Vishnu, known as Dashavatara. Here is a brief description of each avatar and its purpose:

1. Matsya (Fish Avatar): The first avatar appears as a gigantic fish to save humanity from a catastrophic flood and recovers sacred scriptures stolen by demons.

2. Kurma (Tortoise Avatar): Shri Vishnu incarnates as a tortoise to support Mount Mandara during the churning (Manthan) of the cosmic ocean to obtain the elixir of immortality (Amrit).

3. Varaha (Boar Avatar): He Takes the form of a boar to rescue Goddess Earth (Bhudevi) from the clutches of the demon Hiranyaksha and restore balance and order.

4. Narasimha (Half-Man Half-Lion Avatar): Shri Vishnu transforms into a man-lion to destroy the demon king Hiranyakashipu and protect his devotee Prahlada.

5. Vamana (Dwarf Avatar): Appears as a dwarf Brahmin to suppress the power of the demon king Bali and restore the authority of the gods.

6. Parashurama (Warrior Avatar): Shri Vishnu takes Avatar as a fierce warrior to rid the world of evil and restore dharma (righteousness) by eradicating corrupt rulers and warriors.

7. Rama (Prince Avatar): The most popular avatar, Shri Vishnu incarnates as Prince Rama, the protagonist of the epic Ramayana. He defeats the demon king Ravana and establishes a just and righteous rule.

8. Krishna (Cowherd Avatar): Known for his playfulness and divine teachings, Lord Vishnu assumes the form of Lord Krishna to guide and inspire humanity through the epic Mahabharata and the Bhagavad Gita.

9. Buddha (Enlightened Avatar): In this avatar, Shri Vishnu appears as Gautama Buddha to teach the path of enlightenment and liberate souls through non-violence and compassion.

10. Kalki (Future Avatar): This is the final avatar yet to come. Lord Vishnu is prophesied to appear as Kalki, riding a white horse, to cleanse the world of evil and restore righteousness at the end of the Kali Yuga, the current age.

Each of these Avatars represents a form of divine intervention, bringing balance, protection, teachings, and deliverance from evil forces during different periods of time during evolution of the earth and civilization.

Apart from the ten Avatars (Dashavatara), there are other Avatars mentioned in Hindu scripture. These may be called partial-Avatars. Some of these include:

11. Mohini: The female avatar of Lord Vishnu who appeared during the churning of the cosmic ocean.

12. Hayagriva: The horse-headed avatar of Lord Vishnu who retrieved the Vedas from the demon Hayagriva.

13. Dhanvantari: The physician avatar who emerged from the cosmic ocean with the elixir of immortality.

14. Vyasa deva: The author of the Vedas, Mahabharata, Bhagwat, and other scriptures. The sage and one of the Chiranjivis (immortals).

15. Nara-Narayana: The twin sages who are a joint incarnation of Lord Vishnu in the epic Mahabharata.

16. Kapila: The founder of the Samkhya philosophy, who is considered an incarnation of Lord Vishnu.

17. Four Kumars – First four conscious beings created by Lord Brahma

18. Rishabha: The first Tirthankara (enlightened being) of Jainism, considered an incarnation of Lord Vishnu.

19. Balarama: The elder brother of Lord Krishna, known for his strength and loyalty.

20. Narada: The celestial sage who travels between realms and imparts knowledge and wisdom.

21. Dattatreya: Also known as Trimurti, is a sage and the Master of Yoga with three heads representing Brahma, Vishnu, and Mahesh.

22. Yajna: An incarnation of Vishnu who emerged during a great ritual sacrifice to restore order.

23. Prithu: The first king according to Hindu mythology, who was an incarnation of Lord Vishnu.

24. Matsya-Narasimha: A combined form of Matsya (fish) and Narasimha (man-lion) avatars, Lord Vishnu took this form to defeat a demon who hid in the ocean and on land.

The number of avatars varies in different Sanatani (Hindu) sects and traditions. I have mentioned only some of the commonly mentioned avatars in Vedic scriptures. Some scriptures mention Adi Purush as the first Avatar. However, as we have mentioned Shri Krishna as the Creator, we consider Him as the Adi Purush.

Shri Krishna Avatar

Here we will discuss only a bit about the Krishna Avatar. Lord Krishna's Avatar occurred during a time of turmoil and evil on earth during the Dwapara Yuga. The main purpose of Lord Krishna's incarnation was to restore righteousness, uphold moral values, and guide humanity towards the path of righteousness.

He taught important life lessons and provided guidance through his teachings, actions, and divine activities, as described in epic scriptures the Bhagavad Gita, Shrimad Bhagwat, and others.

Shri Krishna emphasized the importance of fulfilling one's duties, practicing non-attachment, and surrendering to Paramatma (the Creator). His Avatar is also a pathway for devotees to establish a deep and personal relationship with the divine and attain spiritual enlightenment (Moksha). Additionally,

Krishna's incarnation highlighted divine love, compassion, and grace, making him an object of devotion and reverence for millions of devotees in their daily life.

It is interesting to note that across diverse global regions, countries, and cultures, individuals interpret the concept of the Supreme Being (God), often referred to as the Original Creator, in diverse ways.

Some view this Supreme Entity as the Original Father (masculine), the Original Mother (feminine), or a blend of all genders, understanding that **the Original Creator exists beyond any specific gender, form, or name.** These perceptions align with regional, cultural, and spiritual beliefs.

Within the realm of Vedic (Hindu, Sanatan) Dharma, different manifestations of the Supreme Being, the Creator is worshiped under different names.

In the male form, this entity is revered as Krishna, Vishnu, Brahma, Mahesh, Narayana, Venkatesha, Param-Pita, Parameshwar, Ishwar, Bhagwan, Shiva, Ram, and others.

Part-1, Chapter 1: Krishna the Creator

The female form is celebrated through names such as Radha, Lakshmi, Durga, Kali, Saraswati, Jagat-Janani, Aadhya-Shakti, Adi-shakti, Para-Shakti, Sita, Jagat-Mata, Maa, and more.

In a combined male-female depiction, the divine couple is revered as Radha-Krishna, Lakshmi-Vishnu, Lakshmi-Narayan, Rukmini-Krishna, Uma-Maheshwar, Gauri-Shankar, Shiv-Parvati, Shiva-Shakti, Sita-Ram, Prakriti-Purusha, and so forth.

It is crucial to understand that regardless of the perceived name or form, followers of Vedic Dharma believe that the Original Supreme Creator is the omniscient, omnipotent, and omnipresent infinite existence beyond any name or form.

While individuals of various beliefs worship the Original Creator in different names and forms, like millions other Krishna-devotees, I personally find it captivating to recognize the Original Supreme Creator as **Krishna** during my earthly existence. For the devotees, the name 'Krishna' encompasses all the aforementioned titles and depictions.

Throughout the ages, the Creator has manifested in numerous Avatars, with one of the most recent being around 5100 years ago, known as Krishna Avatar.

Born as the son of Vasudeva and Devaki in Mathura, Bharat, Krishna is acknowledged by spiritual leaders and great souls such as Mahaveer Swami, Guru Nanak, Gautam Buddha, belonging to different branches of Sanatana Dharma including Jainism, Sikhism, and Buddhism. Their holy scriptures also point towards the same Creator or Absolute Existence.

Krishna, during his incarnation, exhibited extraordinary charisma and supernatural abilities, along with a strong connection to humanity. Through his pure divine love, captivating personality, and exceptional acts of public welfare, he touched the hearts and minds of countless individuals in his era and continues to do so over countless generations.

Krishna, in His earthly form, exhibited awe-inspiring qualities and divine powers, captivating both the natural and supernatural realms. His immaculate love

Pic. 5: Different names of the Creator Lord Krishna.

charming personality, and extraordinary charitable endeavors endeared Him to millions throughout his generation and beyond, a legacy that will span countless future generations.

Fully comprehending and documenting the entirety of His wondrous acts, pastimes and experiences is a near impossibility. However, even our limited knowledge of Krishna evokes a profound sense of love, enlightenment, divine energy, confidence, admiration, and devotion, as we discover His divine presence within ourselves at our very essence, at our core, in our Innermost-self.

CHAPTER 2
INFINITE UNIVERSES AND WE

All beings enter My Nature at the end of a Kalpa (universal cycle); I send them forth again at the beginning of (the next) Kalpa!
(Krishna - Gita Ch 9: 7- sarvabhutani............myaham)
Animating My Nature, I repeatedly send forth all this multitude of beings, who are helpless by the force of Nature.
(Krishna - Gita Ch 9: 8 - prakritim............vashaat.)

This is the current Universe we reside in, which is just one among an infinite series of Universes that are created, expand, contract, and eventually disappear or merge into the Creator. It is widely accepted in scientific circles that this Universe began with the Big Bang approximately fourteen billion years ago and continues to expand rapidly, giving rise to countless visible and invisible galaxies. This is the present Universe in a series of infinite Universes, characterized by the cycle of creation, expansion, contraction, and eventual disappearance.

At a certain point, this expansion will come to a halt and the Universe will gradually contract, eventually returning to a state of Singularity (Adwait) where all matter is condensed into an infinitesimal point at the time of Big Crunch or cosmic dissolution (Kalpaant or Pralay), as in

Part-1, Chapter 2: Infinite Universes and We

Pic. 6. This marks the completion of one Universal cycle (Kalp)*.

Subsequently, another Big Bang will occur, initiating a new Universal cycle (Kalp) as in Pic. 7. This process of creation, expansion, and dissolution has occurred infinitely in the past and will continue infinitely into the future, forming and transforming countless Universes. *[*Kalp: based on Krishna's revelation in Gita Ch 9: 7]*

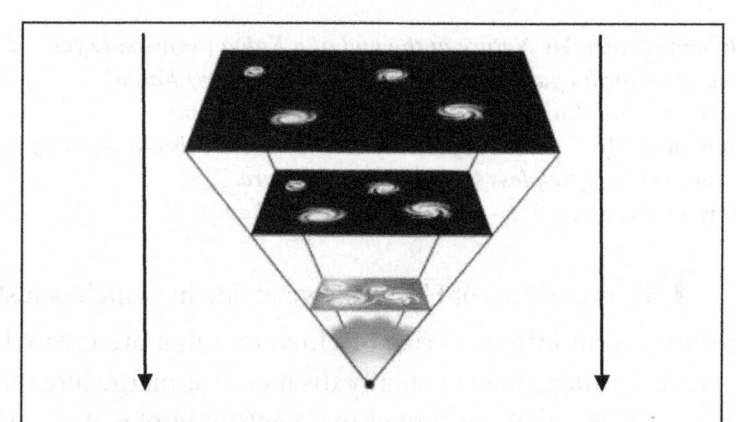

Pic. 6 -The Big Crunch (Kalpa-Ant), condensing Universe to an infinitesimal point at the bottom (Reverse of expansion - Top to bottom). *Picture Courtesy: Wikipedia*

It is possible that this may not be the first instance of my expression of these thoughts, or your first encounter with them. Such actions might have likely occurred countless times in the past, and likely continue to occur countless times in the future, within different periods of billions of years between two Big Bangs known as Kalpa. Additionally, these same actions might repeat in each of the

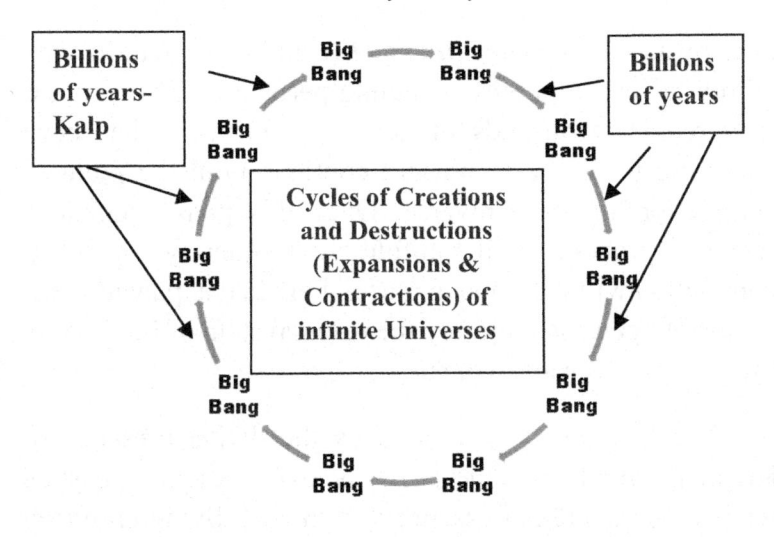

```
     Billions           Big ----- Big            Billions
     of years-         Bang      Bang            of years
       Kalp       Big                      Big
                  Bang                     Bang
                        Cycles of Creations
                         and Destructions
                  Big    (Expansions &      Big
                  Bang   Contractions) of   Bang
                          infinite Universes
                  Big                      Big
                  Bang                     Bang
                           Big     Big
                           Bang    Bang
```

Pic 7: Cycles of infinite Big Bangs triggered by the Creator (Krishna)

infinite Universes and Kalpas, if the governing laws remain consistent across all Universes in each Kalpa *(as mentioned in Gita Ch 9: 7, 8).*

We all are expansions of Krishna

There is no Truth superior to Me. Everything rests upon Me, as pearls are strung on a thread.
(Gita Ch. 7:7 - mattah parataram..........manigana eva).

We must recognize that we are all manifestations of Krishna. There is no higher truth than Krishna, and everything depends on Him as pearls depend on a string *(Gita Ch. 7:7 - mattah parataram..........manigana eva).* At the beginning, Krishna intended to multiply Himself, leading to the occurrence of the Big Bang and the emergence of desire. Through this desire, Krishna initiates His expansion project, ensuring that the necessary reproduction takes place within a being. At the appropriate time, He influences that being to turn inward, *to become introspective* and strive to unite with Him at its core, thereby regaining perfection. This process may require thousands of years and births. It has been occurring in the past and will continue until the point of contraction in the Universe. Once this phase begins, a reverse process will unfold subsequently. Gradual contraction will continue in place of gradual expansion, and ultimately getting smoothly the original state of Perfection, Singularity (Adwait), Oneness or Ekatva.

The Universe is pervaded by the divine presence of Krishna, which includes His beloved Radha. Krishna represents the eternal essence within each living entity, in perfect union with His latent energy, Radha. Krishna unites with His latent energy Radha through boundless love. The divine energy of Krishna resides within every individual as their immortal Soul, also known as Atma or Purush.

The physical body, mind, and intellect, collectively referred to as the ego, represent the transient and illusory (Mithya) aspect of Nature known as Prakriti or Maya. The Maya is a manifestation of Radha's creative energy. Radha is Krishna's latent energy. Prakriti is perishable and created by the influence of Radha's energy.

When a person transcends the limitations of Prakriti, they get awaken to their true nature as the radiant Atma, the observer within. Such a realization indicates a person's wisdom, knowledge, and spiritual growth. They are known as yogi, seer, Sanyasi, Apt-Purush, or liberated soul, experiencing fulfillment, happiness, contentment, inner peace, and bliss. In this state of perfect Krishna-consciousness, they attain a state of perfection.

Essentially, each of us carries the divine essence of Krishna within our nucleus, but as we navigate the influences of Prakriti (Maya), represented by ego and ignorance, we become entangled in the illusory and impermanent aspects of the universe. Once we transcend the influence of Prakriti, we are in the divine field of Krishna. Thus, we have the Creator (Krishna) at our core (nucleus). As we come out of the nucleus due to mysterious forces of Prakriti (Maya), we get shrouded by ego & ignorance, and become a part of perishable & illusory universe. It has been further explained below.

Our Nucleus and the Universe

As mentioned earlier, the universe originated from a single point known as singularity, and as it expands, we also have originated from a singularity at the core of our being. This core, the nucleus, is referred to as the Innermost-self, the dwelling place of Krishna or Paramatma, which is always shining with eternal, infinite cool-light-energy, wisdom, and awareness (Pic. 8). This expansion plan involves the emergence of ego and other components of nature, such as ignorance, material world, and desires (Maya). Thus, as per the expansion plan of Krishna: coming out from the core is the start of 'ego' and all related instruments of nature (ignorance, material world, desires, or Maya).

Initially, the ego manifests subtly, followed by the development of the mind and intelligence, which form the subtle body (Sukshma Sharir). Eventually, this progress leads to the solidification of the ego into the physical body (Sthool Sharir), which becomes subject to the cycle of Karma. To achieve the reunion or Yoga with Krishna, individuals must revert and transcend their identification with the body and material consciousness and then endeavor to delve deep within to reconnect with the nucleus, reversing the process of expansion.

**NUCLEUS OF THE BEING & THE UNIVERSE
[YOU, ME, ALL & THE COSMOS]**

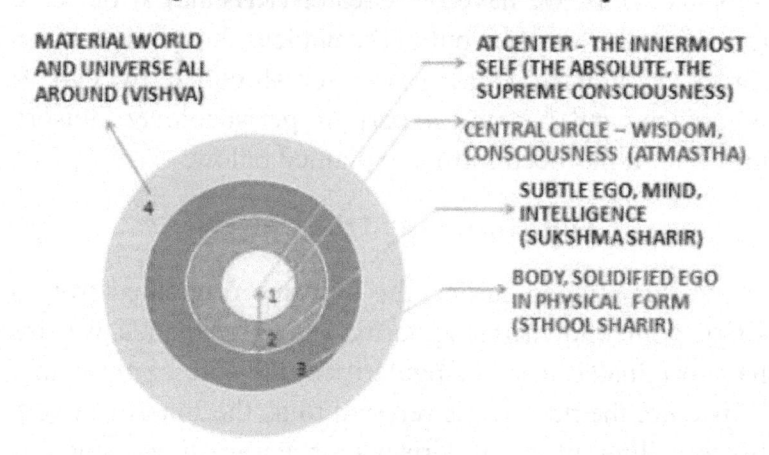

MATERIAL WORLD AND UNIVERSE ALL AROUND (VISHVA)

AT CENTER - THE INNERMOST SELF (THE ABSOLUTE, THE SUPREME CONSCIOUSNESS)

CENTRAL CIRCLE – WISDOM, CONSCIOUSNESS (ATMASTHA)

SUBTLE EGO, MIND, INTELLIGENCE (SUKSHMA SHARIR)

BODY, SOLIDIFIED EGO IN PHYSICAL FORM (STHOOL SHARIR)

Pic. 8 - Nucleus of a being and the Universe

Illusive worldly love v/s Radha-Krishna's Divine Love

These two (My higher and lower Natures) are the womb of all beings. I am the source and dissolution of the whole universe.
(Krishna - Gita Ch.7:6 - etad yonini....pralayastatha).
Know Me (Krishna) the eternal seed of all beings; I am the intelligence of intelligent; the splendor of the splendid objects am I!
(Krishna - Gita Ch.7:10 - bijam mam ....aham).
At the last of many births the enlightened person comes to Me, realizing that all this is Vasudeva (Krishna); such a great soul is extremely hard to find.
(Krishna - Gita Ch.7:19 - bahunam janm......sudurlabhah).

A man who has not yet attained a higher level of consciousness and a deeper understanding of inner vision, or whose readiness for Yoga or Moksha has not yet arrived, is drawn towards external distractions by the allure of worldly pleasures, thereby reinforcing his ego. He becomes physically attracted to another woman, seeking a fantastical union akin to Rukmini or Satyabhama, in pursuit of companionship or fulfillment. This pursuit often leads to establishing a relationship with a girlfriend or wife. In society, marriage or forming relationships becomes a social construct and obligation aimed at maintaining societal harmony for procreation.

The divine essence of Krishna exists within every female as well. Inspired by Krishna's cosmic energy Maya, she too is motivated to attract or be attracted to a male counterpart, to partake in Krishna's grand plan of multiplication. She experiences the desire to create and nurture offspring, utilizing the innate maternal instincts and abilities bestowed upon her by nature. This desire of theirs is an extension of Krishna's original 'Will' (Sankalp), transformed into desires, to multiply Himself and expand the divine creations. Thus, it is all part of Krishna's divine plan that, for a certain period, males and females look outside themselves (being extroverted) in search of their ideal partners or unions, as Krishna ultimately seeks to multiply and expand Himself through this union.

According to the ancient Vedic literature, after individuals, irrespective of their gender, fulfill their responsibilities in procreation and growth, they are guided towards other endeavors or responsibilities determined as per norms set by the Creator Krishna. It becomes apparent that according to Krishna's expansion plan, facilitated by the illusionary influence of Maya, individuals feel compelled to witness the union of their children and grandchildren in marriage and subsequent procreation, ensuring the continuation of creation and expansion. This process continues until an individual's consciousness reaches a heightened level, enabling them to recognize the presence of the Creator (Krishna) within themselves and attain liberation, known as Mukti, Moksha, or Nirvana.

Furthermore, pervaded within the intricate layers of DNA lies the inherent capability for evolution and growth, propelling each being towards a state of higher consciousness and improved manifestation. As we traverse the passage of time, we witness the gradual progression of all life forms (including plants and animals), as they ascend towards the next stage of their evolution as per their genetic makeup. This incredible progression ultimately culminates in the apex of existence – the human form. Undeniably, the human form holds a special place within the cosmic design, for it is here that individuals are bestowed with the sacred responsibility of expanding their consciousness and fulfilling their destined obligations. It is within human life that profound opportunities for self-realization arise, leading individuals towards the path of liberation and ultimate union with Krishna, the Creator.

A Meera is self-sufficient and does not require a romantic partner, as she has already achieved a deep connection with Krishna and is fully absorbed in Him. Similarly, a Vivekananda or an authentic Sanyasi or genuine Saint or a genuine contemplative individual does not feel the need for companionship, as they have attained inner realization and have merged with the Divine. These individuals have already fulfilled their worldly duties in previous lifetimes and in this lifetime or birth, they are tasked with uplifting the consciousness of the masses or specific groups of people. Their goal is liberation or Moksha.

This inherent system is present in every being and must be followed. There is no option. It is a part of the Creator's Maya, a divine illusion created for expansion and multiplication, leading eventually to disillusionment, and merging with the Divine. This is also known as the Divine Play (Leela). It gives us hope and immense inspiration.

We are all extensions of the Divine (Krishna), so it is obvious that we have Krishna within us. When we realize the presence of Krishna and His latent energy Radha within our core, realize our true essence, we attain perfection, liberation (Moksha). It is Krishna's Leela that all beings must pass through illusive worldly love and ultimately immerse in Radha-Krishna's Divine Love having perfection, Moksha.

We all are moving towards perfection

Let us reflect on our previous conclusion. Our origin is rooted in perfection. We were once perfect, but through the event of the Big Bang, we became fragmented into countless imperfect components. Since then, we have been fulfilling our roles in the universe's creation and expansion. In doing so, we have been progressing towards perfection by adhering to numerous universal laws established by the Creator.

Within the vast expanse of the universe, everything is in constant motion, except for the Creator, the Supreme Being, Supreme Existence, or the Supreme Consciousness, we refer to as Krishna. In a state of equilibrium, characterized by singularity known as Adwait, Krishna and

Part-1, Chapter 2: Infinite Universes and We

His latent energy, Radha, are indistinguishable. They exist in perfection, embodying absolute peace, absolute energy, and absolute bliss. This state is also inherent to our true nature, as we all emerged from it.

During the process of creation, Krishna multiplied Himself and resides at the core of every infinitesimal particle, entity, and existence as the spiritual energy, or Purusha. Accompanying this spiritual energy is His material energy, or Prakriti, which represents nature's energy.

In the concept of duality (Dwait), our ego (which encompasses the physical, mental, and intellectual aspects) creates a sense of identification with our body, mind, and intelligence. This leads to feelings of dissatisfaction and a perception of incompleteness as either a male or female being.

Consequently, we seek external sources for fulfillment in the outer world. This pursuit often results in the entanglement of our mind, ego, and desires in various activities, leading us through a multitude of challenges and experiences, including joys and sorrows, victories and defeats, successes and failures, and other contrasting aspects of life's dualities.

Within Krishna's illusory energy, known as Maya, we find ourselves naturally attracted to the allure of the opposite gender, wealth, and fame, as represented by Kamini (attraction towards romantic relationships), Kanchan (attraction towards material wealth), and Kirti (attraction towards recognition and fame).

Some individuals seek a romantic partner in different bodies or minds to feel complete and fulfilled (Kamini), while others pursue wealth as their path to fulfillment (Kanchan). Additionally, some individuals endeavor to attain power, status, respect, and fame in society in their quest for fulfillment (Kirti).

In pursuit of spiritual growth and enlightenment, individuals may adopt various approaches. Some may resort to employing cruelty, anger, deceit, intoxication, and unconventional practices. These Tamasic methods are considered highly undesirable.

On the other hand, others may choose to embrace love, compassion, philanthropy, assisting others, and engaging in social causes. These Rajasic practices are seen as a more favorable path.

However, the most esteemed and effective approach involves embarking on an inward journey through austerity, selflessness, self-discipline, self-sacrificing and charitable acts, the practice of Yoga and meditation, detached engagement in worldly affairs, and embracing a life of renunciation (known as Sanyas), or self-surrendered devotional services to the Creator.

These Sattvic practices are highly regarded as most optimal means to spiritual growth according to the wisdom outlined in Vedic literature.

These practices aim to achieve the highest level of spiritual growth and unity with the divine essence, often represented by Radha-Krishna or the union of Prakriti (Nature) and Purusha (Soul, Spirit).

Part-1, Chapter 2: Infinite Universes and We

Pic. 9: Beyond Maya (Kamini, Kanchan, Kirti) is Krishna or Moksha

The goal is to attain a state of perfection, absolute unity with our Innermost-self, and complete absorption in the divine. This can also be referred to as liberation, enlightenment, freedom, perfection, or salvation. This journey towards perfection or Moksha offers a source of hope and inspiration for all living beings.

CHAPTER 3
THE CREATOR MAINTAINS EQUILIBRIUM

(of three qualities and two tendencies)

In the beginning of creation, the entities of Purusha and Prakriti were brought into existence, accompanied by the element of time. Prakriti, representing nature, was created with three qualities known as Gunas: Sat (the quality of purity and truth), Raj (the quality of passion and activity), and Tam (the quality of darkness and inertia). Every aspect of the material world, from subatomic particles to celestial bodies like the sun, earth, moon, planets, and galaxies, operates under the influence of these Gunas, while the Purusha silently provides the necessary energy. Furthermore, all living beings possess inherent inclinations or tendencies known as Swabhava, which can either be a Deva tendency (associated with virtues, righteousness, and inner peace) or a Danava tendency (associated with malevolence, evil, and causing suffering).

Both tendencies (Swabhavas) play a significant role in the expansion and evolution processes. While some beings exhibit a mixture of both inclinations, there is always a

Part-1, Chapter 3: The Creator Maintains Equilibrium

predominant tendency within everyone. The Creator ensures a harmonious balance of these tendencies (Swabhavas). The Purusha (Soul), acting as a catalyst, influences these processes without actively participating in any activities. The Creator designs automated plans and programs, akin to software programming, to maintain equilibrium by regulating the Gunas (qualities) and Swabhavas (tendencies) present in all beings.

Pic. 10: Krishna maintains equilibrium of three qualities Sat, Raj & Tam, and two tendencies Deva & Asura

The Creator skillfully exercises control over the various qualities (Gunas) and tendencies (Swabhavas) inherent in nature and beings, utilizing them to foster the expansion, evolution, and wellbeing of the world and all living creatures. It is important to note that these qualities and tendencies are interconnected in a complex manner, extending from the tiniest subatomic particles to the vast expanse of galaxies.

This interconnection has existed since the very moment of creation, persists today, and will continue until the eventual dissolution of the Universe. Even in the unified state that follows this dissolution, a perfect balance is maintained. The subsequent cycle of creation and expansion commences after a deliberate disturbance and swift equilibration of divine energies.

During this process of expansion and evolution, in any given epoch (Yuga), when the balance of these qualities and tendencies becomes slightly disrupted (albeit as part of the Creator's plan), the Creator incarnates as an Avatar according to predetermined arrangements, taking corrective actions to restore the proper equilibrium between the three qualities (Gunas) of nature and the two tendencies (Swabhavas) of beings.

The Creator's topmost priority lies in promoting goodness, purity, virtuousness, and decency (referring to the Sat-Guna), which are closely aligned with the divine tendency (Swabhav). This emphasis on goodness facilitates harmonious expansion and creativity.

For the Creator there is nothing good or evil. Both good and evil are His creations and the tools. These are necessary forces that balance or complement each other. It is just like positive energies and negative energies complimenting or balancing each other to maintain equilibrium.

He has established boundaries for what is considered good and evil. However, when evil surpasses those boundaries, he takes action to eliminate the excess and restore balance.

This may occur through the intervention of Avatars, nature's gifts, natural disasters, accidents, or other means, all of which are already part of his plans. This was true in the past, it remains true today, and it will continue to be true in the future.

The equilibrium of the three Gunas (qualities)

The influence of the three modes or qualities of Mother Nature affects everyone. Initially, many individuals exist in a state of tamas (darkness, ignorance). There are two types of tamas: dull and violent. In the dull tamas state, individuals are lazy, intoxicated, and prone to procrastination or a combination thereof. In the violent tamas state, they are aggressive, deceitful, restless, and exhibit dictatorial tendencies. (Fig. 11).

Material nature consists of the three qualities - goodness, passion, and ignorance (Sat, Raj, and Tam). When the living entity meets nature, he or she becomes conditioned by these modes. (Krishna - Gita Ch. 14:5 - satvam rajah....avyayam.)

The mode of goodness conditions one to happiness, passion conditions one to the fruits of action, and ignorance conditions one to madness or insanity. (Krishna - Gita Ch. 14:9 -satvam sukhe....atyuta.).

Those situated in the mode of goodness gradually go upward to the higher planets (consciousness); those in the mode of passion live on the earthly planets (action-reaction); and those in the mode of ignorance go down to the hellish worlds (darkened mindsets). (Krishna - Gita Ch. 14:18 - urdhvam.....tamasaha.).

GOODNESS, PASSION, DARKNESS (SATVA, RAJAS, TAMAS) TRANSFORMATION

Pic. 11: Satva, Rajas, Tamas transformation

The Three Gunas (Qualities)

Every individual possesses three inherent qualities (Gunas). Typically, one quality tends to be dominant while the other two remain latent. These Gunas are Sat, Raj, and Tam.

Sat: Individuals with a predominant "Sat" quality are characterized by honesty, truthfulness, morality, compassion, selflessness, holistic thinking, love, and forgiveness. They display kindness and spread love and happiness to all beings. Such individuals are often referred to as "Sattvic" (closest to Deva Swabhava), embodying saintly qualities and demonstrating a willingness to sacrifice their own interests for the benefit of others in need.

Raj: In individuals with a predominant "Raj" quality, passion and activity are prominent. They are called "Rajasic." These individuals harbor various desires, greed, selfishness, fear, and other impurities associated with worldly pursuits. While they engage in worldly activities, they also partake in acts of charity and assistance to others, often expecting something in return. Most individuals in common households exhibit Rajasic tendencies.

Tam: Individuals with a dominant "Tam" quality have a larger tendency towards ignorance, lethargy, aggression, violence, and darkness. Their lives bear resemblance to those of animals. Such individuals are referred to as "Tamasic," as they experience numerous limitations and bondages. These individuals experience a heightened sense of negativity and hostility.

Ego and divinity

Every individual possesses varying degrees of ego.

A thick ego is detrimental. It limits one's thoughts and actions to their own body or immediate surroundings. A common ego is acceptable. It allows for thoughts and activities that extend to one's limited social circles. A thin ego is preferable. It enables thoughts and actions that have a global impact. However, the goal is no ego or divinity.

The path to divinity begins with shedding one's ego. An egoless individual engages in thoughts and actions that transcend boundaries and reach a cosmic level.

Divinity serves as a gateway to connect with one's innermost self or the Divine. Thus –

Thick ego is bad. The thoughts and activities of a person with thick ego - are confined to their own body or to the nearest ones.

Common ego is fair. The thoughts and activities of a person with common ego - spread within his or her own limited social circles.

Thin ego is better. The thoughts and activities of a person with thin ego - spread globally.

No ego or Divinity is the best, the goal. Egolessness is the start of divinity. The thoughts and activities of an egoless person - are cosmic, spread infinitely. Divinity is the gateway to the Core, Innermost-self, or Krishna.

Relation between three qualities and ego

Just to summarize: A person with a divine nature possesses zero ego, while a person with a Sattvic nature has extraordinarily little or thin ego. On the other hand, those with a rajasic nature possess an average or common ego, and those with a tamasic nature have a thick ego. Thus -

Divine person has: **Zero ego** (egoless)
Sattvic person has: extraordinarily little or **'thin' ego.**
Rajasic person has: **'common' (average) ego.**
Tamasic person has: **'thick' ego.**

Each of these qualities holds significance in various stages of life. They may fluctuate over time. However, our aim should be to attain divinity, which is accomplished by first embracing a Sattvic nature. This realization leads us towards liberation, the ultimate truth, or perfection.

Individuals with these three qualities Individuals possessing the three Gunas, or qualities, exhibit differing degrees of ego and therefore fall under the influence of Nature (Maya). However, those who transcend ego and exist in an egoless state are no longer subject to the control of Maya/Nature. When ego dissolves, one becomes attuned to divinity and connected directly with the Paramatma (Krishna).

Equilibrium of two tendencies (Swabhav)

Following the explanation of the three Gunas, let us delve into the concept of the two tendencies or inclinations.

The divine/virtuous qualities are conducive to liberation, whereas the demonic qualities make for bondage.
(Krishna - Gita Ch.16:5 – Daivi.....Pandava)

In this world there are two kinds of created beings. One is called the divine (virtuous) and the other demonic (evil). I have already explained to you at length the divine qualities. Now hear from Me of the demoniac.
(Krishna - Gita Ch.16:6 - dwau bhut......me shrunu.).

The first is the divinely inclined, characterized by virtuous qualities that pave the way for liberation and spiritual growth. Conversely, the second tendency is marked by demonic attributes, which often lead to bondage and hinder one's spiritual progress. Thus, the two tendencies (Swabhav) are: Sur and Asur (or Deva and Danava).

Sur or Deva Swabhav means: good, decent, divine, saintly, virtuous nature.

Asur or Danav Swabhav means: demonic, evil, tormenting nature.

Again, these tendencies, Sur and Asur or Deva and Danava, encapsulate contrasting aspects of human nature. Swabhav, the propensity known as Sur or Deva, represents virtuous, divine, saintly, and morally upright behavior. Conversely, the disposition termed Asur or Danav portrays malevolent, wicked, and tormenting characteristics.

A comprehension of this delicate balance between these two inclinations can provide valuable insights into societal dynamics. The equilibrium between contrasting tendencies is crucially maintained by Krishna, the Creator.

Furthermore, any imbalances that may arise are intentionally orchestrated and accompanied by corrective measures as part of a greater plan. By embracing the inherent nature of divine or Deva Swabhava and offering prayers or engaging in karma without attachment, one can approach a state of closeness to Krishna and attain a deeper understanding of the Absolute Truth.

CHAPTER 4
KRISHNA – AN AVATAR
(Yesterday)

As previously discussed, in our lives, Krishna is realized in two ways: As the Creator 'the Formless Eternal Existence' and as a 'Krishna-Avatar' in the human form. Formless Krishna is realized by advanced Yogis, Sanyasis and Rishis (scientists). Krishna in human form is realized by Bhaktas (devotees) or spiritually aspiring humans, aspirants. In either way of realizing Him, it is only the difference in our perception, not in His existence. *For ordinary humans it is difficult to perceive or visualize Him as the Formless. It is easier to perceive, realize or visualize Him by commons as an Avatar-Krishna in human form, and to relate with Him.*

Thus, we perceive Krishna in His two forms:

1. **Krishna as the formless "Supreme Creator"**

2. **Krishna as an "Avatar" in human or worldly form**

1. Krishna: as the formless "Supreme Creator"

Krishna is the Original Creator, synonymous with Absolute Truth, Eternal Existence, Absolute Purity, Perfection, Eternal Consciousness, Absolute Energy, Absolute Peace, Absolute Knowledge, Absolute Bliss, and All-these-in-One. He is, in fact, nameless. So, with or without the name "Krishna," He is the same Original Creator, Absolute Truth, Absolute Existence, Absolute Purity, Absolute Energy, Perfect, Absolute, Eternal.

Different religions or beliefs throughout the world perceive Him (the Creator) in different names and forms. However, no matter how we realize Him, He and only He is Perfect. Perfection cannot be multiple; it is whole, the only, the One. He is omniscient, omnipotent, and omnipresent, existing everywhere. There is no space in the universe where He is not present. He exists in every drop of water, each spark of fire, every particle of air, dust, sand, and all material. He is present in all atoms and sub-atomic particles of the material world, in void and cosmic space. Beyond imagination, He is limitless and bound by nothing, absolutely Free.

He pays meticulous attention to everything. He perceives every detail, whether it is visible or hidden, near or infinitely far. He listens attentively to everything, whether near or infinitely distant. He touches everything, whether it is close or infinitely distant. He detects all fragrances from all places. He has control over all actions taking place throughout the universe according to His divine plan. He influences all beings and their actions on Earth and beyond, according to His predestined plan. He is the creator of our solar system, the Milky Way galaxy, and countless other stars, planets, and galaxies. At every moment, He orchestrates their activities according to His predetermined plan. This has been happening since time immemorial and will continue for eternity.

Shri Krishna has an inherent ability to generate active positive energy for creation, sustenance, granting blessings, and providing benefits to His devotees. Those who truly comprehend Him, connect with Him emotionally, surrender to Him, have a deep understanding of Him, and exhibit devotion towards Him experience the flow of this energy. By submitting themselves to Lord Krishna, individuals and groups automatically open themselves up to this positive energy.

Additionally, He also possesses and manages negative energies, using them for the purpose of destruction and to punish evil forces and individuals with negative karma. In doing so, He maintains balance and harmony in the Universe. The Universe is an amalgamation of both positive and negative energies.

Lord Krishna's utilization and integration of these energies is beyond common comprehension and perception, which is why it is often referred to as the Illusive energy, the Latent energy, or the YogaMaya in Vedas. It should be noted that Mother Nature (Prakriti, Maya) is also a component of His YogaMaya.

2. Krishna as an "Avatar" in human or worldly form

As discussed earlier, an incarnation, or Avatar, is a profound and deliberate manifestation of the Divine by the Creator. It occurs during a unique and significant period. Throughout the billions of years since the creation of the

Shri Krishna: Yesterday, Today and Tomorrow

Pic. 12: Krishna's Positive Energy keeps flowing to his devotees

universe and the evolution of life on Earth, exceptional circumstances have arisen at various moments that necessitated extraordinary solutions beyond the capabilities of ordinary humans.

Avatars are the embodiment of these solutions, predestined by the Creator as part of His governance over the Universe.

The Creator takes on various forms and appears as Avatars in different ages and millennia to conduct essential actions (Leela) during critical periods and specific situations, ultimately benefiting humanity.

Part-1, Chapter 4: Krishna – An Avatar

~KRISHNA AVTAAR~

TO BENEFIT GOOD HUMANS AND SAINTLY PEOPLE

TO NEUTRALIZE ANNIHILATE EVILS

TO PROTECT RIGHTEOUSNESS, ORDERLINESS

TO DESTROY WICKEDNESS

Pic 13: Creator's Krishna-Avatar in Dwapar-Yuga

The various incarnations (Avatars) have distinct roles in fostering the development of civilization, humanity, and upholding societal order and discipline (Dharma). These incarnations safeguard righteous individuals and eradicate wicked individuals and their groups, thereby ensuring lawfulness, ethics, peace, progress, and a healthy environment on Earth.

The entirety of DNA and genetic codes, ranging from single-celled organisms, viruses, fungi, amoebas, and ultimately the complex human brain of both present and future generations, have all been formulated by Him. Births, accidents, and deaths are all under His control, meticulously planned and implemented.

A state of normalcy, smoothness, peace, and prosperity is also part of His plan. However, social disturbances, conflicts, anarchies, hierarchies among rulers, presidents, prime ministers, ministers, secretaries, military commanders, and all other officials at various levels, spanning from entire nations to metropolitan cities, small tribal villages, families, and individuals, exist to regulate them - all of which have been orchestrated by Him alone.

The strategic planning of diverse Avatars by Krishna indicates His foresight in anticipating exceptional or challenging circumstances throughout different periods of time. Krishna-Avatar emerged during a critical juncture in the Dwaper-yuga, approximately 5100 years ago, when the lives of countless virtuous individuals were in jeopardy. Further insights into the Krishna Avatar will be explored in subsequent sections.

The magnificent Krishna Avatar

Krishna, as a manifestation of the Supreme Creator Himself, assumes human form. His omniscient nature entails an awareness of all occurrences within the cosmos. He possesses an intimate comprehension of the innermost thoughts, life-cycles, and actions of each individual. Krishna's incarnation on Earth represents a beacon of benevolent love, wisdom, and positive energy, aligning with the promotion of virtue and morality, as well as the elimination of evil, malevolence.

Krishna's human embodiment as an Avatar serves a multitude of extraordinary purposes. These include supporting the well-being of righteous humans and saintly individuals, safeguarding principles of goodness and order, while simultaneously subduing or eradicating evil and those who perpetrate it, ultimately erasing wickedness from existence.

In His incarnation as Krishna, He was born from ordinary humans (approximately 5200 years ago), experienced the stages of childhood, youth, and adulthood. He entered matrimony, had children, and actively participated in societal affairs. Throughout His life, He performed extraordinary feats, bringing joy to His family, friends, society, and devoted followers, executing the various purposes for which He had descended as an avatar.

As an Avatar, throughout His life Krishna never worried about anything. Worries are worldly. Krishna is divine. Krishna as an Avatar wrote the script of His life, and of all the events and persons around Him. As an Avatar He had to function as an ordinary human, to be perceived by the commons as one of them, but extraordinary enough to remain always above all of them, remain a winner, victorious or successful at the end. Success means achieving whatever was thought or planned to be achieved.

Successful Krishna achieved whatever and whenever He wanted to achieve. Whenever He faced a problem, He had the solution. All was scripted by Himself. So, under all the circumstances He kept on smiling, even in the battlefield, where death danced everywhere, every moment. Everything has been scripted by Him, played, and executed by Him.

An Avatar is born with these capabilities. A bit about His life, activities and pastimes are given in the scriptures like the holy Bhagwat (Shrimad Bhagwat), Mahabharat, Vishnu Puran and many other scriptures. Krishna's philosophic message is summarized in the holy book Geeta or Gita (Shrimad Bhagwat-Geeta), a small book (of eighteen chapters and 700 verses), a part of the great scripture 'Mahabharat.'

When His objectives were accomplished and His divine play completed, He voluntarily relinquished His mortal form and merged back into His original divine essence. The vast expanse of literature contains countless stories about Him, comprising numerous volumes. However, we shall focus on specific aspects of His incarnation pertaining to safeguarding humanity and upholding righteousness, known as Dharma.

Krishna-consciousness

Krishna-consciousness refers to the state of awareness of the ultimate perfection that Krishna represents. In this understanding, everyone has a core that is divine, but it is often obscured by external materialistic influences known as impurity or Maya. These external influences trap the mind in pursuing worldly pleasures and create a cycle of experiencing dualities such as happiness and sadness, success, and failure.

Krishna, through His teachings in the Gita and His divine actions (Leela), imparts the wisdom that the evolution of a being occurs through performing righteous actions over multiple lifetimes. As these impurities are gradually dissolved, the brilliance of the inner core becomes more apparent. Eventually, when all impurities are eliminated, the ego vanishes and Maya is transcended, leading to a state of complete absorption in the blissful perfection and ultimate Truth within.

When we engage in contemplation or meditation on Krishna, we immediately feel a sense of connection with His captivating smile, beauty, and the enchanting melodies of His flute. This connection brings about a feeling of absolute protection, alleviating any worldly fears or concerns. We experience a profound sense of peace, fulfillment, and bliss as if we are surrounded by heavenly gardens filled with fragrant flowers, adorned with colorful butterflies, and buzzing bees, accompanied with friendly birds filling the air with their melodic chirping and songs.

In our surroundings, we are immersed in the beauty and abundance of various trees and plants, adorned with seasonal flowers, fruits, and vegetables, emanating delightful fragrances. The weather is equally pleasant, as we witness a harmonious coexistence between nature and a diverse range of harmless animals, while songbirds fill the air with their melodic and cheerful chirping. This atmosphere elicits feelings of love and peace among both humans and other living beings.

Furthermore, we strongly sense the presence of Krishna, offering protection and solace amidst the challenges and uncertainties of the world. His blessings manifest as love, joy, hope, vitality, and strength, permeating our beings. This empowers us with positive thoughts, energy, and emotions, enabling us to extend support and care to one another without selfish motives or expectations.

Inwardly, we experience a sense of purity, self-discipline, and liberation, fostering a state of genuineness and spiritual freedom.

We experience a profound spiritual connection and a sense of being immersed in ultimate truth. We envision ourselves as individuals who have achieved remarkable success, wealth, and fulfillment, and are readily available to help those in need.

Pic. 14: Krishna gives feeling of protection, fearlessness & divinity

We transcend mere physical pleasures and enter a state of divine consciousness, realizing our interconnectedness with the entire universe, from the tiniest subatomic particles to expansive galaxies and beyond. We feel a deep sense of universal love and unity and experience a profound sense of liberation and freedom. This transformative and blessed state is the result of being fully immersed in Krishna Consciousness.

Floating in Krishna's divine love

As we are surrendered to the boundless love of Krishna, and as Krishna takes hold of our thoughts and consciousness, we are enveloped in a sense of purity, positivity, vitality, confidence, and solace. A profound sense of peace, both within ourselves and in our surroundings, washes over us. Our breathing becomes deep, cool, and regulated, providing comfort and tranquility. Our heartbeats follow a steady rhythm, offering reassurance and calm. Our countenance becomes illuminated with self-assurance, radiating an aura of holiness and divinity.

Krishna's memory invokes a sense of divine atmosphere, where majestic Nature exudes safety, harmony, and love. Within ourselves, we perceive the eternal melodies of His flute as a silent resonance (Anahat Naad), enveloping our entire being in blissful vibrations. Life becomes an orchestration of gentle music and transcendental serenity, as an auspicious aura permeates both our external and internal realms.

We find ourselves gracefully floating amidst positive energy in the vastness of space, where our body, senses, thoughts, emotions, and every aspect of our existence bask in divine bliss.

Deeply recollecting Krishna, we immerse ourselves in Krishna-consciousness, experiencing heightened levels of positive energy and creative inspiration. Our consciousness naturally ascends to a meditative state, even as we diligently fulfill our daily responsibilities. We sense an eternal quality within ourselves. With Krishna infused in our thoughts, our hearts brim with an ocean of pure love, perceiving His presence in every being. We are moved to share and spread this love to all those we encounter. Recognizing Krishna as the purest and most exalted existence, we undergo internal transformations, reflecting His smile, beauty, and love in our outward demeanor, internal system, consciousness, and overall existence.

In a state of deep awareness and understanding of Krishna-consciousness, we exude unwavering self-assurance, evident through our bright and joyful expressions. We experience a profound sense of security and protection from the eternal essence, and consequently extend this sense of security and protection to those in our circles who hold affection, trust, and respect for us.

With Krishna's presence deeply felt within our innermost being, we feel an elevated sense of achievement and endless possibilities. Our minds overflow with numerous ingenious, achievable, and high-quality ideas, even if their realization may take centuries. No task seems insurmountable to us; we possess multiple solutions for every problem that arises. Problems dissolve effortlessly in the vast sea of opportunities and solutions we perceive.

In Krishna consciousness, we are liberated from all forms of fear. Fearlessness becomes our inherent nature, empowering us to fearlessly uphold and speak the truth. We readily offer assistance and support to friends, individuals seeking help, loved ones, and marginalized groups deprived of justice or basic dignities.

This courage prompts us to bring wrongdoers to justice, uphold fairness, instill discipline within families and communities, as well as establish 'rule of law' within our nation.

When we reflect upon Krishna, we experience an inner connection to Him and a sense of immortality. We perceive our physical body as a tool to fulfill the activities determined for us by Krishna, based on our past actions and in accordance with His divine plan. This understanding grants us a realization of the eternal nature of our soul and fosters detachment from material cravings and desires (Vasanas).

Consequently, our pursuit of transient pleasures associated with our perishable body diminishes. Rather, we prioritize the proper care of our body, recognizing it as a precious gift from Krishna, and endeavor to transcend identification with the physical self to become absorbed in Him and work in His service.

In this state of Krishna consciousness, we experience a profound connection to the entirety of the universe. We perceive ourselves as present within all galaxies, in every expanse of empty space, and in both known and unknown realms.

We sense our presence within every particle, atom, and subatomic particle, as if it were our very own abode. We feel a part of all space, ranging from the grand void (Shunya) to the infinite expanse (Anant). Detached from attachments to individuals or things, we experience our singular, universal omnipresence as a detached observer.

With a deep connection to Krishna, as our desires are eliminated, controlled, or managed, anger, anxiety, worries, and subsequent stresses diminish or become manageable. Consequently, our minds become calm, serene, and balanced, enabling unbiased thought processes, supporting wisdom, and facilitating accurate decision-making for a harmonious existence on personal, social, national, global, and universal levels.

By experiencing unity with Krishna, we attain a sense of abundance and fulfillment. We perceive ourselves as possessing a detached sense of stewardship over the universe, while still maintaining an observer's detachment. We attain a state of complete peace, tranquility, serenity, and bliss bestowed upon us by the ruler and creator of the Universe, all the while being aware of the concept of emptiness or nothingness (Shunya).

We recognize Krishna's presence within all living beings, our interconnectedness with the entire natural world. Moreover, we exude kindness, mercy, benevolence, forgiveness, love, and compassion when we engage with the practicalities of life in a Krishna-conscious mindset.

CHAPTER 5
KRISHNA: HIS CHARM, LOVE AND SMILE

(Yesterday)

Krishna, as an Avatar, possesses a captivating and charismatic personality characterized by virtues such as decency, fearlessness, confidence, and natural grace. His physical appearance exudes attractiveness with his curly black hair and modest attire, accompanied by an aura of compassion and a perpetual, friendly smile. These external qualities belie his immense strength and courage, which he demonstrated by triumphing over powerful adversaries such as elephants, horses, bulls, formidable wrestlers, and demons during his time.

Moreover, Krishna's love knows no bounds and his wit, intelligence, and sharp memory enable him to tackle numerous challenges and provide solace to his family, friends, and the wider community. This unique combination of beauty, charm, intellect, and bravery continues to captivate people and devotees from different corners of the world, simultaneously thwarting the efforts of jealous opponents, enemies, and hypocrites.

Furthermore, Krishna's magnetic persona attracts the attention and affection of women—regardless of their marital status—who end up harboring deep admiration, adoration, purity, and devotion towards him. In return, he blesses them with boundless love, peace, bliss, and the ultimate liberation, Moksha.

Krishna's love and divine bliss

The mere thought of Krishna recalls a sense of love, joy, transcendent bliss, and spiritual enlightenment. It signifies a connection with a sacred presence that supports and directs us throughout our lives.

Krishna embodies love in its purest essence, an inseparable companion of our existence. His name is synonymous with various expressions of love - sincere, untainted, universal, and timeless. He represents true love, cosmic love, and an everlasting love that transcends time. Devotees feel that Krishna is love, and love is Krishna.

Furthermore, Krishna personifies divine bliss, an inseparable quality that defines Him. He is synonymous with eternal bliss and the divine ecstasy that emanates from Him. It is impossible to conceive of Krishna without envisioning boundless love and divine bliss intertwining harmoniously. Devotees also realize that Krishna is divine bliss. Divine bliss is Krishna.

Krishna's smile

Krishna is eternally adorned with a smile, which serves as a constant companion to him. This smile symbolizes Radha, his beloved consort, and represents his untapped potential. It is impossible to envision Krishna without his smile or to separate him from Radha. Their union is inseparable.

In all situations, even amidst the intensity of battle, Krishna never fails to exhibit this divine, ever-present smile. It signifies his immense reservoirs of positive energy, unparalleled self-assurance, and infinite capabilities. Krishna's smile serves as a window into his boundless wisdom, everlasting joy, and eternal nature.

Can we maintain a constant state of happiness in our daily lives?

Regrettably, that is not possible. We encounter a multitude of situations throughout our existence that elicit a range of emotions and intellectual responses. These experiences include both positive and negative aspects, such as joys and sorrows, accolades and depreciations, acceptances and rejections, successes, and failures, along with a multitude of conflicting circumstances.

We try our best to cope with varying circumstances and situations. In this process our brain remains busy finding solutions with different options available. Mental calculations keep on going considering various permutations and combinations of methods of solutions. Though all this happens within a few seconds, it consumes lots of our energy.

Consequently, our facial expressions and body language continuously fluctuate, displaying an array of emotions and reactions. Our smile fluctuates during this process. Most of the time when we are not sure of the solution, our smile vanishes. However, there is an exception

Shri Krishna: Yesterday, Today and Tomorrow

Pic. 15: Krishna's Beauty, Brain, Bravery & Love rejoices all

To this human experience - Lord Krishna. The Avatar Krishna, with His eternal and unwavering love, possesses a perpetual smile on His face.

His infinite wisdom and omnipotent nature render Him unaffected by the dualities and upheavals of the material world, as these facets are His own creations.

The Truth, Soul, and Presence of Krishna

The essence of our existence lies in the realm of the Soul (Atma). Deep within our innermost self, Krishna (the Supreme-Soul, Paramatma) is present, representing eternal truth. Krishna embodies and encompasses the absolute truth within our inner sanctum. This divine truth and Krishna are inseparable entities. Krishna is the Truth. The Truth is Krishna. These can never be separated.

Often, our perception becomes clouded amidst the distractions and obligations of daily life, making it difficult to recognize Krishna's presence deep within us. However, when we find moments of calm and introspection, a glimpse of Krishna at our core is revealed. By directing our focus to this inner space, we gradually uncover a clearer image of Krishna. We can then experience the loving aura, magnetic pull, and complete unity with Krishna.

Ultimately, Krishna is not only within us but within the core of our very core. It is as straightforward as that. Thus, we attain a sense of union (Yoga) with Krishna at our deepest level, realizing our inherent oneness with Him.

In the practice of Yoga with Him, we attain a state of oneness with the ultimate truth and experience the abundant essence of the entire universe, as well as the emptiness of nothingness (Shunya). The profound realization of "Soham" meaning "I am That Cosmic Truth" gradually emerges within us, establishing itself and shining brightly.

We feel we are owner of the whole Cosmos, occupying whole of the infinite Cosmos, while still residing in the brightest grand-void (Shunya) in our Innermost-self united with Krishna. Through this realization, we gain a sense of freedom and perfection. We are completely content, abundant, and detached from any attachments, including our physical, mental, and egoistic aspects.

We sense ourselves as the custodian of the entire cosmos, encompassing the vast infinity, while also residing in the radiant emptiness within our innermost self, united with Krishna.

In this state of enlightenment, we gracefully abide in our eternal abode (Dham) of peace, bliss, divine luminosity, and boundless wisdom, which have always been and will eternally be our very own.

Most valuables: Only within

Krishna blesses us with opulence. If we want partial happiness, partial truth, partial wealth, partial satisfaction, we can find anywhere outside in the material world. But when we are looking for the most valuables - infinite bliss, absolute truth, infinite wealth, infinite love, infinite satisfaction, infinite energy, infinite peace, and complete fulfillment, where else can we find these except in our Innermost-self, at our core's Core (with Krishna).

In fact, these most valuables already reside within us all the time, yet due to our ignorance or obsession with worldly desires, we try to find these outside in the material world through various vague thoughts and activities, destined as per our previous Karma, and get these fulfilled temporarily and partially with partial satisfaction.

This predicament is the result of Maya (illusion). All must fall into its trap, unless we take shelter with full devotion to our own Innermost-self in Oneness with Krishna, the Creator.

Throughout moments in my personal history, I have experienced periods of profound contentment, satisfaction, and inner peace that were so immersive that I lost track of time. However, I found myself compelled to engage with the external material world, possibly because of my past actions. In these moments, I am reminded of the presence of a higher power and the concept of destiny.

Undoubtedly, destiny is shaped by our previous actions, and there is no escaping its influence. The only way forward is by persistently striving to seek refuge in devotion to our true inner selves through the practice of Yoga with

Krishna. This union can be achieved through surrendering oneself and having unwavering confidence in the Innermost-self. The mind tends to wander outwardly (extroversion), and it is our responsibility to continually redirect it back to our innermost self and allow it to dissolve and merge in harmony with Krishna, achieving a state of unity.

In practical life, it is crucial to strike a delicate equilibrium between extroversion and introversion. Extroversion is essential for socializing, sustenance, and survival, while introversion allows for introspection, analytical thinking, serenity, and overall spiritual fulfillment (Moksha). Different situations and circumstances call for a combination of both extroversion and introversion, as predetermined by our destined path.

In a family, it is often observed that when one spouse is more extroverted, the other tends to be more introverted. This dynamic helps maintain a sense of balance, harmony, and peace within the family unit while fulfilling societal expectations and responsibilities.

Ultimately, the practice of introversion paves the way towards perfection, inner peace, bliss, and liberation—referred to as Moksha or Krishna—the supreme goal of human existence.

Shunya (void) and Anant (infinity): In Krishna's Love

When fully immersed in the love of Krishna, we experience the profound essence of His love. This state allows us to be completely enveloped in the boundless ocean of eternal love, truth, bliss, compassion, vitality, energy, freedom, and devotion.

Shri Krishna: Yesterday, Today and Tomorrow

In this state, the concept of infinity (Anant) merges with the concept of absolute emptiness (Shunya), blurring the distinction between void and infinity. Our individual existence either fades away or transforms into a universal existence. In other words - our individual existence either

Pic 16: Krishna's shelter gives success to both (extrovert & introvert)

dissolves or undergoes a transformation, merging with the cosmic existence of Krishna.

Part-1, Chapter 5: Krishna – His Love, Charm and Smile

Indeed, this is the state of becoming one with Krishna, the Creator, wherein creation is absorbed by the Creator, leaving only the Creator. It is akin to a drop being absorbed by the vastness of the Ocean, leaving behind no dual (Dwait) existence of drop and Ocean, but only a singular (Adwait) existence of the Ocean (Krishna).

No number of words can precisely describe or capture this state. It can only be truly grasped through realization. This realization transcends mere words, rendering them inadequate and confusing. In this state each word is felt like a bondage. Fully liberated, we are immersed in the ocean of infinite peace and bliss. It represents the goal of every being, the pinnacle of realization.

CHAPTER 6

THE COSMIC MANIFESTATION OF KRISHNA AND HIS MAYA

(Yesterday)

This divine energy (Maya) of Mine, consisting of the three modes of material nature, is difficult to overcome. But those who have surrendered unto Me can easily cross beyond it.
(Krishna = Gita Ch.7:14 - daivi hyesha....taranti te.).

In the original creation event, Krishna initiated a colossal expansion of Himself, permeating and manifesting in countless forms throughout the vast expanse of the Cosmos. His omnipresence maintains its full potency at the core of His being, which served as the point of origin for the monumental event known as the Big Bang.

Through profound introspection, diving deep into our innermost selves and connecting with our core (the soul), we come to recognize that the very initiation of the Big Bang originated from within us.

Even after fourteen billion years since the inception of the Big Bang, Krishna continues to exist at our core, having birthed this magnificent Cosmos. At the dawn of creation, we too existed, albeit in a latent form, invisible and traversing various tangible and intangible processes such as physical, chemical, biological, genetic, and countless lives.

It was only recently, a few thousand years back, that we finally evolved into our current human form, meeting the conditions necessitated for the germination and blossoming of these latent "seeds." The abundance of these metaphoric 'seeds' is vast and extends across the vast expanse of the Cosmos, encompassing galaxies, stars, planets, black holes, and even the enigmatic realms of dark matter and empty space.

These seeds serve as the origin points for all forms of existence, including the beings that populate our world today. At the very essence of each being resides Krishna, the all-pervading force. Significant to note is that Krishna's presence extends to the core of every being, illuminating their innermost selves.

It is postulated that numerous planets potentially harbor life in diverse stages of development and various forms, all with Krishna as their core. Scientific exploration, employing its own methodologies and taking sufficient time, may unveil some of these phenomena. Multiple civilizations, including those on Earth, have risen and disappeared over time.

While science provides authentic outcomes, its scope is always confined within time and space limitations. Conversely, the Creator (Krishna) surpasses all limits, transcending time. The realization of Krishna and the subsequent attainment of fulfillment, tranquility, and divine ecstasy lie beyond the confines of science and nature.

The realization of our true identity leads to the dissolution of even the name 'Krishna'. Upon immersing ourselves in the Absolute Truth, we become conscious of our omnipresence from the void (Shunya) to infinity (Anant), without perceiving any distinction between the void and infinity, ultimately realizing our existence.

The phenomenon of Cosmic Time Waves can be visualized through the graph depicted in Figure 17.

It is hypothesized that within a cycle period 'f' of approximately 1000-2000 years, there is a prominent phase of peak Dharma strength (at the crest) and a significant phase of decline in Dharma (at the trough).

In between these two phases, there are minor fluctuations in Dharma (estimated to occur every 50-100 years) represented by ripple crests and troughs. Dharma means ethical duty or righteousness.

The Cosmic Time Waves

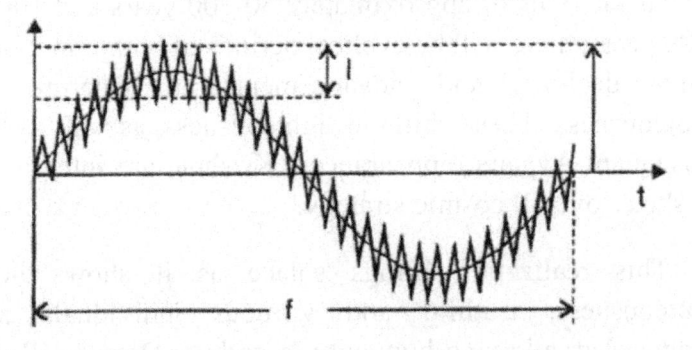

Pic. 17 - **Sinusoidal waves (f~1000-2000 years) with Ripple waves (l = Dharma fluctuation) every 50-100 years)**

When Dharma reaches its lowest point in the trough, Krishna, as the "Major Avatar," emerges to rejuvenate the upward flow of Dharma. Additionally, during the troughs of the ripple waves, Krishna may also manifest as minor or partial Avatars, based on the circumstances.

This recurring pattern has occurred in the past, is currently happening, and will continue in the future according to Krishna's mysterious yet deliberate plans and programs. (In the figure, 'l' denotes the minor drops-rises in the intensity of the Dharma during ripple periods.). We can summarize it as follows:

- Close to the bottommost moment of the trough, Krishna incarnates Himself as the 'Major Avatar' to boost up the upward flow of Dharma. (nearly 1000 to 2000 years).
- In between, during the ripple waves' trough time also, as needed, He comes as 'minor or partial-Avatars.' (nearly 50 to 100 years)

It suggests that Tomorrow (in the future) also, at regular intervals of approximately 50-100 years and 1000-2000 years, there will be cyclical periods of both minor and major declines and advancements in Dharma or righteousness. These shifts in righteousness, as well as the subsequent Avatars (appearances) Krishna, are integral to Krishna's overall cosmic strategy.

This realization brings solace as it shows how righteousness, truthful and virtuous individuals are safeguarded, allowing humanity to endure. Despite all the difficulties, in the end, it is only the Truth that prevails (Satyameva Jayate). It is how Shri Krishna fulfills His mission and promise of incarnating Himself to protest the saintly people and destroy miscreants whenever they grow.

Krishna and his Maya

I am never manifest to the egoist and unintelligent. For them I am covered by My eternal creative potency (yoga-maya); and so, the deluded world knows Me not, who am unborn and infallible. (Krishna: Gita Ch.7:25- Nahm prakashah....avyayam.).

Many, many births both you and I have passed. I can remember all of them, but you cannot. (Krishna: Gita Ch 4:5- bahuni me.... parantapah.)

Although I am unborn and My transcendental body never deteriorates, and although I am the Lord of all sentient beings, I still appear in every millennium, through my Yogamaya in My original transcendental form, by controlling the nature. (Krishna: Gita Ch 4:6- ajo api san.......mayaya.)

Krishna should be perceived as the embodiment of Truth, the ultimate Truth, the supreme Truth, the sole Truth (Eko Sat, Ek Onkar). He existed even before the phenomenon of the Big Bang. He not only initiated the Big Bang but also continues to exist as unwavering, unadulterated Truth despite it. He remains as the singular Truth, the ultimate truth, the enduring truth, and the absolute truth. The universes are repeatedly formed and dissolved at His will.

The physical and metaphysical (visible and invisible) universes have been created out of Him as His Maya (Prakriti or material energy). Whatever has been created is transient, is perishable (Nashvar), is pseudo-truth (Maya). Only He, the Creator (Krishna), is imperishable (Anashvar), undiminished (Akshar) and embodiment of Truth (Satya).

Our physical bodies, as well as all living organisms, natural elements, and even the smallest particles, are manifestations of the Creator's expansive cosmic energy, commonly referred to as 'mother nature' or Prakriti. These expansions are illusory existences we call Maya. The Creator dwells within each existence, empowering them,

Part-1, Chapter 6: The Cosmic Manifestation of Krishna ...

although His presence remains imperceptible. By delving deeply within oneself, one can come to perceive the divine, comprehend the truth, and attain ultimate enlightenment, ultimate Truth Krishna.

The exploration of one's inner self and spirituality, known as Adhyatma, commences with transcending physical and sensory experiences. It involves the rejection of false ego, misguided perceptions regarding the body, mind, intellect, and materialistic pleasures and sufferings. The internal journey towards attaining Eternal Existence involves seeking the presence of the Creator within the

Pic. 18 - Outside is Maya, inside is feeling of divinity, Krishna

Innermost-self, ultimately leading to immortality and the realization of Ultimate Truth Krishna, means Moksha, which stands as the pinnacle objective of human life.

Conversely, the external journey of individuals is influenced by Maya, constantly subjected to the constraints of time and space, engendering various dualities and cycles of birth and death. All things external, physical, material, tangible are essentially Maya (Mithya), an illusion.

As previously discussed, Prakriti, or nature, utilizes three Gunas (Sat, Raj, and Tam) as tools to exert control over all living beings.

However, divinity transcends these Gunas and consequently remains beyond Maya's influence. Divinity pertains to the state of egolessness in an individual, where Maya holds no sway. Divinity ensures that one exists within Krishna's inner realm.

Sat represents the state of minimal ego, with the least amount of control exerted by Maya.

Raj symbolizes the state of average ego, with a moderate level of control exerted by Maya.

Tam signifies the state of significant ego, with the highest level of control exerted by Maya.

Further,

Sat is associated with the color white, indicating sustenance & Vishnu.

Raj is associated with red, symbolizing creation and Brahma.

Tam is associated with the color black, embodying destruction Shiva.

The greater the presence of ego, the greater Maya's control. The state of egolessness, or no-ego, allows one to reside in divinity and seek refuge in Krishna, where Maya ceases to exist. Attaining egolessness involves acquiring knowledge of Truth, surrendering to Krishna, or consistently remembering Him.

When human consciousness is directed towards external worldly desires and materialistic pursuits, it becomes entangled in the transient nature of things, driven by lower tendencies known as Raj and Tam. Consequently, it becomes trapped in the repetitive cycle of birth and death.

Alternatively, when human consciousness is turned inward, it is drawn towards the eternal truth (Sat) and gradually detaches from material desires and impurities. This inward journey leads to a state of neutrality, moving beyond the complexities of the material world.

As one delves deeper into this state of Sat, the mind gradually dissolves, leaving behind only pure existence and divinity.

This transcendence represents liberation from the illusory nature of the material world known as Maya, where there is no longer a sense of ego or illusion. What remains is the realization of pure existence and divinity.

In this deep state of divinity, the consciousness merges with the Innermost-self, the ultimate reality and creative force known as Krishna. Through this merger, one is liberated from the cycle of birth and death, attaining Moksha (Salvation, Ultimate-bliss, Mukti, Nirvana, or Liberation).

Krishna and the concept of time

Krishna, the eternal cosmic energy, is the creator of time and nature, including space. He exists beyond the limitations of time and space and is often referred to as Maha-Vishnu, Maha-Kal or SadaaShiva.

The creation of space and time occurred simultaneously, and both coexist. Furthermore, they will cease to exist simultaneously and merge in Krishna at Pralay or Kalp-Ant.

Our understanding of time is interconnected with our solar system, which represents just a fraction of our vast galaxy, the Milky Way.

From the perspective of the eternal and infinite cosmic creator, Krishna, our solar system is comparable to a minuscule atomic system within the entire cosmos, known as Brahmand.

However, it is important to note that this solar system is also Krishna's own creation. Thus, while He possesses comprehensive knowledge about our solar system and our concept of time, He is not constrained by it.

Across various galaxies, there exist diverse configurations of suns, moons, and star systems, all of which are also Krishna's creations. Each of these galaxies and celestial bodies operates under different individual time systems.

As the omnipresent Creator, Krishna possesses complete awareness of these unique time systems as well. Moreover, He has devised His own scale for measuring time, known as celestial time.

Krishna possesses thorough knowledge of our past, present, and future. He meticulously designed and programmed these aspects for all of us. In fact, as I write these words, I can sense a source of inspiration from Him.

He is observing my act of writing and impelling, energizing, and directing me to continue. Every single moment, all our thoughts and deeds stem solely from His inspiration and divine plan.

As an Avatar, Krishna possesses the ability to recall all His past lives. He is aware of when and why He took on various incarnations and the purposes they served.

Part-1, Chapter 6: The Cosmic Manifestation of Krishna ...

Even in His Avatar form, He remains connected to His eternal divine form. However, as an Avatar, Krishna operates within certain limitations that He has imposed upon Himself, in alignment with the specific mission of each Avatar incarnation.

CHAPTER 7
SIGNIFICANCE OF KRISHNA AVATAR

(Yesterday)

If we take a moment to contemplate the impact of the absence of Krishna in Bharat, we can truly comprehend the significance of his presence. In the hearts and minds of Bharatiya people, particularly the Hindus, Krishna's absence would have resulted in a different religious landscape. Lord Rama would undoubtedly continue to serve as the quintessential figure for upholding family values, discipline, commitment, sacrifice, the ideal of Rama-Rajya, simplicity, ethics, morality, justice, bravery, citizen welfare, duty, and devotion.

However, the absence of Krishna's divine character in the history of Bharat would have undoubtedly deprived us of the epic Mahabharata.

This monumental tale provides a multitude of captivating elements, including thrills, adventures, bold advancements, stimulating entertainment, vibrant life, dynamism, vitality, profound wisdom from the Gita, enduring beauty, the epitome of all phases of life - childhood, youth, and adulthood, eternal love, captivating music and dance, ecstatic experiences, appreciation of nature, harmonious relationships with cows, animals, and the environment, the contrasting lifestyles of villages and cities, the complexities of life in palaces and humble huts, miraculous occurrences, the dynamics of relationships between the rich and the poor, profound friendships, divine connections between gods (Devatas) and devotees.

Further, one can confidently attest that the absence of Krishna from Bharat's historical narrative would have resulted in a considerable loss in our understanding of fundamental concepts such as Dharma-Adharma, Yoga, sacrifice, violence, non-violence, and the intricate nuances of ethical and moral dilemmas faced in everyday life by kings, aristocratic families, and common folk alike.

The significance of Krishna's presence extends far beyond these matters, encompassing a vast array of topics that have shaped our society.

Krishna has played a significant role in various aspects of Bharatiya society, both historically and presently, through individuals who embody Krishna-consciousness or Sanatan-energy. This is why Krishna holds immense importance in the realms of public life, private life, politics, religion, morality, spirituality, monarchy, professions, family, and the lives of ordinary individuals. Krishna is widely recognized as a Purna-Avatar - a perfect incarnation of the Creator.

Krishna transcends the narrations, histories, anecdotes, divine plays (Leela), teachings, and activities mentioned in scriptures like the Mahabharata, Shrimad-Bhagavatam, Bhagavad Gita, Vishnu Purana, and many others.

While Lord Rama holds a special place in the hearts of Hindus and humanity alike, Lord Krishna holds a pervasive influence on the practical lives of Hindus and humanity.

[Illustration: Krishna with halo labeled "PURNA AVATAR" surrounded by words: THRILL-ADVENTURE-DARING-ADVANCEMENT-ENTERTAINMENT-VIBRANT-EXCITE-DYNAMISM-DIPLOMACY-LIFE; VITALITY-GEETA KNOWLEDGE-KAMA PRINCIPLES-ETERNAL BEAUTY-ETERNAL MUSIC-ETERNAL DANCE-ECSTASY-ETERNAL LOVE. Below figure with outstretched arms: KRISHNA-CONSCIOUSNESS FOR PROTECTING INDIA, HUMANITY AND WORLD]

Pic. 19: Shri Krishna - A Purna Avatar

These forms represent different manifestations of the same Creator Krishna, who not only inspires the spiritual upliftment and liberation of Hindus and Bharat (India), but also extends to the entire world and humanity.

Characteristics of Krishna

Krishna personifies the ideal for all virtuous humans. He embodies perfection, truth, and the ultimate reality. Krishna symbolizes boundless potential, possibilities, inner peace, and profound bliss. His name is synonymous with love, a love that is pure, divine, and universal. It is an unconditional and liberating love, devoid of attachment.

In the Krishna-avatar, Krishna has exuded numerous exemplary qualities and virtues. His remarkable deeds and extraordinary abilities are widely known among Hindus and devotees worldwide. Krishna holds an esteemed position in

Vedic literature, Indian mythology, and folklore, commanding immense adoration and reverence.

Parents aspire to have a son embodying Krishna's virtues, while virtuous individuals long for a companion, relative, or mentor akin to Him. His captivating persona appeals to women who seek a charismatic husband, brother, or friend.

It is an insurmountable task to list all the thousands of qualities of the Avatar Shri Krishna. Still, based on my observation and limited knowledge, I have enumerated a few below. Countless instances or examples of these characteristics can be found in scriptural texts and Vedic literature, and related works.

- Childhood is full of fun, naughtiness, and miracles.
- Youth and adulthood full of charm, love, heroism, victories, and miracles
- Eternally handsome, charming, blissful, and smiling
- Flute artist and entertainer
- Kind, loving and compassionate gentleman
- Ideal friend, husband, and lover
- Defender of own people and dependents
- Progressive, practical and breaker of superstitions
- Maker of Strong and United Bharat
- The brave fighter and fearless leader
- Skilled diplomat and strategist
- Knower of past, present and future
- Effective motivator, preacher, and performer
- Protector of family values and relationships. Defender of Dharma (discipline, truth, justice, noble virtues, ethics, and morality)
- Punisher of wicked, evils and miscreants

- Savior of simple and saintly people
- Protector and liberator of devotees
- Embodiment of love, compassion, tenderness, and humanity
- Invincible and ever victorious
- Perfect Yogi and Guru
- Originator of the Gita wisdom
- An incarnation of the Creator Himself
- Respectful to elders, saints, and teachers
- A role model for people of all ages
- Cowherds-man, the King, and the Kingmaker
- A practical and perfect person
- Lover of animals, plants, and nature
- Multitalented, Multidimensional charismatic personality
- Divine protector of Bharat and Sanatan Dharma
- Champion of Vasudhaiva Kutumbakam
- Hundreds of other positive characteristics

There are countless examples to support these observations. In accordance with the narratives found in the Sanatani scriptures, Vedic texts, and other related literatures, the stories of Lord Krishna can be delineated showcasing various aspects of his divine persona. During his childhood, Lord Krishna engaged in activities brimming with mirth, playfulness, and extraordinary miracles. For instance, as a child, he effortlessly lifted the Govardhan mountain with his little finger, protecting the people of Vrindavan from a deluge caused by Indra's wrath. Another compelling example lies in his youthful and adult years, where Lord Krishna epitomized charm, love, heroism, and achieved victories through his extraordinary prowess.

Notably, his divine enchantment captivated the hearts of all who beheld him, demonstrating his eternal handsomeness, blissful persona, and ever-present smile. Additionally, Lord Krishna's mastery of the flute highlighted his exceptional musical talent, rendering him an unrivaled entertainer. Moreover, his gentle nature permeated each interaction, exemplified through his kindness, love, and unwavering compassion for every being. Such characteristics combined with his divine exploits and teachings have embedded Lord Krishna as an iconic figure and a paradigm of virtue and enlightenment.

Krishna serves as the archetype of an ideal friend, husband, and lover, embodying traits such as loyalty, compassion, and deep emotional connections. For instance, his unwavering friendship with Arjuna in the Mahabharata and his tender love for his wife, Rukmini, in Bhagavata Purana are illustrative of his profound interpersonal bonds. Secondly, Lord Krishna assumes the role of a defender not only for his own people but also for his dependents, actively safeguarding their interests and ensuring their well-being. His defense of the inhabitants of Vrindavan against various adversities, including the wrath of Indra and the atrocities of demons such as Kamsa and Aghasura, portrays his unwavering commitment to protecting and preserving the welfare of those under his care.

Furthermore, Lord Krishna emerges as a progressive and practical figure, adept at challenging and debunking prevailing superstitions and dogmas. Through his teachings, such as those found in the Bhagavad Gita, Krishna encourages individuals to seek a deeper understanding, question traditional beliefs, and engage in practical implementing of religious and spiritual principles.

Lord Krishna exhibits impeccable diplomatic and strategic acumen, as demonstrated through his negotiations and maneuverings during the Kurukshetra war in the Mahabharata. Krishna, through his profound understanding of political alliances and the psychology of his opponents, successfully brings together different factions, resolves conflicts, and ensures a favorable outcome for his devotees. The Vedic scriptures illustrate Lord Krishna's omniscience, with numerous instances where he accurately predicts the future and reveals hidden truths. For example, in the Bhagavad Gita, Krishna imparts profound philosophical teachings to Arjuna, foreseeing the consequences of his actions and providing guidance for his spiritual transformation.

Lord Krishna is a charismatic motivational speaker and performer, captivating audiences with his enchanting flute melodies and mesmerizing dance known as Raas-Lila. Through his divine charm and wisdom, he motivates individuals to recognize their true purpose in life and pursue self-realization. Krishna also serves as a guardian of familial values and relationships, prominently portrayed in stories such as his childhood exploits in Vrindavan. He safeguards and nourishes the bond between family members, emphasizing the importance of love, respect, and harmony within the household.

According to Shrimad Bhagwat (Skandh 1), among His 64 qualities, Shri Krishna has forty main qualities (Gunas):
(1) Truthfulness
(2) Cleanliness
(3) Intolerance of another's unhappiness
(4) The power to control anger

(5) Self-satisfaction
(6) Straightforwardness
(7) Steadiness of mind
(8) Control of the sense organs
(9) Responsibility
(10) Equality
(11) Tolerance
(12) Equanimity
(13) Faithfulness
(14) Knowledge
(15) Absence of sense enjoyment
(16) Leadership
(17) Graciousness, Politeness
(18) Influential
(19) The power to make everything possible
(20) The discharge of proper duty
(21) Complete independence
(22) Dexterity, Agility, Handiness, liveliness
(23) Fullness of all beauty
(24) Serenity, Calmness
(25) Kindheartedness
(26) Ingenuity
(27) Gentility
(28) Magnanimity, Nobility
(29) Determination
(30) Perfection in all knowledge
(31) Proper execution
(32) Possession of all objects of enjoyment
(33) Joyfulness
(34) Immovability, Stability
(35) Fidelity, Loyalty, Reliability
(36) Fame
(37) Worship, Reverence
(38) Pridelessness, No ego
(39) Being (as the Personality of Godhead)
(40) Eternity

A few examples of Lord Krishna's some of the qualities as per stories in the Bhagavatam and other Sanatani scriptures are:

Truthfulness: In the story of the Mahabharata, Lord Krishna never deviates from the truth. He always advises his devotees and friends to follow the path of truth. One example is when he functioned as a charioteer for Arjuna during the Kurukshetra War. He constantly reminded Arjuna to fight for truth and righteousness.

Cleanliness: In the Bhagavad Gita, Lord Krishna describes himself as being pure and free from all material contamination. He emphasizes the importance of internal and external cleanliness for spiritual growth and self-realization.

Intolerance of the devotee's unhappiness: Lord Krishna is known for his compassion and empathy towards all living beings. In the story of Draupadi's disrobing in the Mahabharata, Krishna immediately came to her rescue when she called out for help and ensured her dignity was restored. He cannot tolerate the unhappiness or injustice faced by his devotees. Another example: As Arjuna became filled with grief and anguish at the prospect of fighting his own relatives, Krishna counseled him and guided him towards understanding his duty. His intolerance of Arjuna's unhappiness motivated him to provide guidance and support.

The power to control anger: In the story of Lord Krishna and the demon Kamsa, Krishna showed great restraint and control in the face of Kamsa's attempts to kill him. Despite Kamsa's repeated attempts to kill him, without losing His temper he coolly waited for the opportunity to punish him.

Self-satisfaction: In the Bhagavad Gita, Lord Krishna displays self-satisfaction during the Kurukshetra war. He remains calm and composed, completely satisfied within Himself, as he guides Arjuna in his duty as a warrior and imparts spiritual knowledge.

Straightforwardness: Lord Krishna's straightforwardness is evident in the story of Draupadi's humiliation in the Mahabharata. When Draupadi seeks justice for herself, Lord Krishna openly criticizes the actions of the Kauravas and supports Draupadi's righteous cause.

Control of the sense organs: In the story of Lord Krishna's childhood pastimes, he is often portrayed as mischievous and playful. However, he always remains in control of his senses, as seen when he effortlessly defeats powerful demons like Putana and Bakasura.

Responsibility: In the Mahabharata, Krishna took on the responsibility of guiding Arjuna and ensuring the victory of righteousness in the Kurukshetra war. He functioned as Arjuna's charioteer and provided him with valuable guidance and wisdom throughout the battle.

Equality: In the Bhagavad Gita, Krishna preached the message of equality and emphasized that all living beings are equal in His eyes. He treated everyone with equal love and respect, regardless of their social status or background. One example is when Krishna accepted the invitation of Vidura, who was of a lower status, and dined at his house.

Tolerance: In the Bhagavad Gita, Krishna showed immense tolerance towards the insults and persecution he faced from the demons and evil forces. He patiently endured their actions while protecting and guiding His devotees.

Equanimity: In the Mahabharata, during the infamous game of dice, Krishna maintained his equanimity, remained calm, and composed. He advised the Pandavas to accept their defeat gracefully and not succumb to anger or despair. His equanimity and wisdom helped the Pandavas navigate through their trials and tribulations.

Courage and fearlessness: Fear is not at all associated with Krishna. Krishna's valor and fearlessness are exemplified in his role as the charioteer of Arjuna in the Mahabharata. He fearlessly faces numerous challenges and battles during the war, displaying his remarkable courage.

Wit and intelligence: Krishna's wit and intelligence are displayed through his playful interactions and pranks with his childhood friends, the cowherd boys.

Faithfulness: One example of Lord Krishna's faithfulness can be seen in his relationship with his devotees, especially the Gopis (cowherd girls) of Vrindavan. Despite being married to Queen Rukmini and having numerous other queens and consorts, Krishna always held a special place in his heart for the Gopis with whom he danced and did Raas-Lila, fulfilling their spiritual desires and providing them with unconditional love and protection.

Wisdom and knowledge: Lord Krishna is known for his supreme knowledge. In the Bhagavad Gita, Krishna imparts profound wisdom and knowledge to Arjuna, enlightening him on various philosophical and spiritual concepts. He guides Arjuna in understanding the Dharma, the nature of the soul, duty, and the path to liberation.

Absence of sense enjoyment: Although Lord Krishna is the supreme enjoyer and controller of all senses, he is not attached to material sense enjoyment. He demonstrated this quality during his pastimes in Vrindavan, where he would playfully steal butter and yogurt from the homes of the cowherd villagers. Despite having all opulence and power, Krishna displayed a childlike innocence and detachment from material possessions.

Leadership:
1. Motivation through the Gita: One of the most famous examples of Lord Krishna's leadership qualities is during the Kurukshetra war when Arjuna was overcome with doubt and moral dilemma about fighting his own family members. Lord Krishna, as his charioteer, provided him with guidance and enlightenment, reminding him of his duty as a warrior and urging him to fight for righteousness. Krishna's wisdom and strategic counsel displayed his ability to lead and guide others even in the most challenging situations.

2. Gopis' Love for Krishna: The stories of Lord Krishna's interactions with the Gopis (cowherd girls) in Vrindavan highlight his leadership qualities of compassion and inclusiveness. Krishna is shown as a charismatic leader who effortlessly attracts and captivates the hearts of the Gopis through his divine love.

His ability to create a sense of unity and devotion among his followers demonstrates his leadership prowess in creating a harmonious and supportive community.

3. Lifting of Govardhan Hill: The incident of Lord Krishna lifting Govardhan Hill on his little finger to protect the villagers of Vrindavan from the wrath of Indra is an example of his strength, bravery, and willingness to protect his followers as the responsible and effective leader.

Graciousness, Politeness: Lord Krishna treated everyone with respect and kindness, regardless of their social status. He patiently listened to and answered the questions and doubts of his devotees.

Influential: Lord Krishna's teachings and actions had a profound influence on the people of his time and continue to inspire millions of people today. He had the ability to convince and persuade others through his wisdom and charisma.

The power to make everything possible: Lord Krishna displayed his divine powers by performing various miracles, such as lifting the Govardhan hill to protect the residents of Vrindavan from torrential rains. He helped Arjuna achieve victory in the Kurukshetra war against all odds.

The discharge of proper duty: Lord Krishna emphasized the importance of fulfilling one's duty without attachment to the results. He set an example by playing distinct roles in his life, such as a prince, a friend, a guide, and a philosopher, all while fulfilling his divine mission.

Complete independence: Lord Krishna demonstrated complete independence by making his own decisions and taking actions for the greater good. He showed his complete independence when he inspired all villagers to worship Govardhan Parvat and not Indra. Then He single-handedly lifted the Govardhan hill to protect the people of Vrindavan from heavy rain and floods. He did not need anyone's help or support to perform this miraculous feat.

Handiness: Shri Krishna is always available at the calling of His true devotees. He immediately helped queen Draupadi when she prayed to Him at the time of her Cheer-Haran. In childhood He kept on helping His friend Gopas whenever some demons bothered them. When His childhood friend Sudama wanted His help during his tough times, He helped him with prosperity.

Dexterity: In the Bhagavad Gita, Arjuna witnesses Lord Krishna's remarkable dexterity on the battlefield of Kurukshetra. Despite having numerous arrows raining down upon him, Krishna skillfully maneuvered his chariot, dodging each arrow with grace and precision.

Agility: In the story of Krishna stealing butter (Makhan Chor), he exhibits his agility by effortlessly climbing walls, balancing on narrow ledges, and slipping through small openings to reach the pots of butter hidden by the Gopis.

Liveliness: In the Leelas of Lord Krishna as a child (Baal Leela), he would often engage in playful activities with his companions, such as stealing their clothes while they were bathing in the river, or engaging in mock battles with wooden sticks, displaying his lively and mischievous nature.

Fullness of all beauty: In the Shrimad Bhagavatam, it is described that Krishna possesses unparalleled beauty. In various scriptures and paintings, Krishna is described as having outstanding beauty. His charming smile, enchanting flute-playing, and beautiful dark complexion have attracted devotees for centuries. Krishna's beauty is not just physical but also reflects his divine qualities and all-encompassing love.

Krishna's serenity: In the Bhagavad Gita, Krishna displays immense serenity even during the battlefield of Kurukshetra. Despite the chaos and violence around him, Krishna remains composed and peaceful, guiding Arjuna with words of wisdom.

Krishna's calmness: In the story of Govardhan Hill, Krishna calmly lifts the entire hill on his little finger to protect the villagers of Vrindavan from the wrath of Lord Indra. His calmness in the face of adversity highlights his divine power and ability to remain composed in any situation.

Krishna's kindheartedness: Krishna is known for his compassion and kindhearted nature. In the story of Sudama, Krishna greets his childhood friend Sudama with utmost love and respect, despite Sudama's poverty. Krishna showers him with wealth and material abundance, displaying his benevolence towards his devotees.

Ingenuity: In the story of the Govardhan Hill lifting, Krishna uses his ingenuity to save the residents of Vrindavan from the wrath of Indra's thunderstorm. He cleverly lifts the entire Govardhan Hill on his little finger to provide shelter for the villagers from the torrents of rain.

Gentility: Krishna's interactions with the Gopis (cowherd girls) in Vrindavan highlight his gentility and charm. He engages in loving exchanges, dances with them, and plays sweet melodies on his flute to captivate their hearts.

Magnanimity: In the epic Mahabharata, Krishna displays magnanimity by becoming the charioteer of Arjuna, a lesser warrior, during the Kurukshetra War. Despite being the omnipotent Supreme Lord, Krishna willingly takes on a humble role to assist and guide his devotee.

Nobility: Lord Krishna's conduct in the Mahabharata depicts his nobility and adherence to righteousness. He serves as a witness and mediator during the Pandavas' and Kauravas disputes.

Humility: Krishna displays humility and modesty throughout his life. In the Bhagavad Gita, he refers to himself as a servant of his devotees, emphasizing the importance of humility in the path of spiritual growth.

Determination: One of the most famous incidents that highlights Lord Krishna's determination is the battle of Kurukshetra. Despite various attempts at peaceful resolutions, Lord Krishna stood firm in his determination to establish righteousness and fought alongside the Pandavas against the Kauravas.

Supreme knowledge and wisdom: Lord Krishna displayed immense knowledge and wisdom from an early age. He revealed profound spiritual truths and wisdom in the Bhagavad Gita, a conversation with Arjuna on the battlefield of Kurukshetra. He is enlightening him about various aspects of life, duty, and the nature of the self. His teachings are considered a comprehensive guide to living a righteous and fulfilled life.

Divine birth and appearance: Lord Krishna is famously known for his divine birth in the town of Mathura. He appeared as the eighth avatar of Lord Vishnu to rid the Earth of evil forces and establish righteousness. His birth was accompanied by divine signs and celestial celebrations. Lord Krishna's birth is marked by several miracles and divine events that establish him as a divine avatar. For example, he is born to Devaki and Vasudeva in prison in Mathura, and miraculously, all the guards fall asleep, and Vasudeva can carry baby Krishna to safety out of the prison.

Divine charm and beauty: Lord Krishna is described as having exquisite charm, beauty, and an enchanting smile. His attractive appearance captivated the hearts of all those who met him. He is described as having a delightful and captivating form. His beautiful blue complexion, charming smile, and sweet melodious voice are described in the scriptures. He attracts the hearts of devotees through His divine beauty.

Divine Love and Compassion: Lord Krishna's interactions with his devotees, such as the Gopis (cowherd girls) and his childhood friend Sudama, exemplify his divine love and compassion. In the celebrated story of the Raas-Lila, Krishna dances with the Gopis, showering them with his divine love and affection. Krishna displays unconditional love towards his devotees, showering them with affection and fulfilling their desires. Lord Krishna is revered for his boundless love and compassion towards all living beings. This is seen in his interactions with his devotees, like the Gopas, Gopis, Arjun, Sudama and all devotees.

Playful and Mischievous Nature: Krishna's childhood stories, especially those from the Bhagavata Purana, depict his playful and mischievous nature. Whether stealing butter (Makhan Chor) from the houses of the villagers or teasing his beloved Radha and the other Gopis.

Also playing pranks on His friends and villagers, and engaging in playful activities, are well-known and depicted in various scriptures. Lord Krishna's childhood is full of divine pastimes and Leelas (playful activities).

He performed various miracles and playful acts such as lifting Govardhan hill, and defeating demons like Putana, Bakasur, Trinavarta, Shakatasure and many others without any effort. He fearlessly fights them and eliminates them, protecting the people of Vrindavan.

Govardhan Lila: In the Govardhan Lila, Lord Krishna demonstrates his leadership skills by convincing the people of Vrindavan to stop worshipping Indra, the rain god, and instead focus on the Govardhan Hill. His persuasive and charismatic nature inspires the villagers to follow his guidance, leading to a miraculous incident where Lord Krishna lifts the entire Govardhan Hill on his little finger to shelter them from Indra's wrath.

Killing the demon Kamsa: Krishna killed His evil uncle, Kamsa, who had been tormenting His parents and the residents of Mathura with his tyranny.

Joyfulness: Lord Krishna is often depicted as a joyful and playful figure in the scriptures. He is known for his love of music, dance, and laughter. One example of his joyfulness is the famous story of Krishna stealing butter (Makhan Chor). In this story, young Krishna would sneak into the houses of the Gopis (cowherd girls) and steal their butter. Despite being caught in the act, Krishna would deny stealing, laugh, and delight in his mischievous actions, bringing joy to everyone around him.

Immovability: Lord Krishna is immovable in his determination and purpose. One example of his immovability is seen in the Bhagavad Gita, where Krishna advises Arjuna during the Kurukshetra war. Krishna encourages Arjuna to fulfill his duty as a warrior and not be swayed by emotions or attachments. He remains steadfast in his guidance, imparting wisdom and urging Arjuna to undertake his responsibilities.

Stability: Lord Krishna is the epitome of stability, both in his physical form and his divine nature. In the story of the Govardhan hill, Krishna lifts the Govardhan mountain on his finger to protect the people of Vrindavan from the rain lord Indra.

Fidelity: Lord Krishna showed unwavering loyalty and fidelity towards his devotees, such as his childhood friend Sudama. Despite Sudama's poverty, Krishna welcomed him with open arms and granted him immense wealth and prosperity.

Loyalty: Krishna remained loyal and devoted to his devotees and loved ones, such as his childhood friends, the cowherd boys. He protected them from evil forces and always stood by their side during times of need.

Reliability: Lord Krishna was known for his reliability and trustworthiness. He fulfilled his promises and never broke his word. For example, he promised to protect and guide Arjuna during the Kurukshetra war and stood by him till the end.

Fame: Krishna's fame and glory spread everywhere through the stories and teachings of the Mahabharata and Bhagavad Gita. People from all occupations revered and worshipped Lord Krishna for his divine qualities and unparalleled wisdom.

Worship: One of Krishna's most famous stories is the Govardhan Lila, where he lifted the entire Govardhan Hill on his little finger to protect the villagers from a torrential downpour sent by Lord Indra. This act of worshiping and protecting the villagers exemplifies Krishna's care and concern for his devotees.

Reverence: In the Bhagavad Gita, Lord Krishna is addressed as "Parameshwara" which means the Supreme Controller. This shows the reverence and respect that is accorded to Him as the ultimate authority and deity.

Pridelessness or No-ego: Krishna is often described as being completely free from any sense of pride or arrogance. In his childhood pastimes, Krishna would often perform various playful activities like stealing butter or curd from the houses of the village Gopis (cowherd girls). Despite his divine nature and extraordinary powers, Krishna would never exhibit any pride or ego.

The Bhagavad Gita is a prime example of how Krishna remains free from ego. In the epic conversation between Krishna and Arjuna, Krishna repeatedly stresses the importance of performing one's duties without attachment to the results, emphasizing the need to transcend ego and focus on selfless service.

Supreme Personality of Godhead: Lord Krishna is described as the Supreme Personality of Godhead in various Vedic literatures like the Bhagavad Gita and the Shrimad Bhagavatam. He is the ultimate source of all creation and the ultimate object of worship.

These are some of the examples highlighting only a few of the qualities of Lord Krishna as described in the scriptures and Vedic literatures. However, it is important to note that Lord Krishna's character is multifaceted and encompasses many other virtues and attributes.

The scriptures are full of countless examples of His virtues and a multitude of all these transcendental qualities that are inseparable from His being. He serves as the ultimate source of all virtues and aesthetic splendor. Those who are devoted to Him and possess wisdom are aware of His boundless qualities, capabilities, and feats.

The great scriptures such as Shrimad Bhagwat and Mahabharat provide highly elaborate accounts of Krishna's attributes, and such accounts serve as a means of motivation and inspiration for humanity. Among these texts, Krishna's enlightening discourse with his friend and devotee Arjuna on the battlefield of Kurukshetra specifically stands out. This discourse, commonly referred to as the Gita (Shrimad Bhagwat Geeta), epitomizes the essence of knowledge contained in the Vedas and Upanishads.

Krishna, Bharat, and human dignity

According to the Vedic scriptures and literature, the stories depict Krishna as the epitome of a dignified Bharat, representing qualities of freedom and fearlessness. Krishna is revered as Yogeshwar, the supreme lord of all yoga practices, including Gyan yoga, Raja yoga, Bhakti yoga, and Karma yoga. He embodies the principles of Anaasakt Nishkaam Karma Yoga, wherein actions are performed with wisdom and excellence, devoid of attachment, desire, and expectations of outcomes. Additionally, Krishna emphasizes the significance of surrendering oneself and all results of actions to the divine presence Krishna residing within the Innermost-self.

Pic. 20: Krishna's miraculous activities from childhood till old age

Krishna supports Bharat's Unity and Integrity

The Rig Veda. X. 191:
san gacchadhvam sam vadadhvam sam vo manamsi janatam,
deva bhagam yatha purve sanjanana upasate.
(Come together! Speak together! Let our minds be all of one accord as the gods of old sat together in harmony to worship.)
samano mantra: samiti: samani samanam mana: saha cittamesam,
samanam mantramabhi mantraye va: samanena vo havisa juhomi.
(Let our speech be one; united our voices! May our minds be in union with the thoughts of the Wise. Sharing a common purpose; we worship as one.)
samani va akuti: samana hrdayani vah, samanamastu vo mano yatha va: susahasati.
(Let our aim be one and single! Let our hearts be joined as one. United be our thoughts. At peace with all, may we be together in harmony.)

According to the narratives found in the Vedic scriptures and literature, there is a notable emphasis placed on the principles of individual autonomy, familial unity, communal welfare, and the prosperity of the nation Bharat. These ideals advocate for the cultivation of personal strength and resilience, enabling individuals to safeguard themselves, their families, their communities, and their nation. The figure portrayed in these stories symbolizes defiance against unfavorable circumstances, rejecting any form of surrender or false sense of superiority. Constructing aesthetically pleasing temples, structures, and cities alone is insufficient; one must also develop robust defense mechanisms for these establishments and communities.

This figure is not one to retreat in cowardice when faced with attacks on personal pride, dignity, or existence. While strategic retreat may be necessary under certain circumstances, which is never seen as a sign of weakness or defeat. Instead, the focus is on achieving success and victories through the implementation of effective strategies, and inspiring colleagues to do the same. This figure exemplifies a warrior mindset that embraces challenges, employing their power, skills, and wisdom to consistently emerge triumphant.

As per Vedic scriptures, Krishna exemplifies traits and principles that are revered in our society. He encourages individuals who identify with the Hindu or Sanatani faith and traditions to embody qualities such as bravery, intellect, industriousness, success, and triumph. He sets an example by living as an honorable human being and as a guardian for his devotees, dependents, relatives, and friends. He inspires and motivates all members of his community and followers to adopt a similar approach.

Furthermore, he advocates for the protection and preservation of the righteous path (Dharma) and the sacred Bharat-Varsha, which symbolizes the homeland. Krishna also serves as an embodiment of the ideals of a skilled diplomat, warrior, king, peacemaker, problem-solver, protector, kingmaker, upholder of Dharma, friend, lover, entertainer, artist, mystic, sage, yogi, spiritual guide, motivator, prosperous individual, wise individual with foresight, family-oriented individual, divine incarnation (Avatar), and liberator (Mukti-Data) - all encompassed within a single entity.

After the disappearance of Krishna

According to the sacred texts of Sanatana scriptures there was a shift in societal dynamics following the departure of Lord Krishna. During the time of Lord Krishna's presence on Earth, approximately 5,100 years ago, a state of ideal harmony and righteousness prevailed. Following the decisive defeat of evil forces in the Mahabharat war, a period of prosperity, abundance, and tranquility ensued. Nature thrived, encompassing fertile crops, flourishing forests, and rejuvenated rivers and ponds.

The ecosystem, comprised of diverse bird and animal species, experienced growth, and vitality. Society embraced a culture of affluence and benevolence, adhering to Dharma, to the principles of righteous conduct and witnessing boundless abundance in all facets of life. The manifestation of Krishna's divinity permeated every aspect of life, fostering positive energies, social harmony, peace and happiness within the collective consciousness, and overall well-being. The Sattvic Guna, representative of purity and harmony, prevailed over the Rajasic and Tamasic Gunas, symbolizing passion and ignorance, respectively. The cosmic rhythm of time reached its zenith during this period.

However, after Lord Krishna's departure, around 5,000 years ago, the influence of Sattvic Guna gradually waned, marking the advent of the Kaliyuga characterized by spiritual darkness and moral decline. Initially, a delicate balance existed among the three Gunas. But, over time, the influence of Rajasic and Tamasic Gunas intensified, and the related negativity started spreading in society. This way, there has been gradual decline of Dharma, which is continuing and will continue for many millenniums.

This decline of Dharma has resulted in the proliferation of negative thoughts among individuals, leading to corresponding negative actions and an increase in sinful behavior within society. In this context, individuals with deceitful, fraudulent, cruel, violent, aggressive, and immoral tendencies gain prominence and wield power within society. This unfortunate situation leaves vulnerable groups, such as virtuous individuals, women, seniors, children, and the weaker members of society, feeling unsafe and subject to various forms of torment.

Furthermore, the media displays tendencies towards greed, partiality, and corruption, disseminating inaccurate information, half-truths, and biased news that favors those who are corrupt in positions of power and influence. The corruption of judges and the judicial system further exacerbates the situation. Although it is ultimately believed that the truth prevails (Satyameva Jayate), there is a delay in the delivery of justice, and the reliability and transparency of judgments come into question. In many cases, nature itself takes its course in delivering judgments and punishing offenders.

This situation is expected to continue until the end of Kaliyuga, which is considered the period of lowest moral values and the trough of the cosmic wave of time. In the Sanatani scriptures, it is foretold that at the culmination of Kaliyuga, a highly significant period spanning approximately 432,000 years, Lord Krishna will once again manifest Himself as the Kalki Avatar.

The purpose of this incarnation will be to eradicate malevolent ideologies, individuals, and wrongdoings, while safeguarding and nurturing virtuous individuals and reinstating righteous principles. This divine intervention will mark the end of Kaliyuga and herald the dawn of Sat Yuga, an era characterized by righteousness, moral integrity, and enlightenment.

However, prior to the advent of the Kalki Avatar, numerous partial manifestations or mini-Avatars of Lord Krishna will arise periodically in times of profound moral decline. These partial-Avatars will emerge from the ranks of Krishna-conscious devotees, the morally upright and devout local populace, and their leaders, tasked with combating malevolence within their respective societies and nations across the globe. Thus, even though Lord Krishna has physically withdrawn, His profound influence will continue to manifest through the agency of these Partial-Avatars until His ultimate reemergence as the Kalki Avatar during the waning stages of Kaliyuga.

Recent one thousand years in Bharat

The past millennium has witnessed a devastating era for the Bharat Nation. The inherent principles of righteousness and moral conduct, known as Dharma, experienced a significant decline, plunging society into a state of disarray. Instances of violent invasions, wars, thefts, pillaging, ravages, human rights violations, degradation, enslavement, shames, and moral degradation occurred, seemingly predestined. However, in recent centuries, there has been a resurgence of Krishna-consciousness or Sanatani-energy, gradually gaining momentum and instilling a renewed sense of hope for the safety and welfare of families, communities, and the nation. This evolving trajectory, following the trough of the cosmic cycle, serves as an encouraging indication of the upward shift in Bharat's destiny, as it gradually moves towards a brighter future.

PART 2
(TODAY)

***

KRISHNA FOR BHARAT (INDIA) AND THE WORLD "TODAY"

***

TODAY: Represents the current few centuries.

Chapter 8 to 14: For the Bharat

Chapter 15:   For the world

Krishna: I am the universal Self in the hearts of all beings. I am the beginning, the middle and the end of all beings.

(Krishna: Gita Ch.10:20 - ahamatma....ev cha).

CHAPTER 8
KRISHNA's PARTIAL AVATAR FOR SANATAN
(Today)

A few words about TODAY

The ancient Vedic scriptures and literatures contain stories that revolve around the concepts of Krishna's role in society and his impact on the intellectual and spiritual development of individuals. These narratives provide insights into the deep philosophical teachings and values that are embedded within these texts, also known as Vedic or Sanatani wisdom. Sanatan Dharma has been the eternal Dharma since the beginning of time.

Considering these values, efforts have been made to find solutions to some previous and current crucial issues in the Bharat (India) and the World. These have been elaborated in chapters 8 to 14 specifically focusing on the influence of Krishna in the context of Bharat, while chapter 15 broadens the scope to include his impact on the entire world.

One of the central ideas conveyed through these solutions is the recognition of Krishna as the Universal Self, who resides within the hearts of all living beings. This signifies his all-encompassing nature and highlights his presence as the ultimate divine entity. Krishna is portrayed as not just a beginning or an end, but as the entirety of existence itself.

The Vedic scriptures and literatures offer profound insights regarding the interplay of past, present, and future. They illuminate the profound truth that our present circumstances are heavily influenced by our past actions, and that our future outcomes are shaped by the combination of both past and present actions. This understanding closely aligns with the universal law of cause and effect, commonly referred to as Karma.

From the annals of history, we can glean invaluable lessons, extrapolating wisdom from the triumphs and tribulations of previous generations to inform our current choices. By consciously integrating the knowledge acquired from the past with our present decisions, we possess the power to architect a more auspicious future.

Through it all, there exists a steadfast presence Krishna - the divine Creator who governs time itself. Krishna permeates the fabric of all temporal dimensions, His eternal existence transcending the boundaries delineating past, present, and future. Immutable and timeless, Krishna's laws, guidance, affection, vitality, and ethical standards, encapsulated within Sanatana Dharma, permeate all epochs, omnipresent and universal.

Part-2, Chapter 8: Krishna's Partial Avatar for Sanatan

Sanatana Dharma, the timeless and universal way of life, upholds these principles established by Krishna. It is a guiding force that permeates all aspects of existence, transcending limitations of time and space.

The teachings and wisdom found in the Vedic scriptures or Sanatan Dharm transcend any limitations or constraints associated with specific cultural or religious practices. They encompass diverse paths and ways of righteous living that foster human growth, harmony, and dignity.

Whatever Krishna said or did all yesterdays, is relevant today and shall remain relevant all tomorrows too, till Kalp-Ant (the end of this creation). These timeless teachings remain relevant not only for Bharat, but for the entire world, embodying the concept of Vasudhaiva Kutumbakam – the belief that the whole earth is one family.

In Part 1 (Yesterday), we explored the creation, foundational principles, and expansion of the universe, as well as the significance of the Krishna Avatar.

In Part 2 (Today), we will delve into the contemporary (a few hundred years) issues that connect Krishna's perspective, philosophy, and mission with Sanatani Bharat and the broader global context.

In accordance with the wisdom found in the Vedic scriptures and literatures, it is important to acknowledge and contemplate upon the significance of every single day, the present moment of our existence. In today's world, we are witnesses to the remarkable advancements achieved by the human intellect. Throughout these present moments, we engage in various actions, create novel inventions, and preserve them within the faculties of our memory.

Pic 21: Sanatan Dharma is the Dharma since ever, forever

engage in various actions, create novel inventions, and preserve them within the faculties of our memory.

Simultaneously, the intricate workings of our physical and mental selves undergo continuous regeneration, with cells and neurons being created and replaced each moment. These activities are guided by an omnipresent and imperceptible cosmic software, which originates from the Creator (Krishna) and permeates both - the universe at large and our individual minds. The entire fabric of existence, consisting of particles, bodies, stars, planets, and galaxies, adheres to meticulously designed plans and programs orchestrated by this divine and infinite intelligence Krishna.

The Vedic (Sanatani) scriptures and literatures contain profound wisdom regarding the nature of stability and the omnipresence of Krishna. According to these teachings, everything in the universe is impermanent and subject to change, except for Krishna who remains eternally stable and unaffected by these changes. He is the Ultimate Programmer, the Absolute Existence, and the Ultimate Truth.

Krishna's stability is not limited to a specific location or time but is omnipresent. He pervades every particle, every being, and every aspect of existence (like space in the universe and water in the ocean). His presence is unwavering and undisturbed, regardless of the actions and endeavors of individuals. Krishna's presence is that of a compassionate observer, inspiring and energizing all activities, innovations, inventions, and developments. He acts as a catalyst, witnessing everything without directly intervening.

While certain events and activities may seem novel or unfamiliar to humans, they are not new for Krishna. As the Creator, He has been responsible for all happenings since eternity. He is the source of inspiration, motivation, and knowledge for all beings. Thus, the scriptures emphasize the stability of Krishna and the transformative power of His presence, which guides and influences all facets of life.

According to the wisdom presented in the Vedic scriptures, Krishna has specific intentions for Bharat (India) and the world at large. Precisely comprehending these intentions remains elusive, as we can only speculate based on the knowledge imprinted in our intellect and the principles of Nature elucidated by Krishna. Additionally, we can glean insights from His words and actions, which serve as exemplary models for our comprehension and emulation.

Considering our limited understanding and perspectives, we strive to decipher Krishna's message or plan for Bharat and the world with the best of our abilities. While our interpretations may not be entirely precise or comprehensive, we discern glimpses of illumination. Hence, it is worthwhile to pursue and follow these instances of enlightening guidance, as they lead us closer to the ultimate source of creation - Krishna Himself.

Bharat Varsha also referred as India

In accordance with the wisdom elucidated in the Vedic literatures, it is worth noting that the original name of the country we now refer to as India is Bharat Varsha, also commonly known as Bharat. These names have been prominently featured in ancient sculptures and literary works of Bharat.

It is widely believed that as invaders (like Arabs), advanced into Bharat from the western front, their first significant obstacle was the river Indus (Sindhu). Consequently, they named this river as Hindu, which was a derivative of Sindhu. Similarly, they referred to the land beyond Sindhu as Hindustan and its inhabitants as Hindus.

The ancient Greeks, on the other hand, designated the people dwelling across the river Indus as "Indoi," meaning "The people living across the river Indus (Sindh)." Meanwhile, when the British and other Europeans colonized Bharat, they found it convenient to label the land as "India." This is the process through which Bharat came to be called India.

It is important to note, however, that in the ancient literature of Bharat dating back thousands of years, the term Hindu was not used in reference to the local inhabitants of Bharat. They were known as Sanatani, Bharatiya, Arya (a noble or a person of high moral character) or Vedic (Vaidik).

Krishna and Bharat

Krishna, as the Supreme Being, transcends the boundaries of the entire cosmos and the creation itself. In the context of Bharat, Krishna assumes various manifestations as the Divine, including Rama, Krishna, Venkatesh, Varadaraja, Vishnu, Brahma, Shiva, Aadi-Shakti, Adhya-Shakti, Jagadamba, and numerous other forms with distinct names (together with their respective consorts or latent energies). These different manifestations represent the same formless, omnipresent, omniscient, and omnipotent Truth (Krishna).

The historical and cultural significance of Bharat as the holy land where Lord Krishna graced its inhabitants with his divine presence is a subject of immense intellectual curiosity and exploration. The transcendental teachings of Lord Krishna, as found in Vedic literature, serve as a guiding light for the intellectual pursuits of scholars and philosophers worldwide.

Not only did Lord Krishna manifest his profound wisdom and knowledge through his words and actions, but he also played a pivotal role in shaping the societal fabric of Bharat. His ethical teachings and principles of righteous living continue to influence and inspire individuals from all occupations. Krishna's emphasis on Dharma (righteousness), love, compassion, and selfless service has had a profound impact on the social consciousness of Bharat, fostering a harmonious and virtuous society.

The sacred texts such as the Bhagavad Gita, Mahabharata, and Shrimad Bhagavatam stand as brilliant testimonials to the intellectual and literary prowess of ancient Bharat. These timeless works not only capture the essence of Krishna's divine teachings but also offer profound insights into the complexities of human existence, the nature of reality, and the ultimate purpose of life.

Bharat holds a unique place of distinction in humanity's philosophic, intellectual, and societal realm, revered as the sacred ground where Lord Krishna, an esteemed Avatar of great significance expertly displayed his extraordinary exploits (Leela) and commendable achievements.

The profound influence of Lord Krishna resonates throughout every facet of life and society, serving as an immeasurable wellspring of inspiration for adherents of the Sanatani/Vedic/Hindu traditions and the citizens of Bharat. This indelible connection between Krishna and Bharat is so profound that Krishna represents the essence of Bharat, and Bharat represents the essence of Krishna.

Though the Supreme Creator is nameless and formless, it is observed that various names and forms are suited to individuals from diverse backgrounds, education levels, beliefs, and societal contexts. They all ultimately elevate to the same Ultimate Truth. This diversity, often referred to as

Part-2, Chapter 8: Krishna's Partial Avatar for Sanatan

"unity in diversity," is at the core of peaceful coexistence, happiness, and prosperity in our society.

Pic 22: Creator Krishna - the Soul of Universe, Avatar Krishna - the Soul of Bharat

In this publication, as previously mentioned, I have chosen to refer to the Creator and the Avatar as Krishna based on my convictions, which are shared by many other Krishna-conscious Sanatanis. However, it is important to respect the diverse perspectives and beliefs of others, allowing them the freedom to use their preferred names without imposing any specific one.

This practice emphasizes the beauty of the Vedic philosophy, faith, or religion, and serves as the foundation for a flourishing faith that embraces the concept of

Vasudhaiva Kutumbakam, recognizing the interconnectedness of humanity as one global family.

The New Krishna partial-Avatar

Krishna Himself has revealed His secret through these three Shlokas in the Gita:

Krishna: Though I am unborn and of imperishable nature, and though I am the Lord of all beings, yet, ruling over My own Nature, I am born by My own Maya.
(Krishna: Gita Ch. 4: 6 - ajo api san.....mayaya.).
Krishna: Whenever there is a decline of righteousness (Dharma), and expansion of unrighteousness (Adharma), then I manifest Myself. *(Krishna: Gita Ch. 4: 7- yada yada hi..........srijomyaham.).*
Krishna: For the protection of the pious ones, for the destruction of the wicked ones, and for the establishment of righteousness, I am born (arise) at every age.
(Krishna: Gita Ch. 4: 8 – paritranay sadhunam....yuge yuge.).

From these, it is certain that Krishna wants Dharma (virtuousness) to be maintained and virtuous people be protected in all the ages. And whenever Adharma (wickedness or sins) increases beyond a certain limit, He incarnates Himself, reforms or destroys the wicked, evils, miscreants, criminals; and protects virtuous people, communities, and establishes righteousness.

Whenever the practice of Dharma declined and practice of Adharma increased, there were major troubles in Bharat, resulting in disintegration of Bharat Varsha, the Great Bharat nation. Hunger for power & prosperity, jealousy, competition, insults, revenge, complacency, deceit, discrimination, rebellion, huge false ego etc. were reasons for the downfall of many kingdoms. At times, greed, and unjust enjoyment of most resources in Bharat by certain powerful bullying sections of the society and discrimination against some weaker sections in the society, atrocities against them and their exploitation was Adharma, which destroyed the social fabric and unity in Bharat. Foreign invaders, attackers and robbers took advantage of this situation.

Circumstances leading to the Krishna Avatar

Throughout history, India (Bharat Varsha) has faced numerous challenges when the principles of righteousness (Dharma) were disregarded, giving rise to an increase in immoral conduct (Adharma). These detrimental circumstances led to the disintegration of the once-great nation of Bharat. Power-hunger, envy, competition, insults, vengeance, complacency, deceit, discrimination, rebellion, and inflated egos were among the reasons that led to the downfall of various kingdoms.

Additionally, the unfair distribution and exploitation of resources by dominant groups, coupled with the oppression and discrimination faced by weaker sections of society, constituted acts of Adharma that disrupted social harmony and unity. This volatile situation also provided an opportunity for miscreants and foreign robbers' invasions.

The cunning manipulation and collaboration with local traitors allowed foreign invaders to successfully conquer multiple kingdoms and regions, establishing their rule over Bharat. Their strategic efforts also involved establishing networks for religious conversion and increasing their numbers in Bharat, leading to a surge in atrocious acts, indecencies, and plundering throughout the land. Consequently, the practice of righteous conduct (Dharma) waned, while unethical behavior (Adharma) flourished.

This parallel continues to manifest, both overtly and covertly, but no action escapes the notice of the omniscient Krishna. Thus, the stage was set for the Avatar of Krishna. Now, what are Dharma and Adharma?

Dharma and Adharma

Generally, the basics of Dharma in Bharatiya (Vedic) philosophy include observing Yama and Niyama.

Yamas are five: Ahimsa (non-violence), Satya (Truthfulness), Asteya (no stealing), Brahmcharya (celibacy, ever-remembering the Creator) and Aparigrah (non-possessiveness, no-over-possession, no greed).

Niyamas are also five: Shaucha (purity), Santosha (contentment), Tapas (self-discipline), Svadhyaya (self-study, inner-search, exploration), Ishvara Pranidhana (surrendering, submission to God).

The opposite to these is called Adharma. Adharma manifests when the above virtuous values are disregarded or violated.

The individuals who adhere to the principles of righteousness in Bharat, or India, are commonly referred to as Bhadra, Sura, Dharmik, Deva, Arya, virtuous, Sabhya, Sadhu, or decent people. Conversely, those who stray from these principles are known as Adharmi, Asura, Daanav, Rakshasa, Asabhya, evil individuals, and so on.

We are all familiar with the events that have unfolded in Bharat over the past millennium, as well as the ongoing occurrences throughout recent centuries and decades. The sanctity of Dharma, or Sanatana, has been relentlessly attacked. Invaders and looters of Bharat have mercilessly slaughtered virtuous individuals and humanity itself.

They have employed unethical methods of cruelty, fear, greed, incentives, persuasion, and deception to either eradicate or convert the tolerant, welcoming, decent, and magnanimous Indigenous Bharatiyas (Hindus, including tribals) to their own religions, which are based on cruelty, terror, greed, and deceit. This has dealt a heavy blow to Dharma and the virtuous individuals who follow Sanatana (Dharma, Hinduism).

This situation significantly impacted the principles and ethical values advocated in the Vedic scriptures and literatures, leading to a decline in the practice of Sanatana Dharma. Consequently, various incarnations of Krishna emerged in different periods and decades as partial avatars to address this issue.

Presently, the manifestation of this partial avatar is prevalent in Bharat (India) and worldwide through Krishna-consciousness or Sanatan-energy.

Krishna observed the proliferation of Adharma, or irreligion, in Bharat over the course of the past few centuries. He became aware of the sufferings endured by the people and identified certain truths:

- The allure of wealth and prosperity in Bharat attracted numerous wicked and envious invaders who conducted repeated invasions and looting from the western and northwestern regions.
- Millions of innocent men, women, and children were brutally killed by these demonic plunderers, some of whom even ascended to positions of power.

- The dignity of millions of Bharatiya women was violated through acts of rape, abduction, forced marriages, enslavement, and trafficking. They were also coerced into nudity and forced to dance before audiences of thousands.
- These cruel invaders consistently sought to undermine the dignity, self-worth, and self-respect of native Bharatiya people, along with their families. They further humiliated Hindu girls and women by defiling their chastity in front of their fathers, brothers, husbands, sons, relatives, and the public. This lamentable practice endured for many centuries.
- The oppression and eradication of countless Indigenous Sanatani saints, scholars, Rishis, Pundits, patriots, soldiers, Dalits, tribals, labors, businesspeople, farmers, farm-laborers, and common people.
- The destruction and burning of invaluable assets: Universities, Ashrams, temples, ancient artifacts, Vedic literature, scriptures, and libraries.
- The decimation of local cottage industries, trades, businesses, and social structures.
- The obliteration of hundreds of thousands of schools, education centers, universities, Ashrams, and Gurukuls.
- The devastation of ancient monuments, sculptures, temples, and places of worship, with many being converted into places of prayer and gathering for their foreign faiths.
- The forcible conversion of millions of native Bharatiya/Hindus to their own Asuri cruel faith, using unethical means.

- Oppressive taxation (Jizya/Jajiya) on Indigenous Hindus for practicing their religion (Sanatan Dharma) in their own land.
- Invasion by Europeans as rapacious businesspeople, exploiting and enslaving the people of Bharat through deceitful business practices and atrocities.
- Engaging in the forced migration of Indigenous Hindus to various countries as involuntary laborers.
- Engaging in deliberate schemes to systematically undermine and distort Hindu native and Vedic culture and history, sowing seeds of cultural discord among the local population of Bharat through the spreading of deceitful information.
- Employing a strategy of division and manipulation to cultivate animosity and division within Bharatiya/Hindu communities.
- Using deceptive business practices to acquire vast lands and territories within Bharat, thereby effectively enslaving the entire nation.
- Dividing Bharat into two separate nations, resulting in the loss of countless innocent lives, widespread sexual violence, abduction, and human trafficking. These actions have severely damaged the social and cultural fabric of the region, leading to significant moral, economic, and social repercussions.
- This pattern of spreading injustice extends to other parts of the world, as well.

In accordance with the Vedic wisdom, it is observed that Krishna, being aware of various instances of unethical behavior, assumed numerous forms (Avatars) to disseminate the concept of Krishna-consciousness or Sanatan-energy amongst millions of individuals worldwide.

It is worth noting that this Krishna-consciousness, which is also inherent in the Bharatiya culture or Sanatan-energy, intertwines the identities of Krishna (Vishnu, Ram, Shiva, Shakti) and Bharat as one.

This Krishna-consciousness or Sanatan-energy has rapidly proliferated, giving rise to numerous non-profit and non-government organizations. These organizations consist of committed, devoted, motivated, and selfless volunteers who strive to unite all Bharatiyas, serve the underprivileged, and foster a sense of unity among Bharatiyas or Hindus to rejuvenate and establish a resilient Bharat as a global force.

These organizations, operating under various names, have multiplied throughout Bharat, and have expanded their presence globally as well. Through their endeavors, these organizations have nurtured and cultivated resolute, patriotic leaders who have willingly renounced the comforts of family life for the greater purpose of serving and exalting Hindustan, the Bharat nation, and the venerable Bharat Mata.

Today's Krishna Avatar

In the current era, it is imperative to acknowledge the significance of the Krishna Avatar. Presently, Bharat (India) operates under a democratic system, wherein the power lies with the people. The essence of democracy lies in governance that is derived from, conducted by, and benefits the people.

Hence, the collective will of the people, as expressed through their votes, holds immense power. In the current democratic landscape, most individuals do not aspire for leaders who resemble dictators or are beholden to specific lineage. Instead, they seek leaders who possess qualities such as strength, intelligence, wisdom, charisma, humility, determination, eloquence, and the ability to make accurate and timely decisions. Moreover, these leaders should possess a keen sense of nationalism and diplomacy.

The ideal leader for Bharat should emerge from within the populace, while maintaining an elevated position above them. This leader should embody the qualities of sacrifice, progressiveness, constructive thinking, and hard work. Such a leader should possess the traits of a renunciate (Sanyasi) or a practitioner of Yoga by displaying a selfless and detached approach towards a luxurious lifestyle.

Furthermore, the leader should be a learned Gyani (Aapt Purush or Nari) and be Mukt (free) from family bondages. The leader of Bharat should be connected to glorious ancient Vedic roots and must be trying for Bharat to be the most advanced, prosperous nation, and shine globally.

In contemporary times, there exists a divergence in people's understanding of Krishna's Avatar compared to the perceptions held during Krishna's incarnation in Mathura over 5200 years ago.

In this age of advanced technology and interconnectedness, people in Bharat and globally are more connected and well-informed. They possess a greater comprehension of various nations, their cultures, political systems, developments, potentials, strengths, weaknesses, opportunities, and threats.

Pic. 23: Bharat's leader ideally: Vairagi, Sanyasi, Aapt Purush, Gyani, Mukt

They have access to a vast ocean of information, constantly updated through computerization, media, social-media, and internet. Consequently, their knowledge base has expanded. They are aware of the nuclear capabilities of multiple countries and the potential for both peaceful and destructive utilization of this power.

Furthermore, they possess knowledge about international politics, diplomacy, alliances, economies, markets, environmental concerns, diverse cultures, terrorism, rogue nations, peaceful nations, the roles and limitations of the United Nations and other international bodies.

Thus, in modern times, an Avatar is not necessarily a singular extraordinary being, as witnessed in historical accounts from over 5200 years ago. *Instead, today an*

Part-2, Chapter 8: Krishna's Partial Avatar for Sanatan

Avatar can manifest through the collective will of the people in a democratic society, where individuals vote for an ideology or a specific political party or coalition that aligns with their aspirations for progress and the upliftment of our nation, Bharat.

In today's era of technological advancements and widespread internet access, this process has become more accessible and has already begun to occur in recent years. We are witnessing the emergence of an Avatar in the hearts and minds of Indigenous Bharatiya Hindus, symbolized by a nationalistic and Vedic ideology. This ideology has garnered support and advocacy from various groups, including political and non-political parties, leaders, intellectuals, saints, patriots, citizens, forums, and social media platforms. Moreover, its influence is not limited only to our nation, as it continues to gain global recognition and followership.

It is conceivable for a devout and simple-minded Hindu (Vedic, Sanatani) from a rural or orthodox background to envision the manifestation of Lord Krishna as a divine incarnation, possessing unparalleled qualities and serving as a leader and liberator for humanity, as was believed to have occurred approximately 5200 years ago.

This perception of Krishna's physical presence complements and aligns with the ultimate purpose of His incarnation. Consequently, when a political party and its leadership achieve success and govern the entirety of Bharat, it brings about tangible benefits and elation among the populace, who feel respected and content under their administration.

Shri Krishna: Yesterday, Today and Tomorrow

Pic 24: Today's Krishna Avatar - Created by "the Power of votes"

This phenomenon may be regarded as an expression of Krishna effectively fulfilling His role as an Avatar through the dedicated efforts of His devotees associated with the party and beyond. In such a leadership and team, characterized by patriotism, righteousness, steadfastness, determination, and uprightness, the people discern the attributes of a partial-avatar, whose actions provide solace and validate Krishna's promise of "Paritranaay sadhoonam, vinashaay cha dushkritaam" (protection of virtuous ones and eradication of wicked ones).

So, Bharatiya citizens and Sanatani Hindus may perceive such leaders and their teams as today's partial-Avatars of Krishna. *It appears that such an Avatar has already dawned in Bharat which has awakened and activated all Sanatanis.*

Today, the partial Avatar has energized the divine consciousness known as the "Collective Vedic-consciousness". This collective consciousness encompasses the ideals, values, and perspectives of authentic Bharatiya ideologists, national activists, organizations, volunteers, thinkers, institutions, philosophers, professionals, intellectuals, artists, religious individuals, and patriotic citizens.

It encompasses the wisdom and insights of the scriptures, as well as the contributions of ordinary individuals who hold a deep love for Bharat (India) and its heritage.

New Krishna Avatar growing, getting stronger

One can observe that this new Krishna partial Avatar, representing a divine incarnation, is currently emerging and gaining strength. This Avatar takes the form of a heightened Krishna-consciousness and Sanatan-energy, permeating the minds and hearts of patriotic Indigenous Bharatiya Sanatanis. The power of the Creator Krishna is being bestowed upon this Avatar, including its leadership and team, young patriots, grassroots workers, local leaders, intellectuals, and common households.

In the context of today's democratic system, this phenomenon appears thoroughly charged, and can also be seen as an influence of Shri Krishna's divine presence, as a partial Avatar.

Krishna observes that the nation of Bharat consists of a diverse population encompassing individuals who possess noble qualities such as goodness, virtue, morality, ethics, decency, courtesy, amiability, honesty, cleanliness, truthfulness, adherence to the law, love for their families, a commitment to peace, simplicity, happiness, philosophical inquiry, analytical thinking, energy, kindness, compassion, education, talent, artistic inclination, scholarly pursuits, a sense of duty, industriousness, a willingness to help others, intelligence, religious devotion, trustworthiness, a spirit of sacrifice, patriotism, affluence, nobility, loyalty, and freedom.

Conversely, there also exist individuals of nefarious disposition who exhibit tendencies towards wickedness, scandalous behavior, corruption, falsehood, hypocrisy, immorality, unethical conduct, criminality, murder, hatred, jealousy, fraudulence, deception, indecency, discord, terrorism, aggression, injustice, anti-national sentiments, treachery, conspiracy, hostility, greed, and mischief.

With an aim to uphold the values of righteousness (Dharma) and eliminate negative elements, this democratic 'partial-Avatar' of Krishna undertakes the responsibility of ensuring the well-being and advancement of virtuous (Dharmik) elements and elimination of rogue elements.

The current partial avatar of Shri Krishna recognizes the existence of diverse characters in various nations across the world. This understanding stems from the acknowledgment of the dual nature of the world, as revealed in the Vedic scriptures, and experienced in routine life.

The creator of the universe utilizes duality as a tool for balance and expansion. It is through the interplay of opposites such as good and evil, righteousness and wickedness, divine and demonic beings that the universe is sustained and propelled forward.

This perpetual cycle of disturbance and restoration is a fundamental aspect of both the divine (Krishna) and natural order. *Disturbing the balance and then again restoring the balance are His and Nature's method or ways.* Throughout history, we have witnessed how this phenomenon of balancing contrasts plays out in various realms, be it in morality, emotions, physical states, or natural phenomena. Ultimately, this process serves the purpose of progress, advancement, and the eventual reunion of the universe in its ultimate singularity.

Krishna's incarnations are dispersed throughout different regions of the world, adhering to His grand plan, and serving the purpose of maintaining and strengthening righteousness, or Dharma. *For this He appears as partial-Avatars in various parts of the world, completes His plans, and disappears again.* It is important to recognize and acknowledge that these Avatars are integral components of His divine governance, and there is no imperfection in His governing system.

The presence of the divine Krishna avatar brings forth an ambience filled with auspiciousness, vitality, confidence, friendship, integrity, fearlessness, happiness, success, opulence, honesty, truth, and divinity.

Krishna Avatar energizing Bharat

This Krishna-consciousness, also known as Sanatan-energy, is already happening, and being manifested within the consciousness of true Indigenous Bharatiya individuals, thereby empowering and reinvigorating the nation of Bharat. With each passing day, Bharat grows stronger as Krishna's influence eradicates the politicized pseudo-secularity and revitalizes the core of Sanatan Dharma. Sanatan Dharma, being Krishna's own eternal path, is being preserved and reinstated by the Avatar Krishna himself.

Recognizing the Asuri (demonic) influences and the agenda to eradicate Sanatan Dharma from Bharat, Avatar Krishna remains aware of the conspiratorial efforts to replace Sanatan Dharma by aggressive materialistic foreign faiths that have entered from the Western and Northwestern regions of Bharat over the past few centuries. He is also aware of the detrimental plot to further fragment Bharat and establish diverse regimes based on various foreign faiths or political ideologies, devoid of true Dharma.

Krishna, as the supreme consciousness-avatar, permeates the consciousness of all devoted individuals, imbuing them with his divine presence, energizing and empowering them in all aspects of their being - their hearts, minds, brains, and bodies.

This phenomenon can be observed as a contemporary resurgence of Sanatan Dharma, which has withstood numerous challenges and attempts to diminish or eradicate it over the course of centuries. However, as it is rooted in the essence of Krishna, Sanatan Dharma remains eternal, possessing the eternal truth at the core of its existence since the inception of the universe.

The influence of Krishna's avatar has been steadily increasing, encompassing all true and Indigenous followers of Sanatan Dharma, whether they reside within the boundaries of Bharat Mata (Mother India) or across the world. This divine inspiration has transcended professions, genders, and ages, motivating the children of Bharat to contribute their skills, resources, and expertise towards safeguarding, promoting, and advancing the growth, security, defense, and excellence of their homeland.

The manifestation of Krishna's energy in the present time is not limited to a single individual but rather extends to a diverse collective of millions of resolute individuals across diverse cultures and countries. The distribution and allocation of this energy varies based on the individual's level of selflessness, purity, sacrifice, honesty, self-discipline, responsibility, sincerity, wisdom, and devotion to their homeland and humankind at large.

Krishna's Avatar: As per Vedic scriptures

As outlined in the Gita, Krishna's avatar is said to appear when the practice of righteousness (Dharma) declines, giving way to the rise of unrighteousness (Adharma). This occurrence is automatic and part of a pre-existing plan. We can observe the prevalence of Krishna consciousness and the influence of Sanatana energy spreading across India and the world for several centuries, working towards upholding righteousness.

According to the scriptures, in approximately 427,000 years, at the end of the current age of Kali Yuga (which commenced approximately 5,000 years ago), there will be the advent of the Kalki Avatar, a full incarnation of the Supreme Being Lord Krishna, marking the beginning of a new era known as Sat-Yuga.

Prior to the arrival of Kalki Avatar, there will be various mini or partial-Avatars of Shri Krishna that will manifest in various parts of the world, particularly in Bharat, periodically. These Avatars will be tasked with eliminating the wicked and malevolent forces, protecting the righteous, and upholding principles such as ethics, morality, righteousness, integrity, order, and peace (Dharma) in Bharat and beyond. As mentioned earlier, today's partial Avatar has already dawned in Bharat.

CHAPTER 9
KRISHNA'S MISSION FOR BHARAT
(Today)

Krishna embodies the quintessence of the Bharat. He is regarded as a paragon of virtuous ideals by the Indigenous population of Bharat, particularly among the Sanatanis or Hindus. Krishna is Yogeshwar, demonstrating traits such as strength, courage, benevolence, wisdom, erudition, resoluteness, tact, diplomacy, affability, perpetual smile, detachment, divine transcendence, and the ability to harmonize the spiritual and material aspects of life.

Krishna serves as the emblematic representation of Bharat, symbolizing the spiritual essence and traditional values that form the foundation of Sanatan Dharma. With an endless spectrum of virtues, Krishna epitomizes the very essence of Bharat's identity, intertwining seamlessly with the collective consciousness of its people.

Krishna's life has been characterized by multidisciplinary endeavors encompassing various aspects of existence. He exhibited unwavering resilience in the face of adversity and encountered numerous challenges. With a strategic mindset, He sought resolutions and emerged triumphant. Krishna is immortal. Krishna's vision also transcends mortality as He aspires for an immortal, thriving Bharat with an expanding sphere of influence.

- His desire is for all Hindus to emulate His life and teachings, ensuring a society that is resolute, disciplined, self-assured, knowledgeable, powerful, courageous, virtuous, educated, unified, compassionate, and proud of their illustrious Vedic ancestors and their profound scriptures, which contain scientific principles and veiled insights for the betterment of humanity.
- Never surrender to odd situations but fight against all the odds and win over the odds. Embrace adversity and strive to overcome challenges rather than succumb to them.
- Never be worried about problems. Problems are part of life's journey. Problems are opportunities for growth and development. In place of worrying, engage in introspection and contemplation to find effective solutions.
- Aim high and constantly strive for personal and societal progress. Foster a spirit of innovation, excellence, enterprise, and exploration.
- Extend a helping hand to those in need, whether individuals, communities, or nations, particularly those who exhibit virtuous behavior and a commitment to combating criminal tendencies.
- Embrace a progressive mindset and disregard superstitions. While honoring and preserving the

rich traditions and positive energy of our Vedic cultural heritage, discard obsolete beliefs and ideas.
- Live life with a sense of empowerment and freedom. Live like a master, not as a slave. Remember that everyone is a soul (Atma) rather than a mere physical body. Atma is perfectly independent. Atma is ever connected with Paramatma and has infinite energy. Connect with the eternal energy of the divine (Paramatma) and tap into the infinite potential within your Innermost-self.

Indigenous Bharatiya Rishis are Scientists

It is recognized that the ancient Rishis were not only scholars but also seekers of truth who possessed profound scientific knowledge. They were exceptional scientists of their time. Their extensive exploration led to the emergence of numerous profound insights that have stood the test of time.

For instance, they professed the concept of the divine presence permeating every particle of existence, the notion that the Soul itself is divine, and the understanding that the entirety of the Earth belongs to the divine.

Additionally, they advocated for the unity of humanity, proclaiming that the entire Earth is akin to a single family. Moreover, they comprehended the profound concept of the individual self being inseparable from the divine entity.

Furthermore, they recognized the parallels existing between the macrocosm and the microcosm, affirming that the principles observed in the human body are reflected in the broader universe.

Pic. 25: Krishna's vision for Bharat and Bharatiyas

Above all, the Rishis beautifully conveyed the truth that, despite the diverse paths taken, all wisdom leads to the same ultimate truth.

Given below are but a few examples among the countless profound truths discovered and documented in the Vedic scriptures over thousands of years. These are used in routine conversations even among the virtuous villagers in India:

- Kan Kan Me Bhagwan (God in every particle)
- Atma So Paramatma (Soul itself is God)
- Sabai bhumi Gopal ki (whole earth is God's)
- Vasudhaiv Kutumba (whole earth is a family)

- Aham Brahmasmi (I am the Brahm)
- Tat Twamasi (You are That/Brahm)
- Ayam Atma Brahm (This soul is Brahm)
- Yatha Pinde Tatha Brahmande (As in a body, so in the universe)
- Ekam Sat Vipra Bahudha Vadanti (Truth is one, wise tell it in diverse ways),

With the partial Avatar of Krishna, Bharat serves as a source of immense positive energy. Any negativity or negative influences that enter its boundaries are swiftly transformed and transmuted into constructive and positive energy.

The divine presence of Krishna ensures that any negative forces seeking to alter the demographic or societal dynamics of this sacred land will either fade away or be converted into positive energies of Sanatan, ultimately harmonizing with the vast ocean of positive Vedic and Sanatani traditions and values.

Countless endeavors have been undertaken throughout history and continue to persist in eradicating the Vedic/Sanatani culture from Bharat and propagating their own corrupted foreign materialistic and greed-driven religion and culture.

While they may have achieved temporary success in certain regions of Bharat, they ultimately succumb and are assimilated into the vast ocean of generosity and humanity that defines the ethos of Bharatiya society, guided by the principle of Vasudhaiva Kutumbakam (the world as one family).

Bharat spreads Positive Energy of the Vedas worldwide

Bharat, recognizing power of the Vedas, aims to disseminate their teachings and positive energy to the world. The prevailing force of positivity triumphs over negativity, righteousness prevails over evil, and the divine surpasses the demonic. The Vedas, along with their profound wisdom contained in the Upanishads, serve as an abundant reservoir of positive energy, fostering peace, love, and harmony across the globe.

More than 10,000 years ago, the Vedas foresaw and boldly proclaimed the concept of Vasudhaiva Kutumbakam, recognizing the interconnectedness of all beings. Regrettably, due to a lack of comprehensive understanding and implementation of the wisdom found in the Vedic scriptures and literatures, various kingdoms, and populations in Bharat (the Indian subcontinent) were unable to maintain unity and strength.

Therefore, they fell under the oppressive rule of invading forces for nearly a thousand years. However, in recent times, there has been a renewed sense of awakening and self-awareness among the Sanatanis/Hindus. They have recognized their inherent pride and identity (Asmita), as well as their untapped potential for growth and development.

Global Excellence of Bharatiya intellectuals and Diaspora

The nation of Bharat, founded on the principles of wisdom enshrined in its ancient Vedic scriptures, boasts a remarkable cohort of intellectuals, professionals, and a vibrant diaspora. The Vedas, embodying timeless truths and the laws of nature, serve as a profound wellspring of knowledge. The philosophical pinnacle of the Vedas is found in Vedanta and the Upanishads, which offer profound insights into the mysteries of existence.

The corpus of Hindu sacred texts, emanating from the Vedic tradition, stands as the intellectual and societal bedrock of ancient Bharat. Composed by venerable Rishis, erudite sages hailing from all corners of the subcontinent, these scriptures offer profound insights into the mysteries of existence and the laws governing the natural world. In addition, they have served as a catalyst in fostering a sense of cultural cohesion and unity among diverse communities, transcending regional and linguistic boundaries.

Among these scriptures, the Bhagwat Geeta/Gita, spoken by Lord Krishna, stands as the quintessential embodiment of the Vedas and Upanishads. Its teachings continue to guide and inspire people across the entirety of Bharat. The wisdom transmitted through the Vedic scriptures and literatures, exemplified by the teachings of the Bhagwat Geeta, holds profound significance in intellectual, societal, and philosophical realms. It is considered as the culmination of knowledge found in the ancient Vedas and Upanishads, with a prominent influence in the cultural fabric of Bharat.

The profound scientific discoveries made by ancient scholars, or Rishis as they were known, were beyond the comprehension of the general populace. Hence, to disseminate this advanced knowledge to the masses, various methods such as anecdotal narratives and practical demonstrations were employed, aligning these teachings with everyday experiences, and facilitating comprehension. This approach, akin to the practices observed in literary traditions globally, employed relatable characters to communicate eternal truths.

Pic. 26: Global excellence of Bharatiya brains due to Vedas

Naturally, individuals with varying levels of intellectual prowess interpreted this knowledge in accordance with their respective aptitudes. The involvement of diverse characters further facilitated the widespread dissemination of this eternal wisdom, tailored to the individual's comprehension and perspective.

The body of Vedic literature encompasses a rich tapestry of intellectual and societal discourse, encompassing a vast array of profound insights and timeless truths. These scriptures delve into the realms of various disciplines, ranging from metaphysics and cosmology to ethics and social organization.

Imbued with deep philosophical contemplation, the Vedic texts provide a holistic understanding of the universe and the human experience within it. Inherent in these scriptures are profound reflections on the nature of existence, the cosmic order, and the interplay between the material and spiritual dimensions of reality.

Furthermore, Vedic literature reveals intricate narratives and allegorical stories that offer valuable insights into historical events, moral lessons, and cultural practices that have shaped the fabric of Bharatiya society.

It is through the study and contemplation of these ancient scriptures that one can glean a deeper understanding of the intellectual and societal foundations that underpin the Bharatiya ethos.

The profound and expansive body of Vedic literature is characterized by its reverential exploration of metaphysical truths and celestial beings (deities), including Brahma, Vishnu, Mahesh, Rama, Krishna, Saraswati, Lakshmi, Parvati, Durga, Kali, Jagadamba, Chandi, Ganesh, Hanuman, among numerous others who personify the divine essence.

Drawing upon the imagery of a pyramid or a cone, we can discern that individual with various levels of understanding, diverse cognitive aptitudes, ranging from the base up to the zenith, engage with and internalize Vedic knowledge in unique manners.

Positioned at the pinnacle of this structure resides the pinnacle of realization - Adwait, the state of non-duality, wherein the ultimate Truth is unveiled.

Represented by the sacred syllable "Om, ॐ" this formless embodiment epitomizes the ultimate Truth. However, as we descend from the apex, the emergence of duality becomes apparent, and individuals at various levels of the pyramid establish profound connections with distinct archetypes, idols, and divine personifications, adhering to their perceptual spheres or comfort zones.

This description elucidates the rich tapestry of diverse spiritual beliefs and intellectual understandings within the cultural context of India. Everyone operates within their own unique perspective, akin to various levels of a pyramid. It is narrow-minded to expect complete comprehension of the apex, or highest truth, while still immersed within the pyramid. However, there is a shared belief among all individuals that this apex, represented by the formless ultimate truth known as OMॐ, exists. This understanding serves as a fundamental aspect of the Indian psyche.

Indigenous professionals and intellectuals with deep roots in Vedic principles and teachings exhibit a greater proximity to the apex. The apex symbolizes perfection, absolute knowledge, the Ultimate Truth, the realm of the eternal and the dwelling place of the Creator (Krishna). Proximity to the apex results in enhanced comprehension, purity, advanced knowledge, innovative ideas, abundant energy, vast possibilities, immense potential, elevated performance, and notable accomplishments. Those situated at the apex possess a holistic perspective encompassing the past, present, and future.

Krishna is at the apex. Closeness to Krishna at apex serves as the ultimate guiding force for all. As a result, professionals, intellectuals, businesspersons, industrialists, and households in Bharatiya society exhibit remarkable qualities such as energy, diligence, adherence to virtuous principles, courageousness, intelligence, and a strong faith in Krishna. They actively engage with their communities, embrace local customs, uphold legal standards, and contribute to social welfare and nation-building.

This positive influence extends to their families and future generations, who learn to follow the righteous path guided by Krishna and the wisdom of the Gita. Although not openly, they embody internal Krishna-consciousness or the essence of Sanatani values. Their deep-rooted belief in the Vedic philosophy of Vasudhaiv Kutumb (the world is one family) engenders a sense of belonging wherever they go, fostering harmonious interpersonal relationships. These qualities are instrumental in the success of Bharatiya intellectuals, professionals, and the global Bharatiya diaspora, despite some exceptions who deviate from this path.

CHAPTER 10
KRISHNA FOR SPIRITUAL BHARAT, NOT SECULAR INDIA

(Today)

Bharatiya Culture and Vedic Philosophy (Wisdom)

The Vedic scriptures and literatures offer a wealth of wisdom that has shaped various aspects of professional, intellectual, and societal frameworks. These ancient texts, which span over 10,000 years, include the Vedas, Upanishads, Shruti, Smriti, Itihas, Puranas, and numerous other shastras (scriptures).

The knowledge contained within these texts is deeply ingrained in the cultural fabric of Bharat and continues to guide individuals in their pursuit of a moral, ethical, and fulfilling life.

The foundation of Bharatiya (Indian) culture lies in the principles of Vedic philosophy, which encompasses the teachings of the Vedas and Upanishads. Embedded within this philosophy is the essence of Sanatan Dharma, also known as Hindu Dharma, a way of life rooted in the pursuit of self-realization and dedicated to the Supreme Creator.

The interwoven nature of Bharatiya culture, Vedic philosophy, and Sanatan Dharma creates a harmonious and mutually supportive framework that encourages individuals to lead virtuous, egoless, joyful, responsible, active, simple, and loving life dedicated to the Supreme (Creator, God).

The primary objective of Sanatan Dharm can be expressed through various conceptualizations, such as the pursuit and attainment of ultimate truth, self-realization, perfection, Nirvaan, Moksha, Mukti, liberation, the visualization (Darshan) of the Creator, and merging with the Creator.

Sanatan Dharma, also known as Hindu Dharma or Vedik Dharma, encompasses these ideals within its eternal teachings. Sanatan Dharm, rooted in philosophy and spirituality, is not only a religion but also a civilization and a comprehensive way of life.

Shri Krishna, in the Bhagwat Geeta/Gita, emphasizes the importance of upholding and reviving Dharma (righteousness) to protect and preserve society *(Krishna: Gita Ch.4: 7, 8 ...Yada yada hi dharmasya....yuge yuge).* Hindu Dharma, the foundation of Bharat, encompasses all religions without any discrimination, making Bharat a nation that embraces diversity.

The true essence of secularism is already embedded in Hindu Dharma and the fabric of Bharat. Lord Krishna is cognizant of the deceitful actions of those who take advantage of their hosts in Bharat, and He aims to rectify, transform, or eliminate such individuals, while steadfastly defending the values of generosity, decency, and hospitality.

Pic 27: Krishna – Core of Sanatan Dharm & Bhagavat Gita

The "Secular & Socialist" label added later in the constitution of Bharat is deemed as an inaccurate or inappropriate phrase, as it does not align with the principles of the Sanatan Dharma - the ancient and foundational wisdom of Bharat.

The term "Dharma" transcends mere religious affiliations and encompasses much more than religion, Majhab, Panth or faith, as it represents a comprehensive ideology of natural discipline, impartiality, secularity and achieving ultimate Truth.

Sanatan Dharma serves as the binding force for the diverse nation of Bharat and has the potential to incorporate additional nations and the whole of the world ultimately.

Conversely, the weakening of Sanatan Dharma leads to a decline in the strength of Bharat and increases the risks of its disintegration, as observed in historical instances.

The notion of "secularism" and its political implementation stands in opposition to the fundamental principles of Sanatan Dharma, the essence of Bharat. The term "secular" implies a focus on worldly and material matters, devoid of spirituality or religious affiliation and practices. Secularism, in its essence, denotes a separation of religious influence from the public sphere, often emphasizing a purely materialistic worldview.

This ideology fundamentally conflicts with the foundational principles enshrined in the constitution of Bharat, which includes explicit acknowledgments and pictures of many Hindu deities. Moreover, it contradicts the essence and framework of Sanatan Dharma, an eternal and all-encompassing belief system that reveres multiple deities, emphasizes discipline and moral values, and integrates with Mother Nature.

Paradoxically, other religions of Western origin, driven by a desire to convert Hindus and expand their own followings, often adopt a "secular" label in the political sphere, aligning themselves with anti-Indian communist ideologies and religious extremism.

The emergence of this brand of "political secularism" seeks to undermine the influence of Sanatan Dharma. Its intentions are clear – as secularism gains strength, Sanatan Dharma weakens, thereby increasing the likelihood of religious-based disintegration within Bharat. Such scandalous 'secularism' is in fact 'separatism.' This form of secularism can be likened to envisioning a plant's survival without essential elements such as water, sunlight, and nutrients.

Pic. 28: No Secularism in Bharat, Only Sanatan Spirituality

Its implementation, therefore, can be construed as divisive rather than inclusive, allowing for the proliferation of foreign religions and potential demands for separate nations. Recognizing this, it is expected that Avatar

Krishna, the eternal divine consciousness, has the plan to safeguard against the disintegration of Bharat once again.

The word secularism has been deliberately introduced through an amendment into the Indian constitution as a political phenomenon. Its underlying motive is to weaken Sanatan Dharma (the eternal religion) and promote Abrahamic foreign religions for political gain and voter support. This trend is already having a detrimental effect on the strength of Bharat.

However, according to the divine promise in the Bhagavad Gita (Chapter 4: 7, 8), Shri Krishna will protect Dharma at every age. Soon, through constitutional amendments or a new constitution, the term "secular" will be eliminated, leading to a stronger Bharat than ever before.

Killing the Soul of Bharat through pseudo-Secularism

Pseudo-secularism is gradually eroding the rich cultural and intellectual heritage of Bharat. The ancient scientific discoveries and achievements of Indian civilization, such as the sacred sound "OM" ॐ, are unjustly labeled as communal or non-secular by narrow-minded secularists, politicians, and anti-Hindu forces. Some even oppose the use of OM ॐ, in yoga, schools, and public prayers. ॐ is the lifeline, the Soul of India.

There have been and continue to be some objections regarding the inclusion of certain prayers or Vedic-verses in the practices of Yoga, schools, and public prayers. Interestingly, these objections often come from ill-intended individuals who espouse secular ideologies or hold an anti-Hindu sentiment.

Pic. 29: The constitution of Bharat will follow Gita/Sanatan principles

Specifically, there is opposition against the recitation of the profound and uplifting prayer: *"Asato ma sat gamaya, Tamaso ma Jyotir gamaya, mrityor ma amritam gamay,"* which expresses a fundamental aspiration: O Creator! "Lead me from falsehood (illusion) to truth, lead me from darkness to light, lead me from death to immortality."

They protest that this is a communal (Hindu) prayer, so should not be chanted in schools in secular India. They object to the inclusion of Sanatan Dharma verses chants in school settings, arguing that it promotes a Hindu-centric atmosphere in a secular Indian society. However, such reactionary and provocative objections under the guise of secularism have had detrimental effects on the progress of the Bharatiya civilization.

Practices such as Yoga, the chanting of OM ॐ, and Vedic prayers play a significant role in nurturing the Indigenous spiritual, social, and cultural fabric of Bharatiya society. Unfortunately, there are deliberate and organized attempts by foreign-influenced religions, communist ideologies, and individuals with anti-national sentiments to erode and dismantle this crucial lifeline of Sanatanis.

In contemporary times, there has been a surge in media reports regarding incidents of young children within educational institutions engaging in acts of violence, resulting in the harm or even death of their peers, by resorting to the use of knives. This alarming trend prompts us to reflect upon the trajectory our educational institutions in Bharat are taking.

Should we allow the practice of prayers that foster and instill ethical values, morality, and good conduct in our youth to be restricted and prohibited, based on divisive lines of religion and secularism? This excessive emphasis on secularity renders the very essence of our students' growth and development, as well as the Soul or essence of Bharat's constitutional fabric, susceptible to manipulations and disregard.

Through the inclusion of the term "secularism" in the constitution, a tool has been provided to certain mischievous individuals who seek to manipulate the very essence of the constitution. This manipulation goes against the concept of righteousness, or Dharma, and it is imperative that it be halted. Shri Krishna has been observing this with vigilance and, in His partial-Avatar, is now inspiring and energizing those who are dedicated to the cause of eliminating the term "secular" from the constitution or formulating an entirely new constitution that honors and uplifts the eternal Sanatan Dharma.

Secularity abuse vs Oriental & Occidental philosophies

The realm of oriental philosophy encompasses a rich tapestry of religious and philosophical teachings originating from the East. Among these, Confucianism, Taoism, and Sanatan Dharma take center stage. The term Sanatan Dharma encompasses a wide array of Bharatiya philosophies and religions, including Hinduism, Buddhism, Jainism, Sikhism, as well as various local and tribal beliefs and traditions.

It is worth noting that Buddhism, Jainism, and Sikhism emerged from noble individuals hailing from Hindu backgrounds, sharing a foundation rooted in the principles of Sanatan Dharma albeit manifesting in distinct ways. Significantly, the Eastern traditions, particularly Sanatan Dharma, have historically embraced an intimate connection with Nature, nurturing a profound symbiotic relationship with Mother Nature over countless millennia. Vedic wisdom serves as the foundation upon which various fields of knowledge in Eastern philosophy are based.

These fields include sciences such as astronomy and mathematics, health sciences like Ayur-Ved, medicinal practices involving the use of herbs, artistic expressions in music and literature, economic principles outlined in Arth

Shastra, architectural guidelines of Vaastu, stunning sculptures, self-defense techniques (martial arts), civilization-building endeavors, as well as the development of diverse lifestyles and cultures. All these endeavors derive their essence from spiritual teachings.

The principles of Sanatan Dharma embrace the belief in the eternal nature of the soul and the concept of rebirth, influenced by one's past and present actions. Sanatan Dharma does not support the idea of expanding its influence through religious conversions. Instead, it emphasizes that the propagation of Dharma occurs organically, through the innate forces of goodness and the fulfillment of genuine spiritual needs within individuals and society.

The religions predominant in the Western world, known as Abrahamic religions, originate from a distinct geographical area far removed from India. These religions encompass Judaism, Christianity, and Islam, and place emphasis on materialism and worldly pursuits, seeking prosperity and sensual pleasures in this current life only (no rebirth).

They also prioritize the expansion of their beliefs and influence, often employing various methods, whether fair or unfair, to achieve their goals. Additionally, these religions generally do not adhere to the concept of reincarnation and focus on conversions to spread their message.

In contrast, the Vedic scriptures promote an ideal form of secularism that is separate from any religion. It does not engage in direct criticism or dismissal of any religious beliefs but instead upholds the principles of Dharma, which encompass natural laws, humanity, and ethical behavior.

This secularism is not antagonistic toward religion itself but rather transcends it.

It recognizes that there is enlightenment and knowledge available in other realms or beliefs too and acknowledges the existence of secular truths guided by Dharma (Nature's laws, discipline, virtuousness), which are inherent in the universal order and perpetually applicable.

The concept of secularism entails the separation of religion from governance. It suggests that the laws and policies should be guided by the principles of promoting the welfare, well-being, safety, security, and development of the people and the nation, rather than being based on specific religious texts. Moreover, it aims to eliminate discriminatory practices based on religion and strengthen democracy by safeguarding the rights of religious minorities.

It is worth noting that in the original constitution of Bharat, a sense of secularism was inherently embedded in governing Bharat. However, regrettably, it was subjected to alteration through a political conspiracy. Curiously, foreign-based religions, which adhere to specific texts, label themselves as 'secular' while tagging Hindus, who follow their own scriptures and ways, as 'non-secular' within Bharat. This violates the inherent secular principles of nature.

There has been a concerning imbalance in the demographic composition of Bharat in recent times, supported by empirical evidence rather than irrational anxieties or phobias. It is important to acknowledge that the concept of secularism has limited applicability in the context of Bharat, and its usage should be approached with caution. While secularism may have value in Western societies, they are free to continue employing it as they see fit.

Unfortunately, in Bharat, secularism has been distorted to serve the interests of certain foreign-origin religions, leading to propagation and a preferential treatment of these religions over Indigenous Bharatiya or Sanatani faiths. This manipulation is driven by political motivations and has sparked a need for critical examination and review of applicability of secularism in Bharat.

Krishna transforming the alien, foreign mindset

The wisdom found in the Vedic scriptures emphasizes the transformative power of Krishna in eliminating or shifting foreign mindsets. Krishna, a divine force that resonates with billions of individuals of Bharatiya origin worldwide, serves as a source of inspiration, motivation, and unity in the reconstruction and fortification of Bharat.

By instilling a deep connection to the ancient and vibrant cultural heritage of India, Krishna guides and encourages confused individuals who may have been influenced by foreign ideologies to embrace their identity as children of Bharat Mata (Mother India).

Those who sincerely align themselves with Krishna's inspiration and embrace their roots contribute to the strength and resilience of Bharat. However, individuals who defy or betray their heritage face the consequences of their actions, as Krishna and the powerful forces of nature (Krishna's Maya) work either to transform them or to remove them from the sacred land.

The partial Avatar Krishna, being all-pervading and supremely powerful, administers rewards or punishments in a just and eternal manner to serve the greater good and protection of Bharat. This process unfolds through the collective dedication and Krishna-consciousness of over a billion Sanatani individuals, with the support of the ever-active executive energy of mother nature.

Krishna-consciousness: The Nature for Sanatani Excellence

Sanatan encompasses a profound and intricate tapestry interwoven with the diverse and profound spiritual traditions of Bharat. It manifests the profound and perennial philosophies that guide and inspire individuals to seek higher truths and attain spiritual enlightenment.

Through the practice and internalization of these profound teachings, individuals strive to connect with the cosmic consciousness and align themselves with the universal principles that govern the harmonious functioning of society.

In this grand tapestry, the partial-Avatar Krishna, the divine manifestation of the supreme, assumes a pivotal role. Endowed with omnipresence and supreme power, Krishna presides over the cosmological orchestration of rewards and consequences, ensuring a just and equitable distribution of outcomes. These outcomes are not arbitrary, but rather intricately intertwined with the welfare and safeguarding of the sacred land of Bharat.

The boundless multitude of more than a billion Sanatani individuals actively participate in the pursuit of Krishna-consciousness, collectively dedicating themselves to the exploration and understanding of the divine principles that underpin existence. Their unwavering commitment to living in accordance with these principles serves as a catalyst for the evolutionary and transformative processes that unfold within them and in the broader societal context. Furthermore, the executive force of mother nature serves as an ever-active agent, facilitating and harmonizing the workings of this intricate cosmic web.

It is through this symbiotic relationship that the intricate dance of karma unfolds, with individuals experiencing the consequences of their thoughts, actions, and intentions in a systematic and just manner. Sanatan, with its depth and complexity, calls upon individuals to transcend the boundaries of the worldly routines and embody the principles of truth, righteousness, and compassion in their daily lives.

By engaging in profound self-reflection and self-discipline, individuals not only further their own spiritual evolution but also contribute to the societal fabric by fostering an environment of harmony and collective growth.

Together, the interplay between the eternal and the material world, the individual and the collective, creates a tapestry of intellectual and societal development that propels Bharat forward on its path of spiritual enlightenment and cultural preservation.

With each Sanatani's dedicated pursuit of Krishna-consciousness and the unwavering support of the executive energy of mother nature, the eternal essence of Sanatan continues to flourish and inspire generations to come.

Protection of Indigenous Bharatiyas, true Hindus (Sanatanis)

The safeguarding of Indigenous Bharatiya community, particularly His devotees, the adherents of the Hindu faith (Sanatanis), is a matter of Krishna's prime concern. It is visible to Krishna that like followers of any other faith, Hindus also face social challenges and strive for various reforms within their communities.

Detractors of Hinduism, who harbor intentions to obliterate or undermine Hindus and their religious practices, often seize upon these challenges to discredit and demoralize Hindus, while conveniently neglecting to address more severe issues prevalent within their own societies and belief systems.

They tend to magnify even minor problems within Hindu society, while minimizing and downplaying significant problems within their own contexts. This approach is both strategically biased and unjustifiable, as it lacks fairness and is contrary to the principles of righteousness (Dharma).

Surprisingly, certain individuals who claim to be Hindus, whether due to ignorance, ulterior motives, politics, or personal interests, align themselves with these individuals who engage in malicious acts against Dharma (righteousness).

Today, it is observable that Krishna, through His partial Avatar, is actively implementing plans to safeguard His devotees, the Hindus, from these acts of Adharma and from Adharmis and Vidharmis, those who engage in them.

Byproducts of 1000 years' slavery of Indigenous Bharatiyas

Over the span of a millennium, Indigenous Bharatiyas (Hindus) have endured a series of invasions, occupations, and subjugation. These repeated acts of aggression and oppression have left deep psychological scars on the Indigenous population. What was once a powerful, virtuous, and prosperous society has transformed into a submissive and fearful community, marked by a culture of escapism and passive endurance due to centuries of intimidation, mistreatment, and derogation by invaders, looters, and tyrants. Their response to adversity has often been one of tolerance and escapism, seeking solace and comfort in superficial devotion.

However, it is important to recognize that this response, while understandable given the circumstances, falls short as a definitive answer to the oppressors and murderers who continue to threaten and intimidate them to this day.

True grace and tolerance should emanate from a position of strength and victory, rather than stemming from a place of weakness and submission.

The current tolerance exhibited by Hindus is a direct consequence of the defeats, tortures, and intimidations inflicted by invaders and their subsequent generations who remain unrepentant on their ancestors' horrible excesses and not interested in their cultural adjustment or refinement.

The innate qualities of forbearance and tolerance, which were once indicative of strength and victory, have now become a manifestation of a weakened and defeated populace. The present-day tolerance of Bharatiyas or

Hindus is rooted in a sense of fear, powerlessness, and an inability to resist or fight back against the injustices perpetuated by successive generations of invaders and their unyielding audacity. This continued subjugation has suppressed their courage, determination, and willpower, leaving them searching for alternative avenues to regain their lost dignity and respect.

The cowards, helpless or defeated people have no option but to tolerate the excesses on them, or on any of their neighbors or relatives by the oppressors, looters and enemies. *The Hindus are surrounded by more enemies within than outside.* This account is yet to be set right at the soonest to neutralize, control or destroy the offenders and enemies, and to regain the lost strength. Then only the tolerance of Hindus will be more gracious and genuine.

Omniscient Krishna knows this, and through His partial-Avatar is now inspiring and energizing Bharatiya (Sanatanis) to be sufficiently decisive, aggressive, hostile, brutal, and vicious against the reminisce of cruel oppressors, invaders and miscreants surrounding them, to protect their own existence, honor, territories and interests of their families, generations, societies and their great nation Bharat and the Vedic culture.

Krishna forgives and shelters their innocent women, children, and old age people. The water has already come up to the nose and continues rising. Krishna is now protecting all Sanatanis.

It is observed that individuals who lack courage or find themselves in a position of weakness must consider adopting a stance of endurance in the face of aggression, exploitation, and injustice imposed upon them or their communities by oppressors or adversaries.

It is essential to acknowledge that the Hindu community faces numerous challenges both internally and externally.

Addressing these challenges promptly and effectively is imperative for reestablishing equilibrium, curbing, or eliminating such offenders and adversaries, and reclaiming our strength. By doing so, the Hindu community's tolerance will be marked by authenticity and grace.

The omniscient Krishna, understanding the current circumstances, is channeling His divine energy through His partial Avatar to ignite an initiative-taking, firm, assertive, and unyielding spirit within Bharatiya Hindus (Sanatanis), enabling them to confront and safeguard against those who seek to oppress, invade, and disrupt.

This is done to protect the existence, dignity, and interests of individuals, families, communities, generations, and the great nation of Bharat, along with its Vedic heritage.

Krishna offers compassion and sanctuary to the innocent women, children, and elderly. It is evident that the situation has reached a critical point, and Krishna is now intervening to protect the Sanatan and His devotees from harm.

Shri Ram's Pran-Pratishtha and the Foundation of Ram-Rajya

After constructing the new Shri Ram Mandir (Temple) in Ayodhya and conducting the Pran-Pratishtha ceremony on 22nd January 2024, the suppressed minds, thoughts, emotions, and self-respect of all Sanatanis gained freedom, inspiration, and joy after nearly five hundred years. The depression of many generations evaporated forever during those auspicious moments, paving the way for the establishment of Ram-Rajya in the minds of all Sanatanis. This vision is gradually and steadily coming to fruition.

Pic. 30: The New Ram-Mandir in Ayodhya, at Ramlala Birthplace

Just as described in the Bharatiya scriptures about the Deva-Danav Sangram (war), the Sanatani people in Bharat (India) were attacked by devilish (Danavi) forces around five hundred years ago.

Many innocent individuals and saints were brutally killed, and the sacred temple at the birthplace of Lord Ram in Ayodhya was destroyed. In its place, a controversial and disputed structure was arrogantly erected just to insult all

Part-2, Chapter 10: Krishna for Spiritual Bharat...

Sanatanis. It did cause immense disrespect and harm to the pride of Sanatani or Hindu community.

Pic. 31: Shri Ramlala Pran-Pratishtha in Ram Mandir Ayodhya

Over the course of these five centuries, the Sanatani people, warriors, and rulers continued their struggle to reclaim the temple from these demonic forces. Countless Sanatanis sacrificed their lives in many battles, but ultimately, the Sanatanis emerged victorious after around five hundred years of struggle. The unlawful and disputed structure was demolished, and a magnificent new Shri Ram Mandir was constructed in its place.

A new idol of Lord Ram was consecrated within the temple, with sacred rites conducted by Vedic scholars and priests, including the Prime Minister of Bharat, on January 22, 2024, in the presence of thousands of dignitaries and devotees. This momentous occasion, which was broadcasted globally, uplifted the spirits, restored the honor, and revitalized the self-esteem and determination of all Sanatanis, paving the way for a prosperous Ram-Rajya that would bring benefits not only to Bharat but to the entire world.

Ram-Rajya

The concept of Ram-Rajya, derived from Vedic (Sanatana or Hindu) mythology and philosophy, is a profound notion that envisions an ideal state of governance. Rooted in ancient texts and epitomized in the Hindu epic, Ramayana, Ram-Rajya represents a societal framework characterized by righteousness, justice, and equality. In this ideal state, governance transcends mere political authority, encompassing a holistic approach to leadership and societal well-being.

At the heart of Ram-Rajya lies the figure of Lord Rama, revered as the epitome of a righteous ruler. His reign exemplifies virtues such as compassion, integrity, and a deep sense of duty towards his subjects. Central to the concept of Ram-Rajya is the notion of Dharma, or righteousness, which serves as the guiding principle for both rulers and citizens. It emphasizes the importance of moral and ethical conduct in all aspects of governance, ensuring fairness and harmony within society.

Lord Rama's governance in the Ramayana serves as a beacon of inspiration, portraying a leader who prioritizes the welfare of his people above personal interests. His administration is marked by accessibility, where the concerns and needs of every citizen are duly addressed. Furthermore, Ram-Rajya embodies the ideal of inclusivity,

Part-2, Chapter 10: Krishna for Spiritual Bharat...

where all members of society, regardless of their social status or background, are treated with dignity and respect. It promotes equality before the law and fosters a sense of unity among diverse communities. Beyond its historical and

Pic. 32: Historic Auspicious & Gracious Moments after 500 years' struggles

mythological significance, the concept of Ram-Rajya continues to resonate in current administration on governance and leadership. It serves as a timeless archetype, inspiring leaders to aspire towards a vision of governance that prioritizes ethical values, social justice, and the common good.

In essence, Ram-Rajya encapsulates a vision of governance that transcends the temporal and cultural boundaries, offering a timeless blueprint for building a just and prosperous society. In contemporary discourse, the notion of Ram-Rajya continues to serve as a guiding framework for political figures and intellectuals in Bharat

(India), promoting a governance model that is grounded in ethical conduct and social cohesion. This concept epitomizes a vision of governance where values of equity, empathy, and righteousness inform the decisions and policies of those in positions of authority.

Ram-Rajya flourishment with Krishna-consciousness

The ideal of Ram-Rajya is situated in the Treta-Yuga era, predating the Krishna Avatar in the subsequent Dwapar-Yuga period by millennia. As the present Kali-Yuga epoch emerged from Dwapar-Yuga approximately 5,100 years ago, achieving the aspirational state of Ram-Rajya anew may necessitate a resurgence of the divine manifestations and teachings of Avatar Krishna. Through His incarnations, Krishna imparts the transformative essence of Krishna-consciousness to followers, empowering them to embody higher spiritual principles and ethical conduct.

The concept of Krishna-consciousness within the Sanatan ethos (including devotion to Ram, Shiva, Devi, and other deities) encourages individuals to introspect and establish a spiritual connection with the Creator in various forms such as Krishna, Ram, and Shiva. Through this exploration of the inner self, individuals can access boundless wisdom, vitality, and happiness. Drawing from this profound source of spiritual insight, individuals can generate novel ideas that have the capacity to revolutionize society, enhance scientific and technological progress, and

Part-2, Chapter 10: Krishna for Spiritual Bharat...

foster communal unity. These innovations hold the potential to bring about positive change not only within Bharatiya (Indian) society but also on a global scale. Thanks to this wisdom, renewable energy sources such as solar, atomic, hydrogen-based, wind and water-based energy sources will become more accessible and affordable for transportation, agriculture, industries, and household use. Additionally, India's space exploration programs will progress, leading to more cost-effective missions that allow for the sending of

Pic. 33: Ram and Krishna are inseparable forms of the Creator

human explorers or scientists to various planets and their satellites. These advancements will enable Indian scientists to explore and communicate with extraterrestrial beings.

Driven by the principles of Krishna-consciousness or Ram-Bhakti, India is poised to establish itself as a leading force on the global stage, excelling across various industries and sectors while also addressing the needs of both its own population and the broader international community. The country's highly skilled workforce, known for its exceptional abilities as well as qualities such as honesty, integrity, innovation, compassion, and leadership, will be in high demand worldwide.

The adoption of a purpose-driven lifestyle rooted in Krishna-consciousness or Ram-Bhakti among ordinary Indian citizens will foster a culture of cooperation, peaceful coexistence, and spiritual growth. Embracing principles such as yoga, simplicity, and moral progress will not only strengthen cultural unity but also promote a dignified and fulfilling life for all members of society.

A renewed focus on communal harmony, understanding, and collaboration will not only benefit the nation domestically but also contribute to global peace and unity.

Outdated practices such as reservation and divisive tactics based on caste and religion will give way to a meritocratic society where recognition and rewards are based on performance, competence, and achievement. This shift will foster a more inclusive and productive society, paving the way for a brighter future for Bharat/India and its people.

The transformation of extremist and misguided factions towards embracing values of enlightenment and reconnecting with mainstream cultural ideals will cultivate unity and harmony among the people of Bharat. This shift will lead to the enhancement of cottage industries, home-based businesses, and small family enterprises, especially in remote rural and tribal areas where the participation of women will be pivotal.

The effective utilization of natural resources for the betterment of society, the nation, and the global community will be a cornerstone of economic development. A thriving job market will help alleviate issues related to unemployment, as individuals find fulfillment in their chosen professions or entrepreneurial ventures. The promotion of Krishna-consciousness and traditional spiritual practices will create a harmonious and content populace.

In the realm of sports, Bharatiya athletes and players will achieve success on a global scale, supported by governmental, societal, and corporate networks. The practice of ethical living, mutual respect, collaboration, economic prosperity, heightened security, and peaceful coexistence will pave the way for the realization of the ideal of Ram-Rajya.

CHAPTER 11
KRISHNA REMOVING DEMOGRAPHIC IMBALANCE OF BHARAT

(Today)

Demographic imbalance dangerous for Bharat's integrity

Since the attainment of independence, Bharat has witnessed a concerning trend in its demographic composition. The proportion of Hindu population has witnessed a significant decline, paralleled by a substantial increase in the population of people adhering to foreign-faiths. This demographic imbalance poses a grave threat to Bharat's social fabric and national cohesion.

1. Impact on Social Harmony and Indigenous Hindus: The soaring population of foreign-faith people in specific regions has led to an exacerbation of social tension, adversely affecting the lives of Indigenous Hindus there. Instances of heightened suspicion, crime rates, and anti-social behaviors have been reported in such areas. The rapid growth of this population group, facilitated by multiple marriages and unscrupulous conversion practices, only adds to challenges faced by Indigenous Hindus.

2. Political Implications: The concentration of foreign-faith populations in certain regions also raises concerns regarding their separatist demands and aspirations for autonomous territories. Historical instances of regional secessionist movements further emphasize the potential risks associated with such demographic imbalances. The likelihood of renewed attempts to fragment Bharat cannot be dismissed as mere speculation, considering past experiences.

This is a potential threat posed by demographic imbalances to the integrity of Bharat. The demographic shifts in Bharat, particularly due to certain foreign-origin religious groups consistently increasing their population through multiple marriages and dubious conversion practices, raise concerns about the social fabric and country's unity.

Regions with a higher concentration of such communities may eventually demand independence, leading to a potential fragmentation of Bharat.

It is a matter of real concern

It is concerning to observe that individuals practicing different foreign-based faiths have not yet embraced the ancient Vedic culture and the honorable people of Bharat. If they were to acknowledge and appreciate the cultural heritage of their own ancestors, who were Hindus, there would be no issue. However, instead of embracing their own ancestral culture, these individuals continue to idolize

Pic. 34: Krishna's energy protecting Bharat from criminals and anti-Sanatanis

and follow those who invaded, murdered, insulted, and plundered Bharat as their heroes.

They persistently strive to eradicate Hindus and the Vedic culture, with the aim of establishing their own faiths based on conversion, deception, cruelty, bribes, and particular books of their faiths throughout Bharat. This issue is applicable to both foreign-based faiths. The preservation and unity of Hindus are crucial for the integrity and cohesion of Bharat. As long as Hindus maintain or increase their population percentage and maintain a keen sense of unity, Bharat remains intact. However, if the population of individuals practicing foreign-based faiths continues to grow, they inevitably start demanding faith-specific laws, freedom, and even separation from Bharat. This trend has already occurred, is ongoing, and is likely to recur if further tolerance is shown.

Shri Krishna, through His partial Avatar, is encouraging and empowering individuals who identify with the Indigenous Bharatiya/Hindu culture and those who hold respect for the Vedic traditions. His aim is to foster a sense of unity and proactivity among these individuals, urging them to collaborate and devise effective and innovative solutions for ensuring population equilibrium and safeguarding the integrity of Bharat.

Krishna inspires for true love, eliminates trap of pseudo love

Krishna's mini-Avatar exemplifies true love and serves to dismantle the detrimental allure of pseudo love. Furthermore, Krishna personifies compassion, wisdom, strength, prosperity, worldly and spiritual power, and divinity.

In contemporary Bharatiya society, the realm of intimate relationships and matrimonial unions has become multifaceted. Notably, certain religious communities of foreign origin incentivize and even promote unions or deceptive entrapments involving young Indigenous Hindu females, with the aim of inducing their conversion to foreign-based faith systems. These innocent Hindu girls, nurtured with ideals of genuine love, often find themselves ensnared in false or superficial affection, enduring lifelong suffering without a viable means of escape.

Unjustly, they prohibit their own (foreign-faith) community's girls and women from marrying Indigenous Hindu youths and men, unless the latter convert to their faith. Such practices, purportedly justified by dictates from their books, raise concerns as these actions appear scandalous, immoral, and unethical, while also being unfair, cruel, and unjustified.

It leads us to question the necessity of relying on the directives of any foreign faith when we already have a constitution in place. It is imperative to establish a Uniform Civil Code that applies to all citizens of Bharatiya, irrespective of their respective faiths.

Many authentic and respected Hindu families experience the anguish, turmoil, and disintegration because of engaging in such scandalous marriages that deviate from their decent cultural lineage.

Such intermarriages primarily serve to bolster the dominance and population growth of foreign-faith communities, particularly those practicing polygamy, which permits multiple marriages for their men and the subsequent procreation of numerous children to increase their population.

It further constitutes a violation of equitable principles and has a detrimental impact on the self-worth of native Hindus, leading to a decline in their population and political influence within the democratic framework of Bharatiya society.

Part-2, Chapter 11: Krishna Removing Demographic Imbalance...

Pic. 35: Avatar Krishna protecting Sanatani women from love jihad

This phenomenon has persisted over centuries. The pressing issue of population has already resulted in the fragmentation of Bharat in recent times, and if left unaddressed, it may lead to further divisions. It is imperative to recognize this as an objective reality rather than an unfounded fear. It is a fact, not a phobia.

Krishna's current partial Avatar serves as a catalyst for a transformative movement focused on promoting fairness, gender parity, and a comprehensive legal framework applicable to all citizens. He empowers the Hindu community, urging them to safeguard Hindu girls and women with their full attention, care, and proper coaching on their Sanatan heritage. Thus, the partial Avatar of Lord Krishna serves as a vigilant guardian, alerting and rescuing Hindu girls from the clutches of such illusory love entrapment.

He further inspires for homecoming of those whose ancestors earlier were Hindus and converted to foreign-faiths due to circumstances. He motivates Hindus to use their true love and genuine affection to attract the willing decent girls and women willing to return home from foreign faiths, welcome them in Sanatan Dharma freeing them from the constraints of polygamy associated with their faiths of foreign origin. Embracing these opportunities is vital for Hindus to reclaim their ancestral heritage, fostering dignity, love, peace, and unity within the broader Bharatiya society.

Partial Avatar of Shri Krishna also serves as a source of inspiration for Hindu women and young Hindu girls, encouraging them to prioritize self-worth, intelligence, and awareness. He cautions against becoming ensnared in the trap of emotional naiveté and mindless submission to gratification of the body or the illusory satisfaction of rebellion against their own tradition-based values.

Krishna motivates and empowers various affiliations, institutions, and individuals to proactively engage in this mission, demonstrating unwavering determination and utilizing all available resources, strength, and willingness to make sacrifices. Together, they will triumph over the obstacles posed by scandalous, cruel, brutal, and cunning adversaries.

He empowers Krishna-conscious or Sanatani people in Bharat and around the globe and makes this mission easier. He thus unifies Bharatiya society and the nation fairly and strongly. The timeless teachings of Krishna's Sanatan Dharma provide solace and preservation to those who appreciate, honor, embrace, and actively follow its principles.

Krishna Inspires for Protecting Indigenous Sanatan Dharma

Bharat is an ancient civilization that has thrived for thousands of years, encompassing a distinct culture and religious practices known as Vedic or Sanatan Dharma. The term Sanatan Dharma reflects the timeless nature of these traditions. Over time, the Bharatiya civilization and religious beliefs have become intertwined, resulting in the emergence of Hinduism or Hindu Dharma. As a result, both Indigenous Bharatiyas within Bharat and the diaspora around the world can be considered authentic Hindus with ancestral ties to the Vedic or Sanatan Dharma lineage.

Some religions such as Buddhism, Sikhism, and Jainism have also originated in Bharat, with their founders coming from Indigenous and pious Hindu families practicing Sanatan Dharma. Additionally, there are various indigenous isolated tribal faiths and religions, as well as atheists. These Indigenous religions and faiths are considered as integral parts of Sanatan Dharma, along with Hinduism, and their followers are recognized as Indigenous Bharatiyas or Sanatanis.

During the colonial era, foreign rulers adopted a divide-and-rule policy to divide Hindus into categories such as Aryans or Dravidians, North Indian Hindus or South Indian Hindus, and East Indian Hindus or West Indian Hindus, and rule over them. They were partially successful in this endeavor during the period of Hindu subjugation.

Now, in the present era of independence, progressiveness, open-mindedness, deeper understanding of Vedic philosophy and Sanatan culture, improved communication, access to information, and connectivity, as well as freedom of thought, professionalism, and financial independence, this division has significantly diminished. Any remaining divisions among Hindus are trivial when compared to the profound and violent divisions often seen among foreign faiths, where conflicts leading to violence and fatalities are prevalent.

It is important to acknowledge that all genuine Hindus in our country are culturally united. However, it is disheartening to witness some politicians attempting to divide the Hindu population for their own electoral gains. Further, there are some name-sake Hindus who have Hindu names but do not follow Sanatan principles and practices, and act against Hindu/Sanatan interests. Krishna, in His partial Avatar, is currently managing this situation.

Additionally, there are other minority groups in our diverse society who follow certain foreign religions or faiths but have embraced Bharat as their home and have mingled with Sanatani culture and traditions. As such, they too are true Bharatiyas. The amalgamation of Indigenous Hindus and followers of foreign religions is often referred to as Hindustani. It is worth noting that in certain Arab countries, Hindustanis of any faith are colloquially referred to as Hindus by the local Arabs.

The Indigenous Bharatiya/Hindu population is apprehensive about the ongoing religious conversions, as they fear that they may eventually become a minority and face the risk of extinction within a century. This would result in Bharat, the only nation with a Hindu majority, becoming a country predominantly influenced by two major foreign faiths, due to the elimination or conversion of Hindus.

There is a concern about potential fragmentation of Bharatiya society into smaller nations influenced by two prominent foreign faiths. This concern stems from a careful analysis of demographic data from the past few decades and the current ambitious expansion efforts undertaken by these faiths. Recognizing this situation, it is important to acknowledge the wisdom of the omniscient and omnipresent deity, Krishna.

Today, Krishna's partial Avatar has emerged to inspire, empower, and mobilize competent individuals, parties, organizations, and groups. Their intended purpose is to address and reverse the population trend, as well as to ensure the preservation, growth, and ascendancy of Sanatan Dharma. This mission, which is supported by collective and conscientious efforts, people's organizations, effective governance, sacrifices, and intelligence, is expected to bring about control over the situation. It is believed that success will be facilitated by the blessings bestowed by Krishna.

Democracy, demography, and numbers game

Within the context of democracy, demography, and the dynamics between majorities and minorities, an unsettling phenomenon is occurring in Bharat. The growth of minority groups appears to come at the expense of the decline of the majority Hindus. Strikingly, this detrimental trend has been constitutionally legitimized in the name of secularism, masking the underlying issues. Two foreign religions, which are not native to Bharat, exhibit considerable aggression in their efforts to convert Indigenous or native Bharatiya individuals, including local tribes, to their respective faiths.

Tragically, these conversions often result in a departure from the authentic cultural and ideological roots of the homeland, Bharat, in favor of embracing beliefs originating from elsewhere. As a consequence, the demographic landscape of Bharat is undergoing deliberate alteration, whereby the Indigenous Hindu population is experiencing a concerning decline, while the number of converted people is on the rise, resulting in significant effects on traditional practices, cultural values, and religious beliefs of the native Bharatiya community, and also unity and integrity of Bharat.

Avatar Krishna is aware of the significance of demographic factors in shaping society in a democracy. With the equal voting rights, the political power of Indigenous Hindus is steadily diminishing, while that of converted individuals is on the rise. This incremental transformation in the balance of power from majority to minority holds crucial implications for the allocation of constitutionally-sanctioned benefits.

Clearly, Minority enjoys certain specific and crucial benefits over the majority as per the constitution. Ultimately, the majority Sanatani group finds itself progressively conceding ground to these minority foreign-based faith factions.

The privileges associated with minority status ought to be limited once it reaches a certain threshold (e.g., 1.5%) of the total population of Bharat, at which point they should be treated on equal footing with the majority Hindus. Failing to do so would lead to a situation where the current majority Hindus are transformed into a future minority. This clearly contradicts the purpose and principles embodied in the Bharatiya (Indian) constitution. It is not desirable to have guests in one's home who continually pose threats, undermine, or marginalize the host population, and eventually take control through enslavement, expelling, violence, or forced conversions to their Foreign-based faith.

The usage of terms such as "converted," "native," or "Indigenous" is not in alignment with political and constitutional correctness, as all citizens of Bharatiya are constitutionally equal. However, variations can be observed in their ideologies and real-life experiences among those who have converted from Sanatan to a foreign faith. These differences will have political, geographical, and cultural implications for the nation of Bharatiya, with the Indigenous Bharatiyas (Sanatanis) being particularly affected adversely.

Therefore, there is an immediate need to consider constitutional amendments or the introduction of a new constitution to address this matter. Shri Krishna is aware of the significant growth of the two Abrahamic religions originating from the West in various states of Bharat. With these religions potentially becoming the majority in some states, there have been past and ongoing demands for secession and the establishment of new nations.

If the demographic growth of these two minority religions is not controlled, Bharat runs the risk of fragmenting into multiple parts, potentially resulting in the emergence of several separate nations. Moreover, Krishna is determined to prevent this outcome. His foremost allegiance lies with Dev-Bhumi Bharat and its Dharma. Shri Krishna recognizes that the continued existence of Bharat is contingent upon the survival of Sanatan/Hinduism.

Shri Krishna has carefully devised a comprehensive strategy to safeguard, advance, and broaden the scope of His cherished Sanatan Dharma and its influence in the homeland of Bharat and worldwide. He serves as a source of inspiration, vitality, and rejuvenation for the majority populace Hindu through His profound spiritual awakening or the indomitable power of Sanatan consciousness. By harnessing the collective strength of His followers,

Krishna fosters a revolutionary mindset and effectively brings about necessary revisions in the constitutional framework, or even advocates for a new constitution, ensuring equitable justice for His Sanatani people. Thus, as a partial Avatar Krishna undertakes the noble responsibility of protecting the interests of Hindus and the timeless principles of Sanatan Dharma in Bharat, consistently fulfilling His sacred pledge and divine 'Will.'

CHAPTER 12
KRISHNA'S PRUDENT GOVERNANCE
(Today)

Avatar Krishna has a foolproof governance system based on the divinity of Dharma. Fearlessly He protects all people with utmost confidence, patience, and tolerance. He uses truth and non-violence as practicable for the benefit of humanity. In younger age Krishna energized His devotees and friends with Baal-Leela and Raas-Leela, but in adult life He motivates all for tough fight in the Maha-Bharat of real life.

Krishna motivates and energizes all Krishna-conscious Sanatani youths, Karma Yogis, scholars and devotees for strengthening and elevating Bharat and humanity.

Krishna inspires equality of all Sanatanis (Hindus and devotees), true Bharatiyas, without any differentiation of caste or Varna. Eternal Superman Hanuman ji is all powerful in this Kaliyuga. He protects His devotees and fulfills all plans of His master Shri Ram, who is present in Avatar Krishna form also.

Krishna's patience and tolerance for Shishupals of today

Currently, there exist a considerable number of individuals (like Shishupal), who harbor envious sentiments towards the growing Krishna-consciousness or Sanatan-energy movement who are leading to the advancement of Bharat. These individuals persistently engage in criticizing the commendable decisions, advancements, and reforms taking place in our nation. It is worth mentioning that these individuals have a history of participating in corrupt, unethical, and antinational practices.

In a democratic society, every individual possesses the right to freedom of expression, which is duly recognized and tolerated to a certain extent. Nevertheless, it is imperative to note that when such expressions exceed reasonable limits, Krishna promptly intervenes and administers severe repercussions, disciplines, or eliminates the offender. Krishna possesses the authority to administer both disciplinary measures and rewards. It is crucial to avoid misconstruing His love, kindness, and compassion as indications of weakness. Likewise, it is equally important to refrain from perceiving the love, kindness, and compassion exhibited by Krishna-conscious or Sanatani individuals as signs of vulnerability.

Those individuals who persistently degrade Krishna-conscious Sanatani practitioners are timely subjected to severe consequences when they exceed acceptable limits. Krishna-conscious Sanatani individuals, while not outwardly displaying their immense power in their daily lives, are the epitome of strength, as they maintain a direct connection with Krishna's boundless energy. Whenever

Krishna imbues individuals with inspiration and vitality, they effortlessly conduct seemingly arduous tasks, akin to performing miracles. Krishna manifests His Partial-Avatars from devout individuals who possess Krishna-consciousness, to fulfill specific objectives, across various locations and time periods.

Tolerance of Krishna

Avatar Krishna embodies an ideal character that epitomizes both strength and gentleness. He demonstrates tenderness and compassion towards children, women, mothers, relatives, friends, lovers, saints, seers (Rishis), righteous and virtuous individuals, innocents, animals, the environment, devoted followers, and those who follow the path of Dharma (righteousness).

Additionally, he possesses an immense capacity to confront and deter individuals of malicious intent, encompassing ruffians, troublemakers, delinquents, malefactors, transgressors, assailants, perpetuators of heinous acts, malevolent, turncoats, manipulators, falsifiers, deceivers, and any other perpetrators aiming to undermine moral righteousness (Dharma) and disrupt the sanctity, cohesion, and harmony of the Bharatiya society.

Krishna demonstrates a lenient stance towards the unintentional mistakes made by His devotees, offering forgiveness upon their sincere repentance. However, He exercises zero tolerance towards deliberate mischief and scandals, duly penalizing the culprits with utmost severity. Krishna tolerated ninety-nine abusive words or mistakes of Shishupal (as promised to his mother) but punished him brutally upon his 100th mistake. Hindus draw inspiration from this example of Krishna in their own conduct.

Krishna exhibits a dual nature in His actions. On one hand, He nurtures and supports those who possess a gentle disposition, love for humanity, progressive thinking, and creative prowess. On the other hand, He firmly confront and dismantles the adverse elements that oppose the well-being and progress of society. Additionally, He offers protection to those who adhere to moral righteousness (Dharma) while simultaneously disciplining and eliminating those who engage in immoral and destructive behavior (Adharma).

While He demonstrates tolerance towards those who uphold moral values, He displays intolerance towards those who undermine them. Krishna has always been committed to upholding and defending Dharma (righteousness), as conveyed in the Bhagavad Gita: *"I will protect the virtuous and uphold the principles of Dharma (righteousness)."* Today, this commitment is embodied in the Avataric forms, infusing the consciousness of billions of Indigenous inhabitants of Bharat (India), and inspiring them with determination and vigor. It means, Krishna's influence can be seen in the collective consciousness of over a billion Bharatiyas or Sanatanis worldwide.

This influence serves to inspire and empower Sanatanis, the Indigenous Bharatiya people with determination and decisiveness. Krishna, known for His true love, compassion, and kindness, also represents strength, protection, and the eternal consciousness of Bharatiya/Sanatani traditions. This is evident through the recent advancements, progress, enhanced security measures, strengthened defense capabilities, increased confidence among Bharatiya nationalists, as well as the growing recognition and appreciation Bharat has received globally.

It is essential to recognize the presence of the Krishna Avatar in our current era. This manifestation is actively evident in the form of Krishna-consciousness, Sanatan Chetana, both within the boundaries of Bharat and globally too.

The softer form of this energy can be observed in the devoted and committed practices of households, temples, public chanting, peaceful demonstrations, nationalistic media presentations, televised discussions, righteous performances, congregational gatherings, and yoga exercises. On the other hand, the sterner dimension of this energy is manifesting through assertive and resolute actions against immoral, inhumane, scandalous, terrorist, and nefarious forces, both domestic and foreign, that oppose righteousness (Dharma) and the best interests of Bharat. It is crucial to acknowledge that both forms are simultaneously unfolding and will continue to do so.

Krishna differentiates between "genuine and fake tolerance"

In the ancient Vedic scriptures, it is emphasized that while tolerance is a virtue, there are limits to its application. After this limit, intolerance becomes a virtue.

Shri Krishna exemplifies this understanding by distinguishing between genuine tolerance and foolish or excessive tolerance. According to Krishna's teachings, it is crucial to demonstrate tolerance towards well-intentioned individuals entering our home, society, or nation as guests.

Welcoming and accommodating them is considered a virtue. However, Krishna cautions against tolerating mischief or harmful actions perpetrated by individuals who exploit the hospitality they receive.

These individuals, driven by greed, may have ulterior motives such as harming or undermining our society, its values, or its inhabitants. In such instances, Krishna advocates for swift action to address the threat posed by these imposters and criminals disguised as guests.

Pic. 36: Krishna does not tolerate invaders, criminals & anti-Sanatanis

The severity of the response depends on the nature of their crimes and the urgency of the situation. Krishna upholds that it is appropriate to expel or eliminate these individuals without hesitation, as opposed to demonstrating passive tolerance or submission in the face of their wrongdoings.

Krishna embodies an unparalleled exemplar of compassion and love. However, as a guardian of His people, He is compelled to manage criminal elements, imposters, and invaders with unwavering firmness and decisiveness. Krishna does not entertain pseudo-humanitarian justifications in dealing with such individuals. He places utmost importance on the practice and preservation of virtuous qualities, whether exercised through tolerance or intolerance, non-violence or violence, peace, or war. Within the framework of Krishna's Dharma, these actions are deemed essential. Today, Krishna is effectively and firmly addressing these imposters and criminals in His partial Avatar form.

Who are Krishna-conscious Sanatani people?

Individuals who revere Shri Krishna in any of His forms, comprehend and abide by the teachings of the Geeta/Gita, have unwavering faith in Krishna's performances and divine pastimes (Leela), perceive His presence in their lives and consciousness, experience His divine energy and blessings in their existence, walk the path of righteousness (Dharma), and are devoted to Krishna and any of His forms are recognized as Krishna-conscious or Sanatani individuals.

Individuals who adhere to Krishna consciousness or Sanatani beliefs perceive Krishna's presence in all Vedic or Sanatani deities such as Brahma, Vishnu, Mahesh, including Venkatesh, Rama, Shiva, Durga, Lakshmi, Saraswati, as well as their various manifestations.

These resolute and virtuous souls, numbering in hundreds of millions worldwide, strive tirelessly to serve humanity, promote the integrity of Bharat (India), uphold its Vedic culture and heritage, preserve its majesty, and safeguard the Hindu Dharma (religion) - the eternal way of life.

Krishna conscious people or devotees can be found across various sectors and social strata. From those residing in the streets and slums, to laborers, security personnel, students, ordinary households, clerks, teachers, traders, businessmen, industrialists, film stars, government and private sector employees, professionals, and also top-ranking officials such as ministers, governors, prime ministers, and presidents, all those who believe in and feel the presence and blessings of Krishna within themselves are classified as Krishna-conscious Sanatani individuals. These individuals are essentially Yogis.

The devotees of the International Society for Krishna Consciousness (ISKCON) are also considered Bhakti-Yogis, as they have achieved enlightenment in Krishna-consciousness and strive to disseminate it worldwide using the mantra, "Hare Krishna Hare Krishna Krishna Krishna Hare Hare, Hare Rama Hare Rama Rama Rama Hare Hare."

Those who worship Lord Shiva and acknowledge his visit to Gokul to catch a glimpse of Bal-Krishna are also categorized as Krishna-conscious Sanatani devotees.

Along with other Yogis, these Krishna-conscious Yogis are actively involved in embracing and disseminating the partial Avatar of Krishna across various regions globally. They are steadfastly fulfilling His commitment to safeguarding the virtuous and extinguishing the wicked individuals and their affiliations, thus establishing the eternal principles of Sanatan Dharma, as assured by Shri Krishna in the Gita.

Krishna's Eternal Energy: Hanuman Ji

In the spiritual realm, it is believed that Lord Shiva reflects the eternal cosmic energy of the Creator Krishna in a masculine manifestation, while the Adi-Shakti represents this eternal energy in a feminine form. Hanuman Ji, revered as the 11th Rudra or a celestial incarnation of Lord Shiva, holds great significance.

The Rigveda venerates Rudra as the epitome of power and strength, "mightiest of the mighty." Therefore, Hanuman Ji (Rudra) can be regarded as the enduring embodiment of the Creator Krishna's eternal energy in its masculine manifestation. Being Chiranjivi or immortal, Hanuman Ji is believed to have an existence that transcends time and will persist as long as the universe exists.

In ancient times, specifically during the Treta and Dwapar Yugas, Hanuman ji played a significant role alongside the Avatars of Shri Ram and Shri Krishna as depicted in Vedic scriptures. Notably, during the Mahabharat war, Hanuman ji, who represented a part of Krishna's divine energy, resided on the flag of Arjun's chariot, with Lord Krishna himself as the charioteer. Hanuman ji's presence proved instrumental in protecting the chariot and Arjun from numerous adversary attacks, ensuring its invincibility.

Even in the present era of Kali Yuga, Hanuman ji, embodying masculine Krishna energy, continues to manifest in the collective consciousness of devoted individuals. Such individuals include

Pic. 37: Hanuman ji defends pious devotees and destroys demonic people

people from diverse backgrounds such as scholars, professionals, politicians, diplomats, intellectuals, saints, businesspeople, police officers, military personnel, defense forces, farmers, laborers, workers, and all other devotees. Therefore, the indomitable power of Hanuman ji operates through the unity of these devoted Sanatani masses, Krishna-conscious minds, and Bhaktas of Ram and Shiva, and those who adhere to Sanatani beliefs. It is important to note that just as Hanuman ji remains undefeated, so too are his faithful followers.

Krishna, the icon of Fearlessness and Dharma

All beings are most scared of the death. This fear partial-Avatar Krishna addresses in a manner that eradicates this fear from the depths of human consciousness. He expounds upon the notion that an individual is not a perishable physical form or body but an immortal Soul, known as Atma, that transcends the boundaries of mortality. This eternal essence, undergoing a cycle of rebirths, seamlessly transitions from one corporeal existence to another, much like individual changing clothes.

So, a being should never fear death or the threats of death. Death is simply a transformation of the soul from this body to the next body. Here the concept of death is redefined as merely a transformative process for the Soul, divesting it from the limitations of the current embodiment and preparing it for a subsequent life in accordance with past and present Karmas. Hence, a person should never succumb to the paralyzing grip of fear pertaining to death or impending mortality, for it holds no true power over the immortal soul.

Understanding this truth grants unlimited fearlessness and propels individuals to discharge their responsibilities with conviction, incorporating principles of selflessness, austerity, and sacrificing for the greater good. Moreover, one can lead a life filled with legitimate joy and gratification while preserving dignity, with no fear about their mortality.

The Vedic scriptures emphasize that engaging in virtuous actions has profound implications on one's future. Charitable deeds can lead to liberation or a positive outcome in the next life, such as being born into a virtuous, affluent, or respectable family, or even as a powerful yogi.

Contributing to the welfare and protection of our homeland, following, and upholding righteous principles, earning wealth through ethical means, and assisting those in need are all significant acts of goodness.

Furthermore, supporting humanitarian causes and prioritizing the safety of humanity, as well as taking care of animals and the environment, are also highly commendable as good Karmas. Moreover, showing reverence and extending assistance to parents, teachers, and elders should also be cherished as good Karmas.

Fear is not only detrimental to one's self-confidence but also undermines trust in the soul's immortality and adherence to righteousness. Lord Krishna inspires individuals to fearlessness, as it is only through fearlessness that Dharma or righteousness can prevail. A truly righteous person is characterized by their unwavering determination, strength, and resilience even in the face of crisis or challenges.

On the other hand, a fearful person easily crumbles under pressure or adverse circumstances. A true Dharmik remains firm, determined, and strong. The follower of Dharma is a righteous, disciplined, and self-confident person, and so is strong and most importantly - fearless. The self-confidence of a Dharmic person who follows a virtuous path, is derived internally, as they understand themselves to be an eternal soul (Atma). Krishna's teachings serve as a reminder that the soul is immortal and eternally connected to the Paramatma (the Creator, Supreme Soul, God, Krishna) at the Innermost-self.

This unbreakable bond between the soul and Paramatma is characterized by perpetual union and harmony. Paramatma represents boundless energy, intelligence, and existence, infusing the soul with unending strength, infinite wisdom, and flawless perfection. A truly Dharmic person always recognizes and embraces this profound truth, unwavering and self-assured. Krishna, being the epitome of fearlessness, serves as a guiding example for them. A Dharmic individual embodies this fearlessness, constantly sensing the presence of the Paramatma within themselves – the Krishna within.

By establishing this connection with Krishna, they achieve a state of harmonious integration, enabling them to navigate life with unwavering confidence and fearlessness, drawing upon the infinite energy bestowed by Krishna. Their unwavering realization, self-confidence, and fearlessness make them resilient and indomitable.

A person of strong moral conviction possesses a fearless outlook towards death. In the Gita Shri Krishna imparts wisdom that death merely signifies the transition from one bodily form to another, akin to changing garments. The essence of one's being, the soul, is eternal and undying. A person grounded in Dharma or righteousness always remains cognizant of their eternal nature.

Their commitment to Dharma does not necessitate a daily compulsory visit to the temple or engaging in daily religious rituals. Rather, it is marked by a genuine and compassionate heart, filled with love for one's family, country, and humanity. Such individuals consistently engage in virtuous deeds and harbor positive thoughts, effectively assuming the role of a yogi or yogini who fearlessly and perpetually remains connected to Krishna.

Krishna inspires for prudent "truth and non-violence"

Krishna encourages individuals in Bharat to embrace the principles of truth and nonviolence for the betterment of society as outlined in the Vedic scriptures and literatures.

The concepts of truth and nonviolence can be powerful instruments in achieving societal objectives, provided they serve to safeguard the nation, uphold righteous conduct, protect citizens, and preserve their dignity and belongings. However, it is essential to exercise discernment and not blindly adhere to these principles when they may result in yielding to cunning and aggressive forces, leading to the loss of lives, property, and the erosion of collective esteem.

For instance, if one possesses knowledge of an innocent person's whereabouts who is being pursued by a malicious individual seeking to harm them, it would be unwise to disclose this information truthfully. In such a scenario, it is better to remain silent, feign ignorance, or even provide false information to safeguard the innocent person's life. Revealing the truth to the aggressor would only contribute to the unjust killing, and one would bear a share of the guilt. Thus, it is crucial to approach the application of these principles with intelligence, analysis, and adaptability, rather than adhering rigidly and stubbornly out of personal ego or a misguided sense of righteousness.

It is essential to exercise discernment, intelligence, and prudence when utilizing the truth. The truth should be employed in such a manner that it aligns with common sense, while also considering the greater good of society and humanity. In line with the principles of Sanatan Dharma, it is advised to speak the truth in a manner that is pleasing to others and avoid expressing unpleasant truths.

Similarly, one must refrain from uttering false statements, even if they may seem pleasant. This adherence to eternal moral values and ethics constitutes an integral aspect of our societal fabric.

In support of this notion, a story serves as an illustrative example. Once, in a desolate location, a group of criminals pursued a frightened woman. Seeking refuge, the woman sought solace in a saint's small hut, where the saint was present. The criminals approached the saint and inquired about the woman's whereabouts. Rather than revealing her presence, the sage directed the criminals away by silently indicating an alternate path. Only when it was safe for the woman to depart, did the sage inform her to exit the hut and continue her journey to safety.

This captivating tale elucidates the significance of judiciously employing tact and discernment in certain situations, particularly when immediate disclosure of straightforward information may jeopardize the welfare of vulnerable individuals. Thus, the truth should be employed strategically.

It is important to acknowledge the prevalence of deceptive tactics utilized in matters of diplomacy and warfare. While it is true that violence should be avoided whenever possible, it would be impractical to assert that nonviolence can always be upheld in the context of war. When it comes to public or political affairs, blindly adhering to a policy of 'truth and nonviolence' without considering the potential consequences, such as the loss of innocent lives, does not serve as a moral principle or an embodiment of righteousness. Instead, it can be viewed as an act of hypocrisy, ignorance, or wrongdoing, rather than a just form of resistance known as 'Satyagraha.'

Those who employ such tactics and subsequently witness the detrimental outcomes should have the integrity to acknowledge their errors, accept the consequences, and respond appropriately to rectify their actions. To persist in these practices without any desire for change would be indicative of hypocrisy and will eventually elicit consequences orchestrated by a higher authority, such as Avatar Krishna, in ways that are beyond our understanding and are fair.

Ultimately, it is those individuals who possess the humility to admit their mistakes and assume responsibility for their actions that are deserving of forgiveness upon showing remorse and making genuine efforts to rectify their actions.

No Raas-Leela for Krishna when there is Maha-Bharat

Krishna's Raas-Leela with His girlfriends (Gopis), which occurs when He is 8-9 years old, is a beautiful expression of juvenile innocence, natural attraction, enthusiasm, beauty, art, purity, divinity, and liberating energy. However, it is unfortunate that some individuals with lustful intentions have distorted this sacred practice (Raas-Leela) into an adult sensual or lustful activity, thus tarnishing the esteemed cultural and artistic heritage of Bharat.

It is important to clarify that Krishna's girlfriends (Gopis) are not driven by sensuality or lust. Instead, they are virtuous, innocent, naturally pure, and filled with divine love. These remarkable women possess strength, energy, spirituality, and noble character. In fact, they embody the qualities of the divine feminine power, known as Devi or Adhya-Shakti. In Vedic scriptures Adi Shakti (primitive natural energy) is represented as Durga, Kali, Laxmi, Saraswati, and other energies.

During Raas-Leela Gopis feel the infinite energy of the divine mother Adi Shakti within themselves, which uplifts devotees and defeats cruel and lustful demons. Through His association with these remarkable girls or women (Gopis), Krishna emphasizes the empowerment of women, fostering the awakening of Nari-Shakti and Devi-Shakti, symbolizing the strength and potential inherent in the feminine energy.

Today, as the transformative revolution unfolds in Bharat, likened to the grand scale battles of Maha-Bharat, Lord Krishna's teachings from the Vedic scriptures resonate deeply. His guidance encourages girls and women for self-sufficiency, self-dependance, and to embrace newfound strength and empowerment. In addition to their devotional pursuits, Krishna enlightens them on the importance of equipping themselves with self-defense tools such as firearms, swords, knives, and pepper-spray, as well as fostering proficiency in martial arts like Judo and Karate. Moreover, He stresses the need to cultivate physical prowess while also sharpening the intellect and vigilance.

Krishna's message ultimately seeks to inspire tenderness and compassion in their hearts towards children, family, elders, animals, plants, and the vulnerable in society and nation. Simultaneously, He advocates for self-reliance, assertiveness, determination, and resoluteness, enabling women to rise above dependence on men or others for their protection.

Women ought to possess self-respect and exhibit fierceness, firmness, and unwavering resolve when it comes to confronting any form of malevolence, rogues, anti-Bharat forces, those who oppose the Sanatani way of life, or any manifestation of Adharma (evil) and injustice.

Let us reiterate that Krishna, through His transcendental manifestation (partial Avatar), has been inspiring for the empowerment of women as per the wisdom revealed in the Vedic scriptures. Today, Krishna's intention is for women to transcend their previous limitations, no longer remaining powerless (Abala) or succumbing to societal stereotypes of weakness, impurity, and immorality. Instead, Krishna encourages women to remember the infinite power of the Aadi-Shakti existing within them, embrace their strength and autonomy, becoming self-reliant individuals capable of defending themselves, their families, communities, and society. Furthermore, this empowered state enables women to confront and conquer adversities they may encounter along their life journey.

Avatar Krishna has also been inspiring that compulsory military training and service be implemented for all people of Bharat for a minimum of three years. This approach aims to foster self-reliance, discipline, and enhance the safety and security of both individuals and the nation as a whole. By equipping citizens with the necessary tools for self-defense, Bharat can fortify its foundations and ensure its strength.

Krishna enlightening the new generation of Bharat

Today, means over a span of recent centuries, and particularly in the last few decades, Krishna consciousness, or the infusion of Sanatan energy, has gradually permeated the thoughts and beliefs of Indigenous Sanatani/Hindus and individuals of Bharatiya origin, both within Bharat and across the globe. The divine manifestations of Krishna's expansions, namely Brahma, Vishnu, Mahesh, along with their consort energies Saraswati, Lakshmi, and Durga (representing various forms of Adi Shakti), have remained actively engaged in this endeavor.

Additionally, the expansions of Krishna as Rudra, Hanuman, Bhairav, Chandi, and Kali have also fortified their presence within the minds of all Bharatiyas who hold faith in them. Their collective mission is to safeguard Vedic culture, Bharatiya/Hindu society, and the illustrious nation of Bharat. Krishna is helping to cleanse the consciousness of the Bharatiya people who have suffered from over a millennium of subjugation and oppression. This oppression was first inflicted upon them by ruthless invaders and plunderers from the western and northwestern regions of Bharat, and later by European powers who arrived as traders, thieves, and manipulators.

The courageous and patriotic Bharatiya population has, in turn, gained a deeper understanding of history, both within Bharat and globally, learning valuable truths and lessons that were previously unknown to them.

The Hindus are now aware of the painful experiences endured by their gentle and simplistic ancestors. These ancestors faced torture, brutal killings, forced conversions, humiliation, insults, and abuse by invading forces, looters, and robbers. It is disheartening to observe that even subsequent generations and followers of these merciless invaders continue to employ the same hostile, deceitful, and tormenting tactics to instill fear and subjugate the original inhabitants of Bharat/Hindus.

Considering this, Shri Krishna's partial Avatar serves as a beacon of inspiration for the present generation of Indigenous Bharatiyas, urging them to draw lessons from history. They must remain vigilant against the avaricious, crafty, demeaning, and divisive influences that seek to undermine and enslave them. It is imperative for the Indigenous Bharatiyas to unite and fortify themselves, fostering strength, freedom, prosperity, happiness, and expansion. It is equally crucial to uphold the noble principles and eternal Sanatan Dharma that have perpetuated in Bharat for millennia.

Krishna's effective and glorious governance

As we remember Shri Krishna, we immediately feel protected, confident, energized, elevated, victorious, peaceful, and smiling. Remembering Krishna, immediately connects us with our Innermost-self, where He resides. We feel His power, which becomes our power. With infinite power and energy, He exists within us. We feel part of that energy and get elevated. We feel strength, piousness, love, compassion, and purity. Good feelings, good thoughts, good emotions, good innovative ideas, holiness, divinity arise in our heart, mind, brain, and consciousness.

We feel new energy and vitality. We feel healthy, cheerful, energized, and empowered. We feel deeply self-confident. We feel like a powerful master in full command.

Krishna's life is full of adventures. He faces many problems, finds solutions, and remains ever victorious. He visualizes the problems beforehand and is always ready with a solution. It is true in His personal as well as social and national life. The governance methods of the Avatar Shri Krishna can be described in the following terms:

1. **Evolutionary Thinking:** Avatar Krishna transcends entrenched traditions and seeks

innovative ways to address contemporary challenges. He identifies obsolete norms, reforms them, and introduces groundbreaking solutions to meet the demands of the times.
2. **National Security and Prosperity:** Avatar Krishna places paramount importance on safeguarding the well-being and advancement of His nation. He is devoted to strengthening the security apparatus, ensuring economic prosperity, and enhancing the global standing of His country.
3. **Cultural Heritage Preservation:** With unwavering determination, Avatar Krishna protects the dignity, lifestyle, cultural practices, and overall prosperity of His people. He recognizes the significance of preserving their rich heritage and traditions, safeguarding them from any threats or external influences.
4. **Guardian of Bharat's Ancient Wisdom:** Avatar Krishna serves as a guardian of Bharat, diligently safeguarding its invaluable ancient knowledge, heritage, and remarkable cultural legacy. He recognizes the tremendous power and wisdom that emanate from his nation's history and takes immense pride in preserving and promoting it for future generations.
5. **Innovation:** Strategically develops innovative systems and revolutionary infrastructure with the utmost commitment to excellence.
6. **Sturdy base:** Establishes a harmonious social order by maintaining a position of strength and power, as true peace can only be achieved when backed by strength.

7. **Strength of Nation:** Fosters the strengthening of our nation, knowing that vulnerability can breed conflicts, while strength garners respect and cooperation from both individuals and nations.
8. **Glorious Bharat:** Striking a careful equilibrium between unwavering determination and adaptable approaches to uphold peace, foster economic growth, and preserve the moral fabric of our great nation. He champions a genuine sense of loyalty and devotion to our country, while promoting an environment conducive to abundance and a sense of accomplishment.
9. **Justice:** Unflinchingly upholding the principles of justice and order through the vigilant enforcement of legal regulations.
10. **Participative governance:** Krishna ardently advocates for the empowerment of individuals, promoting a participatory form of governance, fostering a keen sense of camaraderie among citizens, and nurturing the fundamental building blocks of society, namely resilient families, and tight-knit communities.
11. **Leadership acumen:** Krishna imparts the wisdom of embracing a leadership mindset rather than succumbing to a subordinate role.
12. **Effective strategies:** He employs strategic measures to effectively combat terrorists, individuals disrupting societal harmony, and those working against the nation's interests, thereby dismantling their networks.
13. **Harmony:** He promotes interreligious harmony and resolves conflicts by encouraging individuals to

comprehend and implement righteous principles in their lives.

14. **Decisiveness:** He sternly deals with individuals who exhibit arrogance and repeatedly engage in wrongdoings, like his actions against Shushupals and Duryodhans.

15. **Effective leadership:** Krishna is dedicated to revitalizing and advancing the great nation of Bharat, fostering unity and resilience among its people. He tirelessly works towards upholding the principles of effective democracy, safeguarding the rights and responsibilities of every citizen, establishing excellent governance, and nurturing competent leadership. He is committed to promoting freedom and promoting dignified conduct in our communications and behaviors, while vehemently condemning and taking strict measures against any form of indecency, anti-national sentiments, and harmful practices.

16. **Judicious:** One of Krishna's distinguishing characteristics is his discernment when it comes to the allocation of human rights. He carefully distinguishes between individuals who merit these rights, such as peace-loving citizens, and those who engage in criminal behavior. Furthermore, he is steadfast in upholding the laws pertaining to human rights. Krishna is committed to promoting and implementing good governance practices that are efficient and beneficial for society.

17. **Tough on corruption:** To combat corruption, Krishna implements strict measures to hold individuals and officials accountable for their unethical actions. Those found guilty of corruption

face severe consequences, while individuals who demonstrate honesty and integrity are duly recognized and honored.

18. **In essence:** Avatar Krishna's approach embodies a fusion of visionary thinking, national security consciousness, cultural preservation, wellbeing of people, intellectual stewardship, and divine liberator.

Krishna inspires equality: No castes (Varnas) - Only Sanatanis

Krishna establishes the equality of all individuals in the Bharatiya society. The erroneous concept of separate castes, known as Varnas, is not supported by Him. Instead, Krishna encourages individuals to recognize and realize the characteristics of all four varnas (specialties) within themselves - Brahman, Kshatriya, Vaishya, and Shudra. A person, like the body of the *Puran-Purush (Kaal Purusha)*, has characteristics of all four Varnas.

Thus, all four varnas coexist within everyone, with some particular Varna being more prominent or active than others. In each person Some Varnas (specialties) are awakened or dominant, others remain dormant or sleeping. It is essential to awaken and cultivate the relevant qualities of different Varnas as per the demands of different situations and environments.

Krishna does not recommend caste differentiation. Only one caste - Manava (the human being)! All are Sanatan or eternal.

Like the body of the Puran-Purush, as mentioned in the Vedic scriptures (Shastras) the body of a human is considered in four parts, which signifies as follows:

Head: Brahman (Brain, Wisdom, Vision)

Arms, chest: Kshatriya (Defense, security, Management)

Thigh area: Vaishya (Business, agriculture, Finance)

Legs: Shudra (Field work, support services)

All these four parts form the body and must perform their share of duties for good health, survival, and accomplishment of the goal of a person. It is essential to recognize that when one engages in intellectual pursuits such as teaching, scientific research, planning, creative endeavors, or holistic endeavors, they operate as a Brahman, contributing to the advancement and betterment of society.

When the same person uses his muscle power with brain to defend and support oneself, own family, society or nation, the person performs as a Kshatriya. When he or she grows food, raises animals for milk, distributes commodity products etc., does trading or business for sustenance of family, community, nation, the person performs the role of a Vaishya.

And when the same person does leg or muscle work to support and serve oneself, own family, society, or nation, he or she performs as a Shudra. The weight of whole body comes on the supporting legs. So, the Shudra happily bears the weight of whole body, whole society with the spirit of service or Sewa.

All these four parts cooperate and support each other. All these four parts form a body. None can perform in isolation. All the four parts are equally important for proper health and functioning of the body to think, plan, perform, survive, and achieve the goals. For Krishna there is only one caste, Jati, or Varna, and that is - "Human being." Different Varna, Jati are only various parts and distinct functions of the same body. Different capabilities, specialties and possibilities existing in the same integrated body. Almost every day, a person uses all these four parts (functions) of the body, so he or she is Brahman, Kshatriya, Vaishya, and Shudra all in one, performing all the four specialized functions every day, at various times.

When any person's brain performs better, and is used more often for holistic purposes, he or she is performing more as a Brahman. When he or she is more skilled in defending or managing functions, he or she performs more as a Kshatriya. The same person, when proficient in agricultural matters or business, and performs it more often, he or she is more in the role of a Vaishya. And the same person, when enjoys his proficiency in serving others, helping others, and spends more time and effort in these services, he or she functions more as a Shudra.

So, Brahman, Kshatriya, Vaishya, and Shudra are different functionalities of the same body and are equally important. No part of the body is superior or inferior. Unfortunately, for centuries this philosophy has been misrepresented, misunderstood, and misused. The enemies of Sanatan Dharma and many ignorant or radicals among Hindus have misrepresented this concept of Puran-Purush (Kaal-Purush), which has poisoned the Hindu society for centuries, and divided them bitterly.

The cunning anti-Hindus, anti-Bharatiyas and ignorant politicians are still fueling this divide and are hell-bent to break Hindus, Sanatan Dharma, and Bharat further. But the silver-lining is that Bharatiya/Hindus are much intelligent now and getting more united knowing the integrity of the body, society, Sanatan Dharma (eternal discipline) and Bharat, with Puran-Purush (Kaal Purush) analogy.

Through Krishna-consciousness or Sanatan-energy and the subsequent partial-Avatar of Krishna, all are united as 'one Bharat, one Bharatiya.' Sanatan Dharma shelters all religions. But under the mask of religion, when any political expansionist or looter ideology tries to attack it, it attacks the 'eternal discipline,' and faces the consequences as destined by Nature.

With Krishna's inspiration and energy, the factual knowledge is prevailing and shining; and Bharat is getting integrated as one body. Bharat remains united and integrated as long as it respects and follows Sanatan Dharma, the 'eternal discipline,' the foundation of Bharat, despite temporary difficulties. It is the beauty of this pious land, Krishna's land, the Veda's land - the Great Bharat Varsh!

CHAPTER 13

KRISHNA WELCOMES ALL TO SANATAN DHARMA

(Today)

Shri Krishna welcomes all people to embrace the timeless teachings of Sanatan Dharma, as elucidated in the profound wisdom of the Vedic scriptures. Shri Krishna, the epitome of righteousness and custodian of moral values, continues to inspire righteous people to unite and engage in virtuous actions for the betterment of Bharat and humanity at large. Undoubtedly, the righteous path often encounters various obstacles, yet through sincere devotion, sacrificial efforts, and the application of wisdom, these obstacles can be defeated, leading to happiness and contentment.

Ultimately, the truth triumphs (Satyameva Jayate)! In today's rapidly expanding global consciousness, the principles of Krishna consciousness and Sanatan Dharma have gained significant momentum. People are increasingly drawn to the inclusive nature of Hinduism, which fosters peaceful coexistence and regards the entire world as one vast, united family - Vasudhaiv Kutumbakam. Let us join hands in embracing the timeless wisdom and teachings of

Sanatan Dharma, fostering harmony, unity, and the upliftment of humanity.

The name "Krishna" is synonymous with piousness, righteousness, charm, authenticity, strength, dynamic action, victory, triumphant accomplishments, and infinite bliss. Sanatan Dharma is Krishna's Dharma, based on Vedic philosophy and scriptures. Notably, countless individuals from diverse religious backgrounds have been captivated by the scientific nature of Vedic philosophy, encompassing religion and culture. However, numerous individuals have yet to fully comprehend and grasp its profound significance.

In the same vein, Bharat (India) is synonymous to Krishna. It is a land that welcomes and nurtures various faiths and religions, providing them solace, growth, harmony, and contentment. This harmonious environment is fostered if these religious communities understand and embrace the Vedic philosophy and Sanatan Dharma, which advocate peaceful coexistence, unconditional respect for humanity, and the belief that the world is one big family (Vasudhaiv Kutumba).

Home-coming and New-entries

The phenomenon of individuals reconnecting with their ancestral roots and embracing the wisdom found in Vedic philosophy is getting popularity. It is evident that numerous individuals, whose lineage can be traced to Hindus, possess an inherent affinity and deep reverence for Krishna and the Sanatan Dharma. Despite the influence of external religious systems due to historical impositions or personal choices stemming from misinformation, greed or fear, these individuals ultimately find themselves gravitating towards the principles espoused in their own heritage. Such a development is not only sincerely embraced but also celebrated by the collective global consciousness.

It is foreseeable that, over time, a considerable number of those who, across several generations, converted to foreign-based faiths from Hinduism will **inevitably embark on a spiritual homecoming, returning to the embrace of Sanatan Dharma.** These individuals, upon their reintegration into the Hindu fold, will be warmly received, respected, and nurtured within the framework of Sanatan. However, it is essential to acknowledge that there may be instances where ignorance manifests in an individual's defiance, leading them to adopt a radical disposition. This radical extremism can potentially disrupt the unity, fabric, and harmony of Bharat, endangering its ancient cultural heritage rooted in Vedic principles.

If some such individuals, due to a lack of understanding, choose to dissent and engage in extremist actions that aim to dismantle the cohesion, essence, and balance of Bharat by challenging the principles outlined in Vedic (Sanatan Dharma) scriptures and attempting to erode the heritage of Bharat and its profound ancient culture, they are considered adversaries of Bharat, and thus adversaries of Krishna. Consequently, they are not embraced within the boundaries of Bharat and necessitate appropriate and resolute disciplinary measures.

In accordance with Vedic wisdom, it is believed that in times of crisis and moral decline, Shri Krishna manifests Himself on Earth to protect the righteous people and uphold the principles of righteousness known as Dharma. This sacred Avatar (incarnation) in the form of Krishna Consciousness or Sanatan energy, has been witnessed across the globe, particularly in Bharat, over the past few decades.

However, it is important to note that this divine intervention of today has been happening throughout history. Shri Krishna has taken various partial manifestations (known as mini-Avatars), earlier also to address and resolve challenging periods of turmoil and persecution faced by Dharma and its adherents, both within Bharat and beyond. Presently, it appears that this is the chosen era for His latest partial Avatar.

Furthermore, when one considers the expanse of time since the creation of the universe, estimated at approximately 14 billion years, and the relatively recent existence of humanity on Earth a few thousand years ago, in conjunction with the ancient civilization of Bharat spanning back tens of thousands of years, the span of a few decades or even a few centuries may not carry as significant a weight.

Welcome global Home-coming!

Greetings fellow global citizens! We observe a significant resurgence of interest in Krishna, particularly among millions in Asia and the Middle East who hail from a Sanatani (Vedic, Hindu) lineage but were compelled to convert to other foreign-religions due to factors such as fear, greed, circumstances, torture, or helplessness. A considerable number among them have grown weary of the aggressive, violent, and immoral practices observed in certain foreign-based faiths or religious practices.

Furthermore, others have become disillusioned by the hypocritical and greed-driven behavior prevalent in specific belief systems.

Surprisingly, we witness a similar awakening among countries in Africa, South America, the Middle East, the former Soviet Union, Mongolia, and Europe. These nations share a deep connection with Mother Nature and the principles of Sanatana Dharma. The discovery of ancient artifacts, customs, culture, history, and rituals provides overwhelming evidence of their inherent similarity and intrinsic oneness with Sanatana Dharma.

Moreover, their collective belief in the Vasudhaiva Kutumbakam, the perception of "universe is one family," oneness, serves as a common ground for unity. Implicitly, their genes and cells carry the memory of their historical past marked by love, comfort, freedom, kindness, and peaceful coexistence within the realm of Vedic wisdom or Sanatan.

Individuals are instantaneously drawn to the Sanatani community, resonating closely with the profound wisdom encapsulated in Vedic scriptures. They find solace and serenity in the timeless cultural and philosophical foundations ingrained within themselves. An innate desire arises within them to reconnect with their illustrious ancestral heritage.

Sanatan Dharm, referring to the eternal nature of existence, encompasses the Hinduism, Sikhism, Jainism, Buddhism, which embody the essence of Vedic culture and philosophy.

By manifesting Himself as a partial Avatar, Krishna ensures the joyous reunion of all individuals, facilitating their journey towards rediscovering their intrinsic roots.

The inclusive nature of Sanatan embraces various approaches to truth-seeking, ranging from idol worship to Adwait (non-dualistic) philosophies and even including those who adhere to atheism, as long as they remain committed to the pursuit of seeking and following truth. Krishna, in this context, extends his guidance and protection

Pic. 38: Krishna's attraction encouraging Homecoming to Sanatana

to all who willingly embark on the path towards reconciliation with their heritage, granting them inner peace, solace, and fulfilment in their quest for ultimate truth.

Invasions, conversions, & now reversion or re-conversion

Historical events unfolded around a millennium ago that marked a dark period for Indigenous Bharatiyas (Indians), particularly Hindus, in the region of Bharat. At that time, external forces were enticed by the prosperity, generosity, and glory that Bharat embodied. It must be acknowledged that Bharat was renowned for its riches, benevolence, and peaceful nature. However, the lack of unity, solidarity, and cohesion among the numerous prosperous kingdoms within Bharat left them vulnerable to invasions and subsequent exploitation.

The invaders skillfully analyzed the strengths and weaknesses of Bharatiya kingdoms and their social structures during their repeated assaults. They meticulously assessed the opportunities and threats presented by the region, capitalizing on the divisions, differences, complacency, and lack of unity that prevailed among the kingdoms.

With relentless aggression, they conquered one kingdom after another, subjecting millions of Indigenous Bharatiya individuals to violent acts of plunder, torture, and enslavement. Regrettably, this resulted in the inhumane loss of countless innocent lives, irrespective of age or gender.

There has been a regrettable history of practices that have brought harm to the Indigenous Bharatiya community, particularly those who follow Hinduism. Notably, the destruction of many sacred temples and the subsequent construction of their own places of worship, over the temples or near existing temples, has sought to undermine and belittle the Indigenous population.

Furthermore, the violation and abuse of millions of women, through actions such as rape, kidnapping, forced marriages, degradation, public nudity, and the abhorrent act of selling them into various nations, have only perpetuated a cycle of suffering and injustice. Employing tactics of terror, cruelty, bribery, mental manipulation, persuasion, and intimidation, a considerable number of Indigenous Hindus have been coerced into adopting foreign faiths driven by helplessness, greed, and cruelty.

Unfortunately, some of these practices persist even today, casting a shadow over the harmonious coexistence of different religious communities within society.

They engaged in the act of abducting Hindu women from various families, subjecting them to marriage or exploitation against their will. Conversely, they adamantly prohibited any marriages between women of their own faith and Hindus. It was a commonly accepted practice to ruthlessly eliminate any Hindus involved in such interfaith unions, without any possibility of challenge.

This religious intolerance even extended to committing acts of murder for the slightest disagreements regarding their foreign beliefs. This reign of terror persisted throughout Bharat, with a few exceptions, and continues to exist albeit to a lesser degree even today.

Numerous regions across different states in Bharat remain unsafe for Indigenous Hindus, particularly in areas of high concentration of these gangs or foreign-faith communities.

The converted individuals, having been influenced and indoctrinated, were compelled to adopt the same mindset and cruelty as their oppressive and undeveloped oppressors. They wreaked havoc upon the Sanatanis and Hindus, with subsequent generations still holding onto these same beliefs and creating unrest in various parts of Bharat, even after religion-based partition of the country.

They identify themselves as citizens of Bharat (India) but fail to truly embrace the rich legacy and pride of their Indigenous Hindu culture due to historical influences brought on by ruthless invaders who pillaged, oppressed, and disrespected the native population. These people exhibit a lack of connection to the ancient Vedic philosophy, religion, culture, and heritage.

Furthermore, they display a disregard for the sacred symbols that embody the glory and pride of Hinduism. Their refusal to recognize the profound wisdom and value within the ancient Bharatiya philosophy, culture, and religion has led to a forceful destruction of indigenous faith and customs. While there are a few exceptions, such occurrences are rare.

Thus, it is a critical juncture for Krishna to take Avatar and rectify the injustices inflicted upon the Indigenous population.

Krishna's partial Avatar has already initiated a revival, reversed conversions, and rectified the wrongdoings of recent centuries.

The process of homecoming has begun and will soon accelerate despite any threats or opposition from those who seek to impede it.

Part-2, Chapter 13: Krishna Welcomes All...

Revolutionary transformation: Era of Shift in Consciousness

With the advent of the Krishna Avatar, a significant shift in consciousness has occurred, impacting millions of Hindus worldwide. This transformative positive energy of Krishna has particularly resonated with individuals whose ancestors embraced foreign religions, diverging from the path of Sanatan Dharma or Hinduism. Krishna's positive energy and its benevolent influence has the remarkable ability to cleanse and purify the minds of those who engage with Krishna-conscious or Sanatani individuals.

It is noteworthy that devout Hindus who worship the Creator in various forms, such as Krishna, Ram, Shiva, Adhya-Shakti, or Nirakar (formless), exhibit a deep awareness of Krishna consciousness or Sanatani principles.

Individuals who have inherited a materialistic aggressive foreign-based religion from their ancestors, as well as those who have recently converted, have currently sensed the influence of Krishna, and experience an awakening of their inherent roots in Sanatan Dharma imbedded in their DNA and genes. Subconsciously, they seek opportunities to reconnect with their ancestral and timeless religion and become a part of the sacred tradition of Vedic Dharma and culture.

However, many of these individuals are held back by fear due to the presence of cruel, aggressive, and malicious leaders or goons within their current foreign-based faiths. These leaders or goons may pose threats and even go to the extent of harm, should these individuals choose to return to Sanatan Dharma.

Additionally, numerous girls and women from these foreign religions have a desire to marry Sanatan Dharma men, but they too fear the consequences that may be inflicted upon them by these vicious individuals, who spare no one, be it men, women, or children. Nonetheless, **the influence of Krishna will provide protection and grant their wishes of a sacred homecoming to Sanatan Dharma.**

According to Vedic wisdom, individuals who possess pure hearts and are receptive to the positive energy of Shri

Pic. 39: Avatar Krishna welcomes home-comers, punishes anti-Sanatanis

Krishna undergo a transformative experience, becoming resolute and devoted individuals. Shri Krishna diligently safeguards these individuals through various Sanatan Dharma organizations, platforms, groups, armies, and movements (Dals and Senas), all of which are supported by a revised, amended, or new Bharatiya constitutional framework that is infused with Krishna's spiritual strength.

This framework serves to facilitate the spiritual homecoming of millions of seekers, *providing physical and sustenance protection including legal, defense, security, social, educational, wedding, welfare, and other protections.* This is a testament to the profound impact and potency of the Sanatana or Vedic culture.

During this revolutionary process of transformation and joyous unification, it is possible that there may be instances of violence and loss of some lives initially. However, with time, this process will become smooth, regular, and resilient, will evolve into a peaceful and regular occurrence, in alignment with the predetermined destiny and under the protection and influence of Shri Krishna.

CHAPTER 14
ANTICIPATED CHANGES IN BHARAT DURING 21ST CENTURY

(Today)

No constitution in the world is ever perfect. Some parts of constitutions are in written form, while some are unwritten. It is an inherent characteristic of constitutions to require periodic revisions, as they are influenced by numerous factors such as societal advancements, shifting perspectives, and evolving national and international circumstances.

The current global dynamics, the changing mindsets and needs of the public necessitate a recalibration of Bharat's constitution to effectively address these and other pertinent developments on a global scale. Considering this, there seems to be a pressing requirement for a comprehensive reassessment leading to the formulation of a "New Constitution" for Bharat. Following the nation's liberation from prolonged subjugation, the constitution was drafted, inadvertently incorporating remnants of the past era of servitude and certain personal and communal biases.

Considering the prevailing global spread of Krishna-consciousness or the universal recognition of Sanatana-energy, coupled with the nation's aspiration for virtuousness and ethical conduct, it is felt that more basic changes are essential in the Bharatiya constitution. Bharat will greatly benefit from a fundamental transformation.

Bharatiya Constitutional amendments or a New Constitution

Bharat is a country deeply rooted in spirituality, philosophy, knowledge, action, and holistic growth. All actions undertaken by its inhabitants are influenced by their spiritual, philosophical, scientific knowledge, and developmental perspectives. It is imperative for the discerning Bharatiya citizen to assess any proposed activity or change to ensure it aligns with the Vedic spiritual, philosophical, and developmental foundations that guide our nation.

The ancient scriptures of India contain abundant descriptions of remarkable advancements in various fields such as mathematics, medical science (Ayurveda), surgery (Shalya), astronomy (Jyotish), architecture (Vastu), metallurgy (Dhatu), aircraft science (Vimanan), weaponry (Astra-Shastra), gemology (Ratna), medicines (Aushadhi, Jadi-Buti, herbs), telepathy (Dur-Sandesh), television (Door-Darshan), yoga-meditation, and numerous other domains of knowledge.

These profound sources of wisdom offer insights and guidance for contemplating any alterations to our constitutional framework or formulating a new constitution.

Shri Krishna serves as a revered symbol of unity, enlightenment, and strength in Bharat. The wisdom and philosophy encompassed in the Gita/Geeta fully encapsulate His spirituality. Furthermore, the Gita stands as the distilled essence of the Vedas-Upanishads and has gained widespread acceptance and study worldwide. It is rare to find a devout Hindu (Sanatani) who disputes or disagrees with the Gita's teachings. The Gita serves as a guiding light for ethics, morality, and Dharma in Bharat. Should any constitution imposed upon Bharat deviate from the fundamental principles of the Gita, it will lack stability and necessitate amendments until it aligns with the spirit of Krishna's Gita.

Undermining Sanatan Dharma or Hindu Dharma contradicts the core teachings of the Gita, which emphasize its strengthening. As stated by Krishna in the Gita *(Chapter 4:7, 8 - Yadaa yadaa......yuge yuge)*, the constitution should continue evolving and adapting until it reflects the message and essence of the Gita. Any deviation from the soul/spirit of the Gita will contribute in weaking and ultimately breakage of Bharat.

In the light of this fact, the obvious prediction is that Bharat will remain a firm, strong democracy with no-nonsense responsible and disciplined civil liberties. It can also be predicted that Bharat will undergo significant changes towards a more responsible and disciplined democracy. Under the guidance of Krishna's inspiration and auspicious energy, there will be constitutional amendments or the introduction of a new constitution that will strengthen social cohesion, unity, knowledge systems, and the self-esteem of the Sanatani/Bharatiya community. These

Part-2, Chapter 14: Anticipated Changes in Bharat…

changes, among other fields, will manifest in the following specific areas in the next few decades:

Pic. 40: Bharatiya Constitution should confirm to Soul of Gita

Hindu/Sanatani Nation: Bharat will be officially recognized as a Hindu/Sanatani nation (Sanatani Rashtra), acknowledging its historic Vedik and cultural heritage. Conversion of any Hindu/Sanatani individual to another religion will be categorized as a criminal offense with severe punishments, up to capital punishment.

1. **Anti-Conversion Laws:** Legal measures will be implemented to deter and criminalize the conversion of indigenous Sanatani, Hindu, and any local or Tribal individuals to foreign-based or other religions. Offenders engaged in repeated or extreme conversion activities may face lengthy imprisonment ranging from 20 years to a life sentence, and in some crucial cases, even the death penalty.
2. **Home-coming:** To maintain the population and supremacy of Sanatana, the government will offer attractive incentives for individuals who themselves or their ancestors had previously converted from Hinduism to return to their ancestral religion, the Sanatan Dharma, in a manner akin to returning to one's own home.
3. **Sanatan Dharma** encompasses all Indigenous populations, such as scheduled castes, scheduled tribes, regular Indigenous Hindus, Dalits, Harijans, and other adherents, including Aryas, Dravidians, Sikhs, Jains, Buddhists (Buddha being one of the incarnations of Vishnu), and others. Those obstructing such voluntary repatriation efforts will face severe penalties ranging from 20 years of imprisonment to life imprisonment, and even the death penalty.
4. **Freedom of Religion:** All inhabitants of Bharat, including foreigners, will be granted the freedom to practice and observe their own religions; however, such practices must adhere to the regulations established by the central and local governments (generally limited to personal or designated spaces). Celebrating foreign-based religions should not be at the expense of causing harm to the sentiments,

religious practices, discomfort to local communities, or breach of national laws.

Pic. 41: Happy Homecoming to Sanatana due to Avatar - Krishna

5. **Freedom of Religion:** All inhabitants of Bharat, including foreigners, will be granted the freedom to practice and observe their own religions; however, such practices must adhere to the regulations established by the central and local governments (generally limited to personal or designated spaces). Celebrating foreign-based religions should not be at the expense of causing harm to the sentiments, religious practices, discomfort to local communities, or breach of national laws.

6. **Women empowerment:** All women will be treated with respect, dignity, and decency as per highest Vedic norms. All women will be able to exercise their constitutional rights and fulfill their corresponding duties, thereby contributing to the holistic development of Bharatiya society.

7. **Protection of women:** To combat the pressing issue of sexual violence against women, stringent legal measures will be implemented. Perpetrators of rape, a heinous crime causing immense harm and suffering, shall face severe repercussions. These penalties shall range from a minimum sentence of twenty years of imprisonment, to the ultimate measure of capital punishment, depending on the severity of the offense.

8. **Protection of women (Fast-track trial):** In line with the objective to ensure swift justice, a fast-track trial system will be established that will ensure resolution within a month, thereby timely holding the offenders accountable for their heinous deeds. Similarly, acts of cruelty or violence towards women will not be tolerated. Those found guilty of engaging in such behavior shall be subject to the same stringent punishment measures as those implicated in cases of sexual assault. This inclusive approach aims to safeguard the rights and safety of women across all spectrums of society. On the other hand, mischievous or scandalous women misusing this provision with falsehood will be harshly punished with similar punishments.

9. **Human rights and duties**: The constitution will protect the human rights and duties of all Bharatiyas. The constitution plays a vital role in safeguarding these fundamental rights and duties for every citizen. However, criminals involved in acts of terrorism and anti-social crimes do not deserve the same level of human rights protection as law-abiding citizens. The provision of human rights for terrorists, traitors, criminals, intruders, and

murderers will be abolished. Additionally, it will be ascertained that the authority of international human rights organizations is not superior to the Indian constitutional framework for human rights and duties. To effectively manage and regulate human rights agencies, be it on local or international levels, it will also be ascertained that these fall under the supervision and control of the Bharatiya federal or central ministry/board responsible for such matters.

10. **Mandatory Military Training:** All individuals below the age of thirty, regardless of gender, will be required to undergo a three-year military training program followed by suitable placement in Bharatiya businesses, industries, military, or local and central governments.

11. **Education:** Bharatiya educational system will prioritize teachings on self-defense, self-reliance, nationalism, the pursuit of truth, comprehensive knowledge, own-businesses, research, and innovation. Scholarly works will be revised or penned anew to accurately depict the triumphs, accomplishments, dignity, and glories of Indigenous Bharatiya warriors, rulers, thinkers, scholars, revolutionaries, freedom fighters, and spiritual, social, and political leaders. Students will be imparted with factual (true) and authentic knowledge of Bharatiya and global history. Historical records and stories will be published and widely disseminated to ensure widespread awareness of verifiable truths and facts.

12. **Freedom of Expression:** While ensuring freedom of speech, it will be expected that discourse is conducted with civility, adhering to truth and the

best interests of the nation. Disallowance of unsubstantiated claims, baseless accusations, or derogatory remarks against Bharatiya government officials, ministers, presidents, public figures, saints, ancient deities, culture, monuments, scriptures, symbols, religious leaders, priests, and other revered figures. Violators will face severe penalties ranging from imprisonment of 10 years or more to the ultimate penalty of capital punishment.

13. **Preservation of Bharatiya identity (Heritage & Pride):** In accordance with the revised constitution, the preservation of Bharatiya (Indian) identity, encompassing Vedic philosophies, Dharma, culture, and historical monuments, will become a pivotal objective for all citizens. While tolerance will be upheld within the boundaries of decency and legality, any actions or behaviors that undermine Bharatiya pride will be firmly addressed and the offenders will face severe legal consequences, ranging from minimum 10 years imprisonment to the death penalty. Bharat's rich heritage, cultural legacy, and national sovereignty will be duly respected and safeguarded.

14. **Revision of secular and socialist terminology:** The terminologies "secular" and "socialist" will be omitted from the Bharatiya constitution, and Hindu or Sanatani nation be added along with Gods' pictures as in the original constitution. Given that the essence of secularism and socialism is intricately woven into Vedic culture and Hindu (Sanatan) Dharma, there is no need to explicitly incorporate these words, which have been subjected to misinterpretation and misuse into the constitution.

Their inclusion in the past was driven by external influences and political agendas aimed at weakening Hindu unity and the fabric of Bharatiya society.

15. **Preservation of Historical and Cultural Heritage:** The meticulous conservation and upkeep of all ancient Vedic monuments, sculptures, and sites of natural beauty will be ensured. This will not only enhance the identity and pride of our nation Bharat but also serve as prominent tourist destinations, thereby contributing to our national glory and income, bolstering the economy, and generating employment opportunities for our fellow citizens.

16. **Removal of Controversial Structures:** Any remnants of enslavement and religious dominance inflicted by foreign invaders, evident in certain structures, shall be demolished or refurbished. However, monuments and memorials that promote human dignity and celebrate the glorious heritage of Bharat and Sanatana, inclusive of foreign-rooted religions, will be safeguarded as required. Nevertheless, the supremacy of Vedic Bharatiya culture and religion will always be given precedence as per modified or new constitution. Other irrelevant structures that lack relevance or utility shall be either removed or revamped for more practical purposes.

17. **Minority status:** Once a particular faith or sector's population reaches approximately 1.5 % of the total population, they will no longer retain minority status and the associated benefits. The government's decision on this matter will be final and not subject to any legal or constitutional challenge.

18. **Voting rights:** Voting rights will be governed by specific guidelines on several parameters including legal status, family size, noncriminal status, law-abidance, and patriotism etc. Illegal and undocumented immigrants will not have voting rights, and those found guilty of fabricating or possessing fake documents and involved in unlawful and criminal activities will face severe penalties including imprisonment for a minimum of 10 years to life, or deportation after penalties. They will also forfeit their voting rights.
19. **U.C.C.:** Uniform Civil Code will be legally in place as soon as possible for everyone, without any exceptions.
20. **Reservation:** Reservation policies will be based on the financial and specific circumstances of individuals. All other forms of reservation will be reassessed or abolished. Intelligence, brilliance, and innovation will be duly rewarded, free from reservations based on caste, religion, or any form of discrimination.
21. **Judiciary:** Ensuring a judiciary system that is devoid of corruption and upholds its responsibilities is crucial. The elected government or parliament will establish standards and have authority over the judiciary, preventing any chief justice from behaving as a super prime minister and overturning important government decisions. Effective measures will be devised and enforced to enhance the judiciary's efficiency and eradicate corruption within its ranks. Collegium system will be replaced by a better professional system to employ judges. Judges must know and adhere to Sanatan scriptures

and way of life. They must get its certification through some prescribed and compulsory tests. Judgement on all pending cases will be made within one year. Any new case will be decided within 3 months.
22. **Census:** Caste-based categorization will be eliminated from the census process. Instead, the population will be classified into two categories: Sanatani and Non-Sanatani. The Sanatani category will encompass Hindus, Buddhists, Jains, Sikhs, Dalits, Scheduled Castes & tribes, and all other individuals whose ancestors were residing in Bharat for 300 years or more.
23. **Privileges:** Sanatanis will be entitled to certain privileges and special benefits compared to non-Sanatanis, as prescribed by the new constitution. Any Non-Sanatani who wishes to assimilate into the Sanatan fold will be adequately rewarded.
24. **Freedom of the press & expression:** In accordance with the principles of a democratic society, the Bharatiya Parliament will establish well-defined regulations pertaining to the freedom of the press and individual expression. This includes introducing measures to address concerns related to the dissemination of misinformation, fabricated narratives, biased viewpoints, and unsupported claims. To safeguard national interests, public officials, esteemed personalities, and the practices of the Sanatan way of life, stringent penalties will be imposed on individuals found guilty of engaging in such activities.
25. **Truthfulness:** Telling a lie will be a severely punishable offence.

26. **Temple-centric economy** will flourish and will elevate Bharat to the topmost position.
27. **New Sanatani democratic governance system:** Based on thousands of years old Sanatani philosophy and culture, a new and most effective political and governance system will be designed and implemented. This will be the best custom-made system suited for Bharat (India). It will be universally appreciated and adopted by many other nations, after making certain changes as per culture, customs and needs of those nations. It will include the best of democratic system but without unintelligent mob-mentality. It will have firmness to preserve local culture but flexibility to adopt the best of other/foreign cultures. It will be based on universal or Sanatan moral and ethical values of Vasudhaiva Kutumbakam in which rogue family members are adequately disciplined, reformed, or punished. It will not support unprincipled alliances just to grab power and exploit the people and resources of the nation.

There will be so many other constitutional amendments from time to time as needed for strength, progress, unity, prosperity, and development of Bharatiya communities and Bharat, or there will be a new constitution (based on the soul of the Gita or Sanatana), as inspired and powered by the Krishna through His partial Avatar.

Likely developments in Bharat in a few decades

The spread of positive energy of Shri Krishna partial-Avatar throughout Bharat has been reforming and uplifting the Bharatiya economy and quality of life of

Bharatiya citizens. Supported by the 'Integrated-will' of Krishna-conscious or Sanatani people, as destined by Krishna, some of the developments expected are to be as follows:

- **Scientific Advancements:** Bharat, a nation known for its pursuit of truth and knowledge, will prioritize and support comprehensive and pioneering research across all scientific disciplines. This concerted effort will pave the way for surprising inventions and discoveries, pushing the boundaries of science and technology to unprecedented heights. These breakthroughs will not only unveil new truths but also rectify existing scientific theories and concepts, benefiting humanity.

Pic. 42 : Krishna-empower Soul Nurturing the Excellence of Bharat

- **Improved Quality of Life:** The uplifting influence of Krishna consciousness will significantly enhance the standard of living for all Indians. Adequate provisions will be made to ensure access to basic needs such as food, shelter, and other essential amenities. Additionally, there will be a focus on fostering recreational activities, sports, healthcare services, and holistic development for individuals of all age groups in the nation. The morale of all Bharatiya citizens will be boosted up, financial situation and quality of life of all Bharatiya will be much improved. Poverty in Bharat will vanish gradually, much before the end of 21st century.

- **Businesses & Services:** Numerous pioneering ventures, micro-enterprises, local industries, regional trading enterprises, modest enterprises, food-processing facilities, warehousing establishments, agricultural product processing facilities, handicraft industries, technology-related businesses, aerospace companies, automotive industries, tourism enterprises, and international marketing agencies will flourish and prosper across Bharat. Their offerings will be valued within the nation as well as globally, benefiting various stakeholders.

- **Infrastructure:** Bharat is actively constructing a robust, advanced network of transportation, conveyance, tourism, and other industry-related infrastructures. This development is expected to progress at an accelerated pace.

- **Tourism:** Thousands high-quality tourist attractions throughout Bharat (India) will be developed. These attractions would primarily focus on highlighting the ancient Bharatiya treasures, including exceptional architectural wonders, Vedic and historical landmarks, stunning natural beauty spots, and sacred pilgrimage destinations.

- **Monuments protection and development:** Additionally, efforts will be made to highlight forgotten historical monuments and structures associated with martyrs, revolutionaries, saints, freedom fighters, and scholars who have played significant roles in the country's freedom struggle, as well as the neglected or overlooked Rishis (Vedic scientists) who have brought honor to Bharat. This development plan, conducted through a public-private partnership model, is expected to create millions of employment opportunities, and stimulate the growth of small, medium, and large businesses. Moreover, the local rural villages, towns, and tribal communities will particularly benefit from these initiatives.

- **Startups:** In Bharat there has been a notable trend among educated and skilled youth who are choosing entrepreneurship over traditional employment. They are establishing and successfully running their own enterprises, regardless of their size. This shift in mindset and action is paving the way for India to become a global manufacturing and services hub. With this enterprising spirit, coupled with the country's potential for exponential growth, it is expected that the quality of products and services offered in India will be exceptional and meet international standards. Consequently, there will be a surge in demand for these offerings, resulting in significant economic revenues and job creation. The transformation of India into a manufacturing and services powerhouse will have profound societal implications.

It will nurture a culture of innovation and self-sufficiency, empowering individuals to take control of their economic destiny. Moreover, the rise in employment opportunities will help alleviate unemployment and contribute to overall societal well-being. Overall, this entrepreneurial wave holds immense potential for India, placing it at the forefront of global competition, while also uplifting its people and society.

- **Strengthening Law and Order**: Measures will be taken to enhance the security of our nation's borders by implementing strict control measures. Those who engage in criminal activities will face severe consequences as our justice system will ensure stringent punishments for offenses. Additionally, we will implement robust measures to eradicate corruption, and those found guilty of corrupt practices will be subject to severe penalties. In recognition of their integrity and commitment, individuals who demonstrate honesty and discipline in their respective fields such as employees, professionals, scholars, businesspersons, and common citizens will be duly recognized, supported, and even given opportunities for growth and advancement. To safeguard our nation's interests, any internal adversaries or traitors will face legal action, and the military capabilities of Bharat will be significantly enhanced, striving to position ourselves as a formidable force on the global stage.

- **Gender Equality:** The trajectory towards gender equality is not merely symbolic, but rather an empowering journey that embraces autonomy, self-sufficiency, enhanced safety measures, the cultivation of inner resilience, increased access to knowledge, a heightened sense of societal responsibility, more respected, amplified recognition, elevated professional pursuits, augmented productivity, and greater inclusion in military and defense sectors. Moreover, women will seamlessly embody the fulfilling roles of nurturing homemakers and loving mothers, while concurrently enjoying utmost regard within blissful familial settings.
- **Temple-social-initiative:** Inspired by the partial-Avatar of Shri Krishna, under the government and judiciary protection, but without their and external interference, a "Temple-social-initiative" will be formed. This initiative will bring together representatives from major Hindu temples across Bharat. Volunteers, including devoted followers of Sanatani, Hindu, and Vedic philosophies, as well as professionals from various fields such as law, business, engineering, and finance, will collaborate to form a non-profit organization.

The primary objective will be to create and manage high-quality institutions such as hospitals, free food, educational facilities, orphanages, elderly care centers, and organizations dedicated to the preservation of temples and Vedic heritage throughout the nation. This non-political initiative seeks to selflessly serve society and uphold the principles of Sanatan Dharma. Contributions generously donated by major temples will be entrusted to this organization, ensuring transparent utilization in accordance with the stated plans to advance the cause of Sanatan Dharma and humanity. Parliament may introduce dedicated legislation, make amendments to the constitution, or include provisions in a revised New Constitution to address this matter. The process will ensure complete transparency. Instances of financial mismanagement, corruption, fraud,

Pic. 43 – Krishna elevating Sanatani Bharat to the top of the world

nepotism, and misuse of resources or authority will be dealt with severely, carrying sentences ranging from a minimum of 20 years in prison to life imprisonment. Additionally, substantial financial penalties exceeding the amount of corruption will be imposed. This approach will serve as a

Part-2, Chapter 14: Anticipated Changes in Bharat...

benchmark for other religions worldwide and will have a positive impact on millions of individuals in Bharatiya.

Furthermore, Bharat will emerge as the leading nation in terms of economic, educational, R & D, political, and military power, enjoying widespread respect and maintaining this position for generations to come.

CHAPTER 15
KRISHNA FOR THE WORLD
(Today)

Krishna represents a beacon of hope not only for Bharat, but for the entire world. His unwavering smile and brilliant positive aura demonstrate His indomitable strength and conviction of embracing Vasudhaiv Kutumbakam, the belief that the world is one big family. Krishna serves as an ideal not only for Bharat but for people across the globe, who aspire to live with happiness, peace, and prosperity while fulfilling their duties and contributing to the progress of their families, communities, and nations.

Drawing inspiration from Krishna, people strive to embody qualities such as positivity, confidence, righteousness, selfless-service, and a joyful demeanor. Krishna's enchanting flute music can captivate the masses, and his dance with friends reveals a remarkable expression of ecstasy. He serves as a role model in various roles, including that of a dutiful son, a dedicated student, a loyal friend, an exemplary husband, a loving father, a supportive brother, an accomplished athlete, a visionary leader, an affectionate lover, a progressive social reformer, a valiant warrior, a protector of Dharma (righteousness), and a true family-oriented individual.

Furthermore, Krishna possesses the qualities of a triumphant warrior, winner of all wars, his relentless pursuit to eradicate wickedness, his popularity as a beloved king, his diplomatic skills, his role as a peacemaker, his mastery as a charioteer, his visionary ideas, his profound preaching. Moreover, Krishna is the greatest yogi (Yogeshwar) and the liberator.

Krishna inspires for stronger East

It is evident that Krishna serves as a profound source of inspiration in fostering unity, harmony, and progress in the Eastern hemisphere. In the current global landscape, marked by an alarming lack of coherence between powerful nations vying for dominance, rampant acts of violence perpetrated by terrorists, the misuse of religious ideologies to promote such acts, insatiable greed for material wealth and luxury, prevalent corruption, and the unabated exploitation of the underprivileged and middle-class populations, it is imperative to turn towards the timeless teachings offered by Vedic scriptures.

These teachings shed light on critical issues such as unemployment among youth, widespread illiteracy, substandard living conditions, inadequate healthcare provision, an alarming surge in criminal activities, the demeaning treatment of girls and women, persistent gender disparities, deep-rooted racism, the proliferation of immoral and unethical practices, mounting environmental pollution, and the unsettling fluctuations in weather patterns.

Amidst this troubling scenario, a profound decline in righteous conduct, and the corresponding rise of immoral and irreligious behavior, Krishna emerges as the epitome of salvation and hope for humanity.

Moreover, it is crucial to acknowledge that **Krishna, in His present form as a partial Avatar (incarnation), has already graced us with His presence to protect those who uphold virtuous conduct and preserve the principles of righteousness (known as Dharma).**

We can observe the presence of the Krishna avatar in its initial stages. Comparatively, this is like when Krishna was born in Mathura and spent childhood in Gokul village during the Dwapar-Yuga over 5100 years ago. However, it is crucial to note that the present manifestation of the Krishna Avatar has disbursed His power among His chosen Sanatanis or Krishna-conscious followers. In our present era of democracy and Information Technology, with the widespread influence of the internet, the consciousness of numerous virtuous individuals worldwide has been touched by the Krishna avatar.

This influence has been instrumental in shaping people's mindset and opinions, leading to the formation of positive power groups. These groups, energized by Krishna's essence, collectively fulfill the responsibilities and functions associated with His Avatar.

Moreover, these positive power groups have expanded across the globe, varying in size from thousands to millions, and exist within different countries. Their power is concentrated within their respective leaders, who function as auspicious spiritual Power Centers. All these spiritual

Power Centers function as support-system of the partial-Avatar Krishna, to establish Dharma and eradicate Adharma in their respective regions.

It is important to recognize that as Bharat is the Karma Bhoomi (work-field) of Krishna, He starts His Leela here once again, and spreads the activities in the East Asian and Southern nations to protect the decent, saintly, virtuous people, to neutralize or destroy the evil (wickedness) and establish the Dharma (righteousness).

Krishna inspires for Grand Alliance of Friendly Nations

Krishna inspires to "unite" people and powers of the Eastern countries and form a grand alliance among good, understanding, and cooperating neighboring countries, especially those where Sanatan Dharma including Buddhism had flourished earlier. The aim is to foster unity and collaboration among neighboring countries that have a rich history of embracing Sanatan Dharma and Buddhism. Potential members of this alliance include Bharat, Nepal, Shri Lanka, Afghanistan, Bhutan, Thailand, Myanmar, Bangladesh, Maldives, China, Singapore, Indonesia, Vietnam, Malaysia, Cambodia, Philippines, Japan, and South and North Koreas. It is expected that Bharat will assume a leadership role in this initiative.

The Eastern countries share close ties to the principles of Sanatan Dharma, and Krishna emphasizes the importance of reinvigorating and promoting these principles within Hinduism, Buddhism, and other East Asian faiths. He calls for a greater understanding and alliance among governments and people in these nations, while also encouraging collaboration among the faith-based organizations.

With their similar religious systems based on right conduct, self-control, wisdom, and meditation, these nations possess a solid foundation for peaceful coexistence and are likely to find common ground in their pursuit of harmony.

Pic 44: Avatar Krishn - supporting sane-forces, punishing insane ones

Along with these, Krishna inspires to have broader alliance among Middle Eastern, Global South and other friendly nations worldwide. Many of these nations have the history of ancestral Sanatan heritage before millenniums, and many cultural and social similarities today. These alliances will encompass various domains such as culture, commerce, industry, science and technology, energy, agriculture, defense, intelligence, education, sports, healthcare and so on.

They are anticipated to materialize soon, supplementing the existing partnerships. These expansive alliances based on Sanatana principles will serve as a catalyst for promoting mutual understanding, friendship, commerce, improved quality of life, unity, security, research, and development, as well as transformative innovations and discoveries.

Krishna Inspires for War against Terrorist-mindset

Krishna inspires Bharat to wage and lead the war against the prevailing terrorist mindsets that have caused immense suffering and loss of innocent lives worldwide. These mindsets find their roots in certain ideologies, both religious and non-religious, that are detrimental to the well-being of peaceful and harmonious societies. To ensure the preservation of a peaceful coexistence, it becomes imperative to address and eradicate these terrorist and destructive mindsets, referred to as Asur, Danav, Rakshasa, Adharmic, evil, dirty, mischievous, anti-human, or devilish.

Currently, one faith harbors such destructive mindsets across various regions globally, which has significant ramifications for societies, disrupting their regular functioning and instilling fear among their peace-loving citizens. The threat posed by these anarchic mindsets impedes the natural progression and advancement of societies, obstructing scientific and holistic approaches to development. Through their imposition of obsolete whimsical philosophies and dictatorial practices, they polarize societies and hinder social cohesion. Consequently, an urgent call to action arises, necessitating a determined effort to eliminate or transform these terrorist mindsets, which have permeated numerous nations, causing societal disorder on a global scale.

As promised in the Bhagavad Gita *(Ch.4: 7, 8 "Yada Yada hi ....Yuge Yuge,")*, Krishna has already manifested Himself as a partial Avatar within the consciousness of peace-loving individuals who adhere to principles of decency, discipline, devotion, and virtues. Leveraging technological advancements, Krishna is actively fostering the creation and unification of various social groups and power centers, empowering societies worldwide to organize and stand united against these nefarious and terrorist mindsets. These empowered groups, in collaboration with democratic governments, play a pivotal role in eradicating or transforming the forces of evil, wickedness, and terrorism.

Krishna consistently motivates civic societies and all genuinely peace-loving religions, particularly those rooted in the rich traditions of the East, and some likeminded Western faiths, to unite and strategize concrete plans for eliminating the so-called religious ideologies that fuel terrorism and killing.

If such ideologies originate from certain books, such books should be amended or banned. These plans should be executed with unwavering determination. A global movement is slated to arise. This movement serves as a call to action for people from all occupations to uphold the integrity, sanctity, and sacredness of their families, communities, and future generations.

During this movement, it is likely that numerous individuals will selflessly sacrifice their lives as martyrs to safeguard the honor, purity, and divine essence of their families, communities, and future generations. Simultaneously, millions of individuals adhering to faiths that espouse terrorism may undergo a fundamental transformation, either through persuasion or by being rendered ineffectual or many eliminated altogether. From the perspective of Krishna, both creation and destruction are integral components of nature's cosmic blueprint. These occurrences are regarded as routine events embedded within Mother Nature and the divine design. The religious beliefs that lend support to acts of terrorism shall soon meet their demise in much the same manner as they grew in prominence. Innocent, moral, saintly, and common people must be protected.

Transformation of madness (insanity) into rationality

In accordance with the Vedic wisdom, the world is a mix of sane and insane people, virtuous and devilish people, decent and indecent people. Accordingly, our society is comprised of individuals belonging to various mental states - some exhibiting clarity of mind while others appear to be deprived of sound judgment.

Consequently, sometimes the prevalence of insanity seems to outweigh rationality in certain regions. Those immersed in madness, referred to as Dushta or wicked, violate the established principles and conventions of communal life, hindering the progress of our society.

These individuals, driven by their distorted ideologies, readily embrace violence, inflict suffering upon others, and perpetrate injustices against those who do not align with their irrational beliefs. Such factions tend to foster prejudice, leading to an atmosphere of vigilante justice, without any legal authority. In contrast, the rational ones, known as Sadhus or virtuous individuals, uphold a deep reverence for diverse thoughts, lifestyles, and faiths within our society. They diligently adhere to discipline, peace, decency, and harmony, ensuring every member feels acknowledged and respected.

It is noteworthy, though, that while the growth of insanity may appear swift, it lacks the solid and steady foundations that foster the enduring development of society. Conversely, the path of reason may seem gradual, yet its progression is derived from profound wisdom and a deep respect for diverse perspectives, belief systems, and ways of life. By fostering an atmosphere of discipline, tranquility, and mutual respect, we can ensure that each member of society feels valued and acknowledged. It is through this deliberate and gradual cultivation of sanity that we can achieve peace and prosperity.

All nations are confronted with similar challenges. Some nations, driven by misguided ideologies, support and nurture terrorist groups, which they later employ against their neighboring or other peaceful nations. However, in time, these very terrorists turn against their sponsors or hosts, causing immense damage to peace, harmony, economy, and the reputation of their benefactors.

The Avatar of Krishna emphasizes the eradication of insanity or the conversion of insanity into sanity. While insanity may proliferate rapidly, it can be swiftly eliminated or transformed into sanity. Krishna ensures this transformation, as stated in the *Gita Ch.4:8* - *"For the protection of the virtuous, the destruction of the wicked, and the establishment of righteousness, I am born in every age."* Avatar Krishna is just doing this.

Part-2, Chapter 15: Krishna for the World

Krishna's love for pious and punishment for wicked

Whatever form of God a devotee chooses with reverence, I fix the faith of the devotee in that form.
(Krishna: Gita Ch.7:21 - yo yo yam yam......aham).

To protect the pious and to annihilate the miscreants, as well as to reestablish the principles of religion (Dharma) - I advent Myself millennium after millennium.
(Krishna: Gita Ch.4:8 - paritranay.....yuge yuge).

All sane faiths or religions have their own importance for groups or regions, without any judgment over anyone's superiority or inferiority. In the Vedic perspective, it is recognized that everyone or a group may have different beliefs or religious practices, which contribute to the collective fabric of society. Krishna seeks common ground in love, compassion, support, collaboration, progress, and growth across different belief systems.

These diverse faiths, regardless of their apparent disparities, hold inherent value and significance. In this context, Krishna, the current partial Avatar embraces the idea of unity and mutual support among different faiths. Krishna does not distinguish between various sane faiths, advocating for their harmonious coexistence and collaboration.

However, when a particular faith strays from promoting peace and righteousness and instead engages in acts of violence, deception, or manipulation, Krishna intervenes to rectify such wrongdoing. This intervention may involve disciplining, transforming, or even eradicating those responsible for such misconduct. Krishna's objective is to safeguard the innocent and protect the greater good of humanity.

He works to neutralize or eliminate the fraction of radical or terrorist individuals who, despite being relatively few, wield significant destructive power to harm people. These elements, characterized by their cruelty, violence, and arrogance, pose a grave threat to the well-being and safety of society. Krishna's intervention guarantees the safeguarding of righteous individuals and societies, while concurrently addressing and either transforming or eradicating wrongdoers and malevolent individuals on a global scale.

Krishna is always for Development, Progress & Liberation

Krishna-consciousness, the blissful Sanatana-energy has been propagating amazingly fast throughout the world, which is indicative of presence of the partial-Avatar of Krishna in the world. It is evident that the presence of Krishna brings about positive effects such as development, progress, and liberation. The rapid dissemination of Krishna-consciousness worldwide further supports the notion that Krishna's influence is actively at work in the world. The impact of Krishna's presence is seen in the promotion of goodness, happiness, peace, tranquility, and harmony in various aspects of society, the environment, and nature. Conversely, areas lacking Krishna-consciousness are marked by violence, mistreatment of vulnerable individuals, injustice, and societal unrest.

Krishna consciousness, also known as Sanatana-energy, plays a pivotal role in fostering societal evolution, safeguarding its well-being, ensuring its advancement, and fostering an atmosphere of peace, cooperation, unity, harmony, and compassion.

Part-2, Chapter 15: Krishna for the World

The Avatar of Krishna embodies serenity and joy, consistently engaging in virtuous actions to fulfill the mission of preserving goodness and eradicating evil. It is noteworthy that amidst these endeavors, Krishna remains calm, engaged in the activities (of defending the saints and virtuous people, and destruction of evils) and He is readily available to bring joy to his devotees.

Krishna establishes that development of an individual is the development of the society, the nation, and the world. As per Vedic wisdom, the development of an individual is intricately connected to the welfare and progress of society, as well as the broader global community. An individual with inner strength, characterized by unwavering determination, self-control, and wholehearted devotion, coupled with high ethical standards and good actions, plays a pivotal role in fortifying society's foundation. Conversely, a person lacking these qualities contributes to the weakening of society. Such weak individuals possess traits that stand in contrast to those of a strong individual, and they lack determination, self-control, and moral discipline.

The impact of both strong and weak individuals extends beyond the personal realm, shaping and molding our communities, countries, and ultimately, the entire world. Krishna, the partial Avatar, and symbol of wisdom, urges those with sincere hearts, resolute minds, and indomitable spirits to become agents of positive change within their respective societies. Krishna himself serves as an example of this transformative power, as demonstrated by the occurrence of the Big Bang upon His willful expansion, an event that continues to unfold through the expansion of the universe. Consequently, Krishna bestows the responsibility of executing His grand project on those individuals who are chosen as His worthy instruments.

Krishna inspires good Karmas. But some people, due to their thick ego, desires, greed, anger, fear, hypocrisy, and other weaknesses perform bad Karmas. Individuals who adhere to the principles of righteousness (Dharma) and exhibit virtues such as selflessness, honesty, and compassion are more likely to create a harmonious and prosperous society. On the other hand, those driven by ego, desires, greed, anger, fear, hypocrisy, and other weaknesses tend to engage in actions that disrupt the balance and well-being of society. In this cosmic order, it is understood that the consequences of one's actions, known as Karma, are in accordance with the universal norms established by the highest power, symbolized by Krishna.

Therefore, individuals who engage in virtuous deeds are bestowed with favorable outcomes, such as improved living conditions, a sense of fulfillment, inner peace, and elevated social status. Conversely, those who partake in negative actions are met with unfavorable consequences, including poverty, a degraded existence, and a sense of disgrace. It is noteworthy that individuals who adhere to Krishna consciousness may not overtly display religious or spiritual attributes, nor visibly identify as devotees of Krishna or followers of Sanatan Dharma.

They continuously immerse themselves in Krishna, engaging in meditation and Samadhi, even during their engagement in regular tasks and responsibilities. They maintain a state of detachment from the outcomes of their actions, as well as from people, relationships, and external circumstances. Internally, they strive to elevate their consciousness to a level where they remain calm, composed, and balanced in the face of all situations, including challenging dualities and adversities.

Individuals who adhere to Krishna-consciousness or Sanatani devotion, whether engaging in scholarly endeavors, intellectual pursuits, scientific research, innovation, engineering, medical practice, professional work, social service, business operations, philanthropy, managerial roles, organizational leadership, defense and military command, or governmental positions such as prime ministers or presidents, as well as those who perform more humble roles as laborers, small-scale traders, service providers, security personnel, homemakers, and householders, all exhibit a state of equilibrium, contentment, and tranquility.

These individuals, referred to as Yogis or Yoginis, are instrumental in driving positive changes, progress, and holistic development in the world. They play a significant role in fostering harmonious coexistence and genuine well-being globally. In His partial-Avatar manifestation, Krishna guides and empowers such individuals to fulfill His mission in various parts of the world.

PART 3
TOMORROW
***
KRISHNA
FOR THE FUTURE BHARAT
AND
THE FUTURE WORLD
***

All tomorrows:

as future years, from the next century to the end of creation (Kalpant)

Chapter: 16, 17 - Krishna for the future Bharat

Chapter: 18 - Krishna for the future world

❁ ❁ ❁

CHAPTER 16
KRISHNA FOR FUTURE BHARAT
(Tomorrow)

In the coming years, extending from tomorrow to the forthcoming century until the culmination of creation, it is essential to recognize the wisdom imparted in the Vedic scriptures and literature. These sacred texts offer profound insights applicable to the progress and prosperity of Bharat.

Creator Shri Krishna ensures maintaining the rule of natural laws all the time, throughout the universe. These natural laws are truth-based. Any deviation from the truth is deviation from the natural laws. It is important to note that these natural laws have remained constant since the beginning of creation and will persist into the future till the end of creation. The Creator is the embodiment of eternal truth, and the creation itself is an expansion of this truth. The Creator instantly established these natural laws at the onset of the creation.

As the creation unfolded, various false elements, referred to as impurities, veiled the core (the truth) within each creation. These impurities, in the form of falsehoods or Maya, tend to surround and obscure the singular truth. To attain the truth, it is necessary to peel away these layers of falsehood or illusion and delve deep into the core, the Innermost-self.

The ongoing events around the world confirm that these had been happening as per these natural laws, are happening as per these natural laws, and shall keep on happening as per these natural laws. Adherence to truth is Dharma. Adherence to falsehood is Adharma. An adherence to truth or falsehood affects the balance of Dharma (righteousness).

As Krishna told in the Gita *(Ch 4: 7, 8 - yada yada hi dharmasya....yuge yuge.),* when truth becomes obscured by an abundance of falsehood, righteousness wanes and unrighteousness prevails, as per these natural laws the Divine Creator intervenes manifesting as an Avatar, with the sole purpose of eradicating Adharma (unrighteousness), establishing Dharma (righteousness), and safeguarding those who embody virtue and decency.

The phenomenon of recurring incidents persists indefinitely on a global scale. Tomorrow, even in the near future, these occurrences will undoubtedly persist both within the realm of Bharat and across the world. This intricately designed mechanism is deeply embedded within the fabric of Krishna's plan (Krishna's software), incorporating the concept of Avatars as well.

Consequently, irrespective of all existing circumstances, a sparkle of hope for enlightenment and progress remains steadfast. We conceive 'tomorrow' as an amalgamation of every passing day, spanning across the upcoming century until the ultimate culmination of creation, known as Kalpant.

Krishna and Bharat tomorrow

Krishna is absorbed in the whole of the Bharat. The life and teachings of Krishna have demonstrated their profound impact on the people of Bharat (India). Krishna, the epitome of love, beauty, strength, righteousness, knowledge, honor, triumph, and propitiousness, continues to be revered in homes across the nation and shall remain so for the duration of world's existence.

Despite enduring centuries of subjugation to foreign conquerors originating from the Western, Northwestern realms and elsewhere, the significance of Krishna within the lives of Hindus in Bharat has not diminished.

Instead, His teachings within the Bhagavad Gita have been embraced on a deeper level, enriching lives through the integration of modern scientific advancements, rejuvenated knowledge, and bolstered confidence. The immortal message conveyed through the Gita has been a guiding light for millions of individuals in Bharat, as well as numerous countries worldwide, transcending time and boundaries.

Today Bharat has experienced increased unity, strength, and awareness compared to previous centuries. Looking ahead, there is a trajectory of further strength, growth, and development, with Bharat projected to become even more potent, inclusive, knowledgeable, influential, progressive, prosperous, and secure in the forthcoming centuries. The eternal principles and truths illuminated in the Vedas, as well as the Gita, have played a pivotal role in shaping the society of Bharat and its people at present.

However, any existing flaws or impurities within Bharatiya society can be attributed to previous instances of ignorance, misinterpretation, and inadequate implementation of these profound truths. By gaining a deep and accurate understanding of these principles and diligently applying them in practice, we have the potential to create a future where peace, prosperity, and happiness permeate throughout Bharat, with the potential to extend these positive attributes to our neighboring countries and even the global community.

Furthermore, through the manifestation of Krishna's partial-Avatar, individuals across the world are bestowed with boundless positivity and opportunities. Krishna's energy knows no bounds, as He abundantly bestows His divine blessings upon devotees, elevating their aspirations and contentment, instilling them with the strength to attain their objectives and prosper in all endeavors.

Only the truth prevails

As per Vedic wisdom, it is emphasized that only truth prevails while falsehood is unsustainable. This timeless truth, encapsulated in the Vedic mantra "Satyam ev jayate", underscores the transient nature of falsehood, deception and counterfeit phenomena that permeate our world. In contrast, truth (Satya) remains constant and unyielding throughout the existence of creation. When truth radiates, it dispels the darkness of falsehood and illusory existence, also known as Maya or Mithya.

Shri Krishna created this universe through the Truth, the Absolute Truth. The principle of truth extends beyond the boundaries of Bharat (India) and holds universal applicability. As Krishna perpetually upholds and nurtures truth, it becomes the guiding force for Bharat and truth-seeking individuals, leading them towards peace, prosperity, and happiness. The dissemination of Krishna's truth through Sanatan-energy or Krishna-consciousness serves to enhance the stature of Bharat in the global arena.

The Bhagavad Gita offers profound insights into the fundamental principles of existence, shedding light on the mysteries surrounding the origins of the universe, the intricacies of karma, the pursuit of knowledge, the workings of nature, the complexities of human desires, as well as the interplay between actions and their consequences. It provides invaluable guidance on how to lead a life of grace, serenity, happiness, and fulfillment, ultimately leading one towards spiritual liberation or Moksha. Embracing Krishna-consciousness, which is synonymous with acknowledging the eternal energy that permeates the universe, paves the way towards the realization of truth.

By treading this path of truth, individuals devoted to Krishna-consciousness, as well as the entire Bharat community, are poised for elevation, aided by the radiant aura and divine vibrations that this spiritual pursuit imbues.

Lead me from untruth to Truth (Asato ma sadgamaya)

This prayer is a significant invocation in the Vedic tradition, seeking divine intervention in leading individuals away from falsehood and towards the realm of truth. The wordings of this Vedic shloka, "Asato ma sat gamaya, tamaso ma jyotir gamaya, mrityor ma amratam gamaya," emphasize the desired movement from darkness to light, from ignorance to knowledge, and from mortality to immortality. We hold the belief that dedicated prayers, when offered with sincerity and honesty, are answered by the Creator, represented by the embodiment of wisdom and divinity, we know as Krishna.

It is our conviction that Avatar Krishna ensures the fulfillment of honest and submissive prayers, guiding individuals towards the attainment of truth, illumination, and eternal life. This journey of purification may encompass multiple lifetimes, as individuals strive to eliminate all impurities and embrace spiritual growth. This principle of seeking truth and enlightenment is not limited to a specific geographical region or culture but holds universal significance.

Whether in Bharat (India) or any other part of the world, the cause-and-effect relationship between actions and consequences remains constant. As are the thoughts and deeds of Bharatiyas today, Bharat will be the same tomorrow. Continuance of such prayers and matching good Karmas will result in prosperity, happiness, and enlightenment in Bharat and Bharatiyas in the future. This happiness and enlightenment will be further extended to the populace of whole of the world as a global family.

Bharat: The Future World-Superpower

Spirituality is the lifeline of Bharat serving as the pulsating essence of Bharat's cultural fabric. Upholding the belief in the eternal nature of the soul beyond the transitory decay of the physical form, the virtuous Bharatiya individuals remain imbued with vitality. Additionally, the Vedic truth that acknowledges the soul as Paramatma (the supreme divine entity) further empowers Hindus (Sanatani, Vedic) by acknowledging an infinite reservoir of energy and wisdom residing within.

Part-3, Chapter 16: Krishna for Future Bharat

Central to the Hindus worldview is the understanding that the physical body houses an eternal soul, with the intrinsic presence of the Paramatma at its core. Consequently, devout Hindus are unwavering in their conviction that immense power and boundless knowledge are accessible within their Innermost-selves. Even if fate were to reduce the world's population to a solitary Vedic Hindu couple, armed with such conviction, they would triumph over any adversity, proliferating and disseminating the knowledge and principles of Vedic philosophy and Dharma across the globe.

"Immortality of Soul and infinite power and knowledge at the Innermost-self" - this is the undeniable potency embedded within the Vedic philosophy's teachings of the Soul's immortality and the infinite power and wisdom residing within one's true self. This conviction emphasizes the enduring strength of the Hindu community, enabling them to survive, thrive, and expand, even in the face of historical persecutions of centuries.

This inner understanding remains steadfast, regardless of external challenges, such as subjugation, enslavement, or oppression. Consequently, Hindus continue to maintain an unwavering sense of freedom and hope, as they recognize their inherent connection to the infinitely powerful Paramatma dwelling within them.

This unshakeable belief ensures the perpetuity of the Hindu identity, as even in the event of physical destruction, individuals are reborn with greater vitality and brilliance. Sanatani beliefs revolve around the concept that Paramatma (the Supreme Being or Creator) is the essence of their existence. The formless and timeless Paramatma is perceived by different Sanatani individuals in various forms such as: Krishna, Rama, Shiva, Brahma, Vishnu, Mahesh, Adishakti, Jagat-mata, Durga, Lakshmi, Saraswati, and more. We believe that "Krishna" encompasses all these divine manifestations.

The glory and radiance of the ancient nation Bharat, known for its profound philosophy, prosperity and culture shall remain forever. Although it may face temporary setbacks or challenges, like the sun temporarily covered behind clouds, its essence can never be extinguished. This is what distinguishes the Vedic Bharat, with its timeless inhabitants and their eternal connection to the divine essence that resides within them.

The teachings of Lord Krishna through his incarnation and the profound lessons of the Bhagavad Gita continue to infuse Bharat, providing it with perpetual vitality, empowerment, and enlightenment.

Considering its illustrious history, Bharat is destined to rise above any adversities it faces and radiate as a global powerhouse. The seeds of Sanatan-energy or Krishna-consciousness have already been sown and are rapidly flourishing. More seeds are being planted, which will soon sprout at the opportune moment.

The growth of Bharat is intricately linked to the progress of humanity. Embracing the ideal of Vasudhaiva Kutumbakam, where the entire earth is viewed as one family, Bharat's expansion is widely admired, appreciated, and supported by nations worldwide.

With a deep-rooted understanding of Krishna-consciousness and the emergence of partial Avatar of

Part-3, Chapter 16: Krishna for Future Bharat

Krishna, Bharat not only aspires to reclaim its former grandeur from millennia past but aims to surpass previous

Pic. 45 - "Whole of the Earth is a family" - Sanatan philosophy

boundaries. Anticipated growth in size, power, prosperity, and influence will be leveraged to disseminate happiness and well-being globally.

The Hindu Nation "Bharat"

Krishna's Bharat is renowned as a spiritual land, rooted in the Sanatan Dharma or Hindu Dharma for thousands of years. Despite being considered secular, Bharat has always welcomed and embraced people of diverse beliefs, focusing on the common thread of humanity.

However, it is expected that significant constitutional reforms or the introduction of a new constitution will soon declare Bharat as a Hindu nation, reviving its ancient grandeur.

This transition will epitomize the revival of the dormant intellect and energy within the Bharatiyas or Hindus. Additionally, it will position Bharat as the world's largest Hindu nation, leaving a profound impact on the global Hindu diaspora who will proudly celebrate their religion and ancestral land. Consequently, Hindu organizations worldwide will receive a renewed sense of purpose and dedication to serve the welfare and advancement of Hindus and the Sanatan Dharma, which encompasses all its various branches such as Arya, Dravid, and hundreds of local beliefs.

All religious beliefs will be respected and protected in Bharat, while adhering to the boundaries established by the new constitution. Engaging in any form of conversion of Hindu, tribal, or indigenous individuals to foreign or alternative religions will be considered a grave criminal offense, subject to severe consequences and punishments, as stated earlier.

In general, those who hold an anti-Bharatiya and anti-Hindu stance tend to overlook and disparage the once illustrious and prosperous history of Bharat. They selectively highlight only the period of the past 1,000 years, marked by invasions, looting, defeat, conversion, mass killings, destruction, enslavement, fragmentation, and humiliation of Hindus.

These individuals aim to suppress the knowledge and remembrance of a vibrant Bharat that existed before this era of slavery. Hindering the revival and empowerment of Hindus by disconnecting them from their rich heritage and golden era of a millennium ago is their underlying motive.

The aforementioned individuals or segments persist in belittling, demeaning, and undermining the Hindu community, causing them disrepute, and diminishing their morale. However, as we embrace the wisdom of the Vedic scriptures, and awaken to Krishna-consciousness, we can anticipate a revitalization and resurgence of Sanatan Dharma (Hindu Dharma).

With the current partial-Avatar of Krishna, this revitalization will confront those who engage in unethical behavior and seek to harm Hindus, holding them accountable through appropriate measures such as punishment, transformation, reformation, conversion or exclusion from public influence or life.

Individuals who possess a profound understanding and utmost appreciation of Vedic knowledge, culture, and holistic principles guiding a disciplined way of life shall be privileged with enticing incentives and appealing bonuses. However, individuals who exhibit an antithetical and disloyal attitude towards their nation, specifically those who undermine and deceive the Hindu community, shall be dealt with systematically and resolutely, adhering to the tenets of the new constitution and in accordance with public sentiment.

Bharat's administration and executives will strive to foster an environment of cooperation, empathy, generosity, and humanitarianism. Nonetheless, any forms of indiscipline or mischief will be promptly addressed and firmly corrected. Bharat aspires to manifest itself as an exemplar of liberal sensibilities, while retaining a steadfast commitment to discipline, control, and efficient governance, avoiding the pitfalls of mindless liberalism.

Optimal population management

Efficient policies and regulations will be devised and enforced to ensure meticulous control and management of the population. Both incentives and deterrents will be employed to achieve this objective. Certain foreign belief systems advocate multiple marriages for their men, enabling them to freely father numerous children and burden the Bharatiya society and government with their upbringing, education, and employment. This practice will be curtailed. All will have to follow Uniform Civil Code (UCC) and new laws for responsible behavior.

Furthermore, as these individuals reach adulthood, they are granted voting rights and tend to favor anti-Hindu interests, often voting against candidates aligned with Hindu beliefs. Given their growing numbers, they not only consume taxpayers' funds, but also exert political influence through their increased voting power. The new stringent regulations will effectively regulate and control population growth, thereby ensuring fairness in political dynamics.

Considerations will be made regarding the restriction of voting rights, governmental welfare support, and other measures to uphold population control and assess citizens' responsibilities. Robust measures will be implemented to address refugees, illegal infiltrators, violators of population guidelines, criminals, traitors, anti-national elements, and fraudulent individuals, who will face severe punitive measures and will be denied voting rights.

Improved Governance, Well-rounded Advancement

Krishna's Sanatani Bharat will have unprecedented progress and development on all fronts. To ensure Superior

Part-3, Chapter 16: Krishna for Future Bharat

Governance and Overall Development every village, city, and state will embrace cleanliness and foster healthy living conditions. Exemplary governance will be established with superior management of law and order, resulting in a significant decline in crime rates. In this paradigm, the presence of goons, gangsters, and thugs will be virtually nonexistent. Consequently, the common citizens will feel safe and secure within their surroundings.

Bharat will thrive as a high-functioning welfare-state, actively engaging all its citizens in productive and beneficial endeavors. The government will play a critical role in safeguarding and advancing the economic and social well-being, ensuring a happy and healthy life for all Bharatiyas. Moreover, particular attention will be given to protecting vulnerable segments of society, including children, students, women, individuals with special conditions (Divyang), and senior citizens. The preservation of human dignity will be paramount.

Every individual in society will uphold their inherent worth and dignity. Without exception, all decent citizens of Bharat will peacefully coexist, dignified and proud of their Bharatiya heritage. Hindu Rashtra Bharat will pave the way for enhanced well-being, intellectual growth, and spiritual development, setting a commendable example for the global community at large.

Overall growth of Bharat

In line with the spread of Sanatana-energy or Krishna-consciousness, Bharat is poised for significant growth across various sectors including Science, Technology, Agriculture, Nuclear Science, Power, Artificial Intelligence, Quantum Science, Vocational Training, Transportation, Education, Space Research, Astronomy,

Economics, Finance, Research and Development, Business, Tourism, Heritage Conservation, Study of Scriptures, Media, Public Welfare, Yoga, Health, Spirituality, Women's Empowerment, Child and Elderly Welfare, and Humanitarian Missions as well.

The modernized infrastructure will notably enhance productivity in agriculture and industry, stimulate trade and business, facilitate efficient transportation of goods and people, and optimize power generation and distribution. These advancements will lead to reduced production costs, heightened profitability, and increased exports following sufficient local consumption. Consequently, foreign currency reserves will thrive, substantially bolstering the global position of the Bharatiya Rupee.

Superior Military and Defense Capabilities of Bharat

Ancient Vedic wisdom offers valuable insights into the optimum path for societal development, including in the realm of national security. The main hero of the Mahabharat, Krishna, always defends His people. Sanatan-energy or Krishna-consciousness will inspire and help Bharat to become self-sufficient in all its military and defense needs and capabilities to safeguard its people and assert itself as a self-reliant nation.

Inspired by the partial Avatar Krishna, Bharat aims to achieve self-sufficiency in manufacturing a wide array of defense equipment. Ranging from sophisticated aircraft to submarines, ships, tanks, ammunition, space-war infrastructures and intelligence tools, Bharat seeks to produce these capabilities and instruments domestically, while also exporting them to other nations, as needed.

Furthermore, Bharat will enhance its National Security Capabilities by actively engaging in research and development activities within its Military Research and Development Wings, channeling efforts towards the creation of novel and exceptional warheads and defense products. By cultivating a vibrant research ecosystem, Bharat aims to stay at the forefront of advancements in military, defense, and intelligence technologies.

Additionally, Bharat will also explore collaborations and partnerships with global entities to procure, study, upgrade, and manufacture innovative military equipment worldwide. Make in Bharat will be the main Mantra. Furthermore, Bharat will seek to promote its expertise by exporting its own indigenous military equipment to several friendly nations around the world.

It is envisioned that antinational activities will be demolished, efforts opposing national interests will be dismantled, while endeavors aligned with the progress and well-being of the nation will be promoted and endorsed. Bharat, in its pursuit of harmonious international relations, will engage in robust military alliances with various friendly nations and neighboring countries. Furthermore, there will be active participation in joint military exercises, fostering closer cooperation and camaraderie.

In furtherance of national security, Bharat will establish strategic bases in multiple nations and islands. The deterrent effect of these measures will serve to dissuade any notion of military aggression against Bharat or its allies. Swift and decisive action will be taken to suppress and penalize any reckless and belligerent behavior exhibited by rogue nations.

Merger, Union, Alliance of Many Nations with Bharat

Bharat is poised to emerge as a global powerhouse soon, driven by a consciousness centered around Krishna-consciousness or Sanatan-energy and influenced by Krishna's partial Avatar. Many neighboring nations, which have endured harsh realities such as corruption, suppression, discrimination, missed opportunities, and injustice within their own borders, will increasingly choose to integrate with Bharat and become its esteemed citizens, thus strengthening and elevating Bharat's International Influence.

They will eagerly contribute to Bharat's growth and development, embracing their newfound Bharatiya identity. Additionally, some countries will opt for strategic alliances with Bharat, remaining within its union or orbit for mutual benefits.

A neighboring rogue nation plagued by poverty and authoritarian military rule will undergo internal divisions, disarrayed governance, and interference from external powers. Consequently, it will fragment into multiple smaller entities. Some of these fragmented states may choose to align with Bharat or join the "Bharatiya Union," an alliance of neighboring nations, under the common constitution of the Union.

The Bharatiya Union will be a conglomerate of nations, with Bharat at its helm, working towards shared goals in defense, foreign policy, economy, and other areas of mutual interest. The integration of these neighboring countries within the Bharatiya Union will either aim to preserve their cultural heritage rooted in the ancient Vedic traditions or seek to enhance their socio-economic progress, overall well-being, and technological advancements through collaboration with Bharat.

Many neighboring nations with historical connections to Bharat, whether through ancient rulers, Sanatan Dharma, Buddhism, or other cultural, religious, political, business, or social interactions, share commonalities and prospects. They will establish an alliance with the influential 'Bharatiya Sangh' in areas such as defense, business, technology, agriculture, tourism, yoga, spirituality, education, and culture, working together for their mutual benefit. Additionally, other nations, both near and far, will also actively engage in similar alliances.

Through international diplomacy, negotiations, and power-pressure, a comprehensive approach will be taken to include Kailash-Mansarovar, Tibet, Aksai-Chin, Gilgit, Baltistan, and the entire region of Jammu and Kashmir (including POK) within the Bharatiya Union territory. With increased homecomings, this will address the population imbalances in these areas, while simultaneously fostering their economic and social development under the guidance of diligent and adventurous Sanatani Bharat.

Furthermore, the restoration of road access to Afghanistan, central Asia, Arab nations and beyond to Europe and Russia will forge new road connections to enhance international businesses. Political, economic, cultural, military alliances of Afghanistan and other neighboring countries with the Bharatiya Sangh will happen by the end of this millennium.

The unity initially between Hinduism, Buddhism and Judaism (and later with liberal Christianity and moderate Islam) will experience a significant boost, as these communities will actively engage in promoting mutual understanding, cooperation, fostering social interactions, and implementing welfare initiatives that benefit them all. Together, they will effectively counter the propagation of violent, divisive, materialistic, and deceptive ideologies.

Individuals who, or whose ancestors, were enticed, coerced, or compelled to embrace foreign faiths earlier, will find solace in returning to their ancestral roots. This homecoming will empower them and stimulate their spirited participation in the consolidation of a stronger alliance with Bharat. As a result, the borders of the Bharatia Union will expand considerably, surpassing the earlier borders of Akhanda Bharat.

Due to internal conflicts and external influences from neighboring countries like Japan, China will inevitably experience division, resulting in the formation of four separate entities. Remarkably, all four countries formed out of the division will establish strategic alliances with Bharatiya Sangh, demonstrating a favorable diplomatic landscape.

New Bharatiya Media Power in The World

The global media landscape is predominantly shaped by influential international entities, primarily hailing from Europe and the USA, with varying specific objectives and missions. Some of these entities also emerge from communist and Islamic nations. Supported by substantial financial resources, they successfully disseminate their political, business, cultural, or religious agendas worldwide, impacting the opinions and beliefs of hundreds of millions of individuals.

Their ability to influence extends to altering public opinions, shaping government policies, impacting religious affiliations, determining cultural interactions, and even affecting social harmony, safety, and mental well-being, as well as relationships between communities and countries. However, it is crucial to acknowledge that their coverage can be biased, selective, and driven by motivations, often leading to factual inaccuracies, half-truths, or even the presentation of false narratives.

In this context, it is pertinent to note that throughout history, both during the Mughal period and colonial rule, the media continued to perpetuate the degradation and vilification of Bharat (India) and the Hindu community. Media outlets, particularly those influenced by communist ideologies or foreign religious affiliations, consistently highlight even the smallest incidents that reflect negatively on Bharat or the Hindu populace. They manipulate information, presenting distorted facts and half-truths to discredit and denigrate Hindus and their faith. Numerous instances can be cited as evidence of their biased reporting.

The media outlets are seen to be engaging in biased activities and openly supporting certain political parties, based on influence from foreign religious or political entities or communist headquarters present outside of Bharat. Their involvement in international controversies aims to weaken the nation of Bharat, potentially leading to its fragmentation into multiple regions, including Communist-Lands, Christian-Lands, and Jihadistans. These media giants continue to adopt a mindset reminiscent of foreign invaders and looters who sought to exploit the wealth and resources of Bharat, while subjecting its people to slavery and colonization.

These foreign-controlled media organizations also exercise substantial influence over the Bharatiya judiciary at various levels, including the Supreme Court. The Supreme Court's decision-making process remains influenced by colonial and Mughal-era courts and political patrons, raising questions about the impartiality and integrity of certain judges. In some instances, it appears as though the Supreme Court follows directives from white regimes in Europe, like the practices adopted during colonial times, or favors Jihadi or communist elements due to external pressure.

Through Krishna-consciousness or Sanatan-energy, Krishna has been inspiring and invoking Narada-consciousness in the media persons of Bharat. This divine influence brings forth the essence of Narada, a celestial messenger known for his truthfulness and ability to perceive and report past, present, and future events in the universe. This serves as an opportunity for individuals to make necessary corrections or find happiness. Narada can be likened to an astrologer, informant, messenger, saint, and devotee of Krishna (Vishnu), acting as a well-wisher and guide for humanity's peace, happiness, and liberation.

Looking ahead, the empowered nation of India, guided by the spiritual force of Krishna, will diligently rectify, and transform the media landscape that has been influenced by foreign interests. This transformation will manifest through the establishment of "New Bharatiya media networks," which will receive substantial funding and be staffed by dedicated nationalist individuals and groups utilizing innovative technology.

These networks will not only wield considerable influence within Bharat/India but will also extend their impact globally. The introduction of this innovative media platform aims to uncover accurate historical facts and data from historical documents. It addresses the issue of misrepresentation that has resulted in the degradation, demoralization, and humiliation of Hindus and Bharatiya nationalists, preventing them from embracing their rich heritage and progressing further.

The New Bharatiya Media strives to establish its reputation as the foremost, credible, influential, and globally recognized source of true information. It aspires to achieve financial independence while upholding its patriotic values, as it highlights and advocates for the preservation of Sanatan/Hindu and Bharatiya interests worldwide.

Neutralizing Anti-Sanatani & Anti-Bharatiya Intellectuals

Intellectual individuals who possess an anti-Hindu or anti-Bharatiya mindset can be considered as integral components of a larger group aligned against Bharat. Acknowledging their potential allegiance to foreign-based faiths or their affiliation with pseudo-secular ideologies, it becomes apparent that their loyalty lies not with Bharat or nationalistic principles but with those who offer them financial incentives, awards, and recognition.

These individuals, sometimes resembling motivated activists or intellectual mercenaries, may exploit their talents to disseminate partial truths, misinformation, and incite chaos and confusion. Operating under Hindu names, they can potentially function as both believers and agents of foreign-based faiths, working towards damaging, undermining, defaming, or even eradicating Hinduism and Bharat. Their actions may extend to leaking confidential information and vital secrets of our nation to its adversaries.

With the watchful and alert Krishna-conscious/Sanatani devotees and Krishna's partial-Avatar, tomorrow they will be meticulously neutralized, transformed or punished adequately. The handling of such individuals will be executed with greater efficiency, specifically targeting such intellectuals and those who create mischief while practicing foreign faiths or betraying their Hindu background. Krishna consistently displays profound compassion towards those who follow a righteous path, while demonstrating sternness towards those engaged in malevolent actions (Vajradapi Kathorani, mruduni Kusumadapi – harder than the thunderbolt, softer than the flower).

Managing the Film industry

Films wield a considerable influence over the emotions, mindset, and behavior of the masses and societies, owing to their audio-visual impact on hundreds of millions of people. Unfortunately, there has been an alarming proliferation of morally corrupt and offensive films, both in Bharat and worldwide, which have degraded the tastes of numerous generations and eroded the sanctity of family life. These films, with their shallow narratives solely focused on cheap and indecent entertainment, predominantly promote themes of sexuality, sensuality, base desires, vulgarity, explicit scenes, vengeance, violence, deceit, substance abuse, sexual assault, dishonesty, theft, robbery, and murder.

Regrettably, the motivation behind producing such films lies firstly in the pursuit of financial gain, by appealing to the lower instincts of anti-morality and unethical behavior. Secondly, under the guise of freedom of expression, secularism, and societal reform, some films intentionally aim to denigrate and undermine the deeply-held beliefs of Hindus or those adhering to Sanatani principles, causing immense disgrace and moral degradation. These films often find popularity among communities in other countries that hold anti-Hindu and anti-Bharat sentiments. This detrimental impact erodes the moral fabric and overall well-being of society.

Krishna is inspiring and enabling the leadership through Krishna-consciousness/Sanatan-energy to stop and ban such filthy films from being produced, displayed, or accessed through electronic media. In this regard, it is imperative for leaders and influencers to draw inspiration from Krishna's teachings and embody them in their leadership roles. By doing so, they can effectively curb the creation and dissemination of indecent content. Moreover, Krishna's teachings encourage the promotion and proliferation of films that are not only aesthetically pleasing but also contribute positively to the societal fabric.

These films should uphold Bharatiya (nationalistic) values, embrace Bharatiya culture, and offer uplifting moral stories and meaningful entertainment. It is essential for this vision to counteract the unscrupulous forces driven by greed and bad intent. Therefore, the government of Bharat, guided by the principles of Krishna consciousness, will relentlessly tackle, and overcome any obstacles or opposition that comes their way. They will ensure that the definition of art and freedom of expression remains true to its purpose and that clear guidelines are established for the production and exhibition of films in Bharat. These guidelines will be enshrined in the new constitution of Bharat and will be diligently adhered to.

CHAPTER 17
RESTORATION OF ANCIENT VEDIC GLORIES, AND ADVANCING BEYOND

(Tomorrow)

Bharat (India) possesses the inherent capacity to reclaim its position as a leading nation on a global scale by embracing the Vedic wisdom. It is imperative that we acknowledge and cherish the remarkable achievements of ancient Bharatiya civilization, which surpassed all others in terms of intellectual, societal, and technological advancements.

From expansive knowledge systems to deep philosophical understanding, from innovative scientific discoveries to profound insights into human psychology, the realm of the Vedas encompasses a wealth of wisdom in diverse domains including telepathy, literature, medicine, mathematics, astronomy, sculpture, metallurgy, social sciences, and agriculture. By rediscovering and revitalizing these ancient glories, Bharat (India) can propel itself beyond the confines of its present state and usher in a new era of progress and prosperity.

It can be acknowledged that with the passage of time, various factors such as inflated egos, complacency, lack of foresight, absence of mutual cooperation, unchecked greed, jealousy, unhealthy competition, vengeful actions, betrayal, excessive indulgence in sensual pleasures, negligence, impaired judgment, recklessness, and a decline in moral and ethical discipline have all contributed to the decline of Bharatiya regimes and the onset of subjugation.

This period of subjugation, lasting for nearly a millennium, has unfortunately resulted in the erosion of numerous accomplishments that once adorned Bharat's illustrious history. However, it is imperative to recognize that the rise and fall of civilizations are inherent components of their development and progress. In recent times, Bharat has witnessed a resurgence, albeit with a greater sense of wisdom, self-restraint, and cautiousness.

Vedas, Bharat, glorious past and advanced future

Krishna took avatar in Bharat over 5200 years ago. Before slavery, for a millennium Bharat had been the land of prominence, piousness, and prosperity. Vedas are eternal Truth. Vedas are since the origin of Bharat. Vedas and Bharat are inseparable. Vedic philosophy originated from Vedas. Vedas and their essence Upanishads are the roots of Bharatiya civilization (Bharatiya Sabhyata).

Vedic philosophy is the root of Vedic religion called Sanatan Dharma. Vedic religion (Sanatan Dharma) is the root of Vedic culture (Sanatan Sanskriti). Vedic culture is at the root of Bharat's piousness, prominence, and prosperity.

Thus, the Vedic philosophy, derived from Vedas, forms the very foundation of Bharatiya civilization. Sanatan

Dharma is intertwined with the teachings of the Vedas and serves as a guiding principle for the societal and cultural fabric of Bharat. The profound influence of this philosophical framework permeates every aspect of our lives, contributing to the profound piousness, prominence, and prosperity that characterizes our glorious heritage.

It is important to recognize the significance of Vedic scriptures as they contain the timeless wisdom that has guided Bharat's glorious past and will continue to shape its advanced future.

Embracing and understanding the essence of this profound knowledge holds the key to unlocking the true potential of our society, facilitating intellectual conversations, and nurturing a progressive and enlightened mindset.

The term "Hindu" is not found in the ancient Vedic scriptures and literature of Bharat (India). It was introduced by foreign visitors and invaders to refer to the Indigenous people of Bharat. These invaders, who subjected Bharat to centuries of foreign rule and enslavement, imposed the term "Hindu" on its residents.

Detractors and those wishing to fragment Bharat seek to distance it from its philosophical and spiritual foundation in the Vedas. They aim to transform it into a land dominated by foreign religions and cultures, which have historically been associated with cruelty, torture, exploitation, and the killings of innocent people.

It is surprising that some of these detractors even exist within the so-called secular Hindu community. They have been influenced by a flawed education system, personal

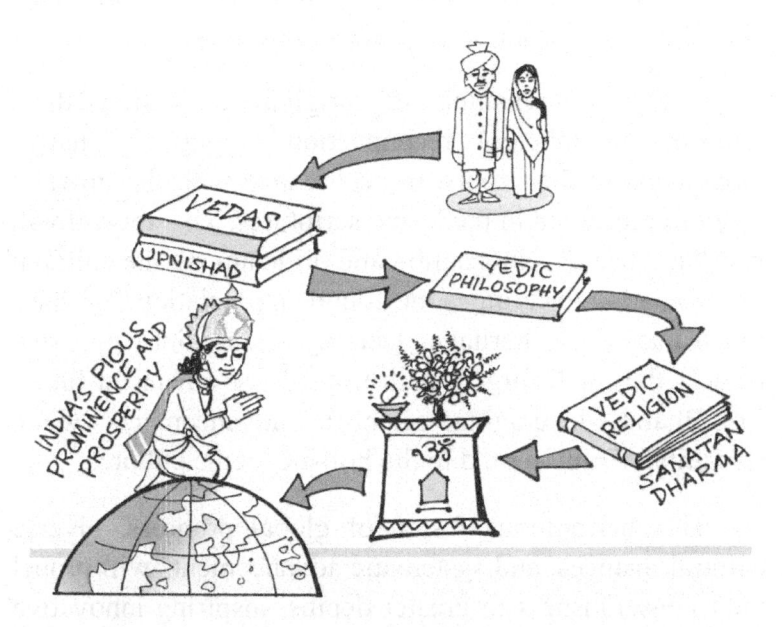

Pic 46 -Vedic scriptures - Roots of vibrant & glorious Sanatan Dharma

greed, fear, ignorance, distorted history books, self-serving and corrupt politicians, international political and religious conspiracies, and media manipulation both before and after independence. With the inspiration of Krishna, the original name "Bharat" has been restored in place of invaders-labeled 'India,' which reminded the slavery of British regime.

Individuals who identify as Hindu may eventually prefer to refer to themselves as Vedic, Aryan, or Sanatani, as these designations accurately capture their true Indigenous heritage and national identity within this revered land. Such redefinitions will immediately align them with the vast wellspring of strength and knowledge contained within the Vedas, as well as reconnect them to the illustrious, magnificent, and prosperous period of the Vedic era. This transformation is already underway.

By re-establishing these original designations, there will be an inherent reconnection among the native inhabitants to their roots, in accordance with the timeless wisdom preserved in the Vedic scriptures. This revival will instill a sense of rejuvenation and pride among the children of this land, fostering a profound appreciation for their illustrious Vedic heritage. Delving deeper into this rich legacy, they will forge a path towards an advanced future for Bharat, leveraging scientific advancements while remaining firmly rooted in the holistic Vedic culture.

This harmonious fusion of global progress, diverse cultural nuances, and systematic advancements will propel their consciousness to greater depths, inspiring innovative ideas and solutions to the multifarious challenges faced by both Bharatiyas and humanity at large. Gradually, the remnants of their past subjugation will be eradicated, enabling them to recognize themselves once again as masters of their own destiny.

Expansion of Sanskrit language across Bharat and the world

The Sanskrit language holds the distinction of being the most ancient and scientifically advanced language not only within India but also globally. Countless scriptures, such as the Vedas and Upanishads, are written in Sanskrit. Additionally, Krishna's revered Shrimad Bhagavad Geeta (Gita) is composed in this illustrious language. The highly scientific, melodious, and computationally-friendly Sanskrit language is poised to make a resurgence within

Bharat (India) after a significant pause of over a millennium.

People across India are showing great enthusiasm for Sanskrit and are eager to embark on the journey of learning it. This educational endeavor begins at the foundational level, starting from primary schools and extending to all educational institutions throughout the country. Sanskrit's popularity will extend beyond national boundaries, leading to its integration into primary schools, universities, and even doctoral research programs in numerous other countries.

It is noteworthy that Sanskrit boasts the largest vocabulary of any language in the world. Engaging in conversations and chanting Sanskrit mantras enhances memory, cognitive abilities, and provides an invigorating effect on brain cells, ultimately fostering a sense of mental tranquility, contentment, and joy. Moreover, Sanskrit can be considered the root of various Bharatiya languages, and foreign languages exhibit influence from its fundamental vocabulary.

Research on Vedic scriptures in Bharatiya languages

Scholars have extensively studied the profound Vedic scriptures, which comprise a vast amount of knowledge. This Vedic treasure of knowledge is many Bharatiya languages including Sanskrit, Tamil, Telugu, Kannad, Odia, Bengali languages. Some European scholars have translated certain scriptures, while NASA has also shown interest in exploring the wisdom of ancient Indian sages (Rishis) for potential scientific inspiration. However, many scriptures remain unexplored, awaiting further research, translation, and interpretation to impart their wisdom to humanity.

It is important to note that the Rishis did not seek personal gain, recognition, or monetary benefits from their truth's revelation. They were not driven by ego or the desire for ownership through branding, copyright, or patents. Their pursuits were based on a holistic and selfless approach, solely aimed at knowing the Ultimate Truth, and benefiting humanity.

Their work was a voluntary and missionary endeavor, rewarding them with immense satisfaction. This selflessness allowed them to delve deeply into their Innermost-self, enabling them to perceive, experience, and realize eternal truth.

It can be observed that some Western scientists often approach their research with materialistic motivations, which unfortunately limits their ability to delve deeply into the fundamental truths. While they do uncover certain truths that serve specific material needs, these truths remain partial and lack a comprehensive understanding. Nonetheless, these partial truths contribute to the betterment of humanity.

In contrast, drawing inspiration from Krishna, research efforts in Bharat and beyond will focus on exploring numerous Vedic scriptures, deciphering the hidden truths within them, and sharing these insights with the public for the collective advancement of humanity. Soon, we can expect numerous discoveries and inventions rooted in Vedic principles both in Bharat and other nations, which will have a global impact and will benefit all.

Bharatiya village scholars, philosophers: Defenders of Dharma

The rural communities of Bharat, blessed with traditional wisdom steeped in the ancient Vedic scriptures and literature, possess a profound understanding of the interconnectedness between humanity and nature. These individuals, although devoid of formal education, possess a comprehensive knowledge of natural laws, the principles of karma, the cycles of rebirth, and various sciences such as Ayurveda, Jyotish (astrology), and Vastu.

Their practical wisdom enables them to navigate life wisely and contribute to the harmonious coexistence of all beings, guided by the belief of Vasudhaiva Kutumbakam (the world as one family). Recognizing the divine presence in every particle and organism, they perceive life's vitality in every plant and creature. They comprehend the correlation between righteous actions and positive outcomes, emphasizing the significance of virtuous behavior in shaping one's destiny. Additionally, their adherence to principles of selflessness, service, and awareness of both natural and ethical paradigms further reinforces their profound understanding of existence.

Certain individuals residing in rural areas have diligently safeguarded the handwritten manuscripts passed down by their ancestors, who were esteemed sages and scholars. Some have committed these scriptures to memory, including verses, prayers, mantras, and entire books, as imparted by their ancestors, parents, teachers, and gurus. They hold these texts in high regard, recognizing the profound wisdom embedded within them and their holistic implications. While they may not have deciphered all these teachings, they continue to preserve and transmit them to future generations.

They are aware that these repositories of knowledge hold truths that can greatly benefit humanity. Such reservoirs of wisdom truly constitute the invaluable assets of Bharat, also known as Vedic or Sanatan wisdom. When young men and women from these lineages enter higher education institutions, they already carry within them the latent potential of this ancient knowledge encoded in their very genes. They possess a deep sense of assurance and pride in the treasures passed down by their ancestors.

As the opportune moment arrives, these hidden dormant seeds sprout and flourish, leading them to make innovative discoveries and unlock the secrets of nature for the betterment of humanity. This enigmatic process occurs effortlessly, harmoniously, and blissfully. It is one of the reasons why a multitude of individuals from Bharat enjoy impressive achievements, prosperity, and admiration across the globe.

Krishna-consciousness will inspire and enable Bharatiya children and youth in awakening the genetic memories dormant in them and will revitalize and enlighten them. Tomorrow, hundreds of thousands of students from the interior villages, as well as different towns and cities of Bharat will become professionals, scholars and scientists in different businesses, universities, and institutions in Bharat and overseas. Their remarkable accomplishments, research, discoveries, and inventions will offer simple yet effective solutions to complex challenges, thereby bringing honor to Bharat and benefiting humanity at large. Krishna-conscious individuals, who align with Sanatani beliefs, exhibit traits of strength, discipline, self-control, progressiveness, and liveliness. They perceive themselves as instruments of Krishna, maintaining a constant awareness of His presence in their consciousness. Such individuals will zealously safeguard and promote morality, ethics, and humanity on a global scale, defending their families, friends, communities, and nations along the way.

They will perpetually be in search of new truths, harness revitalizing energies and employ effective strategies to defend, strengthen, glorify, and enlighten themselves and humanity. They are the partial-Avatars of Krishna, who can manifest Himself in many parts, with each part having the same infinite potency, and who promised to descend on the earth to protect decent people (Sadhu) and Dharma. This way the Krishna-conscious or Sanatani people, defending the Dharma, will always be blissfully radiating joy and peace all over the world.

Satyam – Shivam – Sundaram

In Vedik scriptures there are hundreds of phrases which guide humans to follow the right path in life. The phrase "Satyam, Shivam, Sundaram" is a Sanskrit slogan that translates to "Truth, Goodness (or Godliness), Beauty" in English. It represents the fundamental values and ideals in Hindu philosophy and spiritual teachings.

Satyam (truth) stands for honesty, integrity, and being true to oneself and others. It emphasizes the importance of living a life based on truth and sincerity. **Shivam (goodness or Godliness)** represents righteousness, moral conduct, and doing what is right and just. It stresses the importance of acts of kindness, compassion, and selflessness. It also means divinity, auspiciousness, Shubh-Mangal. **Sundaram (beauty)** signifies the appreciation of aesthetic beauty, inner harmony, and spiritual grace. It encourages a deep appreciation for the beauty in oneself, others, and the world around us.

Together, these three qualities form the foundation for a balanced and fulfilling life, guiding individuals towards living a life of virtue, authenticity, and beauty. This concept inspires individuals to strive for higher ideals and spiritual growth, ultimately leading to a sense of inner peace and fulfillment. Traditional Sanatanis/Hindus and Rishi-Munis used to follow this path of Satyam-Shivam-Sundaram. Inspired by Bharat, in future globally.

Satyameva Jayate

This is one more widely followed phrase of Vedik scripture. "Satyameva Jayate" is a Sanskrit phrase that translates to "Truth alone triumphs" in English. It is a guiding principle that emphasizes the importance of truth and honesty in all aspects of life. The phrase is often used as a motto or slogan and is also inscribed in the national emblem of Bharat. This phrase originated from the ancient Vedik scripture called the Mundaka Upanishad, which highlights the importance of upholding truth and integrity primarily.

It serves as a reminder that no matter the challenges or obstacles one may face, truth will always prevail in the end. In a broader sense, "Satyameva Jayate" encourages individuals to lead a life based on authenticity, transparency, and integrity. It serves as a moral compass, guiding people to make decisions that are aligned with truth and righteousness. Ultimately, the message of "Satyameva Jayate" is a timeless reminder of the power and significance of truth in shaping a just and harmonious society. In future, inspired by Bharat, this will be followed by all humans globally.

Vasudhaiva Kutumbakam

This is another gem from the Vedik scripture. Vasudhaiva Kutumbakam is a Sanskrit phrase that means "the world is one family."

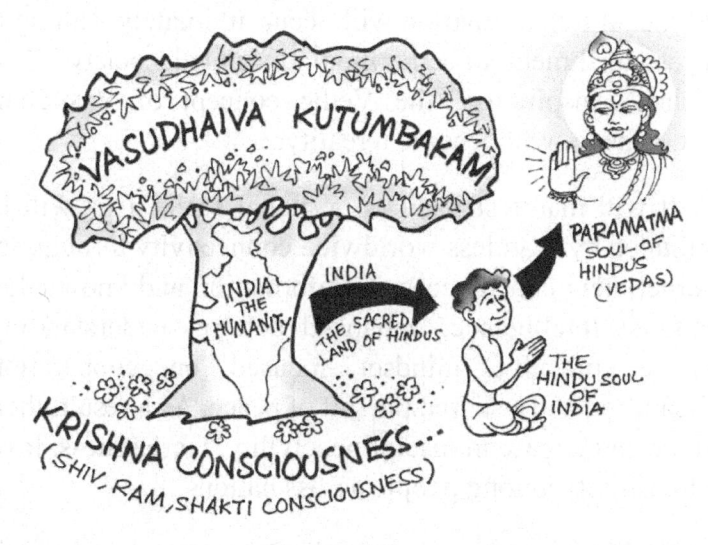

Pic. 47 - Vasudhaiva Kutumbakam - "Whole of the Earth is a family"

It is a concept derived from ancient Indian scriptures and highlights the idea of interconnectedness and the oneness of humanity. The philosophy behind Vasudhaiva Kutumbakam emphasizes the importance of compassion, empathy, and mutual respect towards all living beings, regardless of their nationality, religion, or background. It promotes the idea that we are all part of a global community and should strive to create a harmonious and peaceful world where everyone is treated with love and understanding.

This concept encourages individuals to look beyond their differences and prejudices and to recognize the inherent unity that exists among all human beings. It also assures a sense of unity and solidarity that transcends boundaries and fosters a sense of belonging to a larger, inclusive community.

In accordance with the Vedic wisdom, it is envisioned that global transformation will occur, ultimately leading to the establishment of a harmonious global society. With Krishna's inspiration, the Vedic concept of Vasudhaiv Kutumbakam will become a reality.

It will manifest itself on a global scale. This will be facilitated by seamless worldwide connectivity through the Internet, heightened access to information and knowledge, Artificial Intelligence, enhanced cultural understanding, and a collective mindset focused on cooperation, amicability, and a shared pursuit of peace. As a result, there will be an increase in discipline, civility, fearlessness, love, and positivity among people across nations.

While it is acknowledged that negative elements will still exist, they will predominantly be weakened, marginalized, or confined. Whenever these negative forces gain strength, they will be thwarted by the positive forces within society. In instances where they unite to pose a significant threat, they will be annihilated by the partial-Avatar formed or created by the Krishna-conscious/Sanatani souls at and around the location.

The establishment of a global family will foster the adoption of common international codes that will be universally understood and practiced. These codes will serve as a foundation for mutual understanding and collaboration among nations and their populace. Overall, Vasudhaiva Kutumbakam serves as a powerful reminder of our shared humanity and calls for us to come together in the spirit of unity, love, and cooperation to create a better world for all. This Vedic concept may be adopted in the United Nations Charter or in the charters of other global organizations in the future.

CHAPTER – 18
KRISHNA FOR THE FUTURE WORLD

(Tomorrow)

I know all beings, past as well as present. I know even those who are yet to come. But none knows me.
(Krishna: Gita Ch.7:26- vedaham ... .kashchan).
By delusion of the pairs of opposites arising from desire and aversion, all beings are subject to delusion.
(Krishna: Gita Ch.7:27- ichchha dwesh......parantap.)

The Krishna Avatar holds a position of utmost reverence and serves as a symbol of exemplary human qualities across the globe. From the moment of His birth to His eventual mysterious withdrawal from this mortal realm, every day of His existence was adorned with countless trials, extraordinary occurrences, unforeseen revelations, and infinite potential.

His extraordinary journey encompassed a remarkable lifespan of approximately 125 years, during which He embodied remarkable significance and portrayed distinctive attributes, as briefly touched upon in earlier chapters.

Shri Krishna has an exceptional and remarkable background and accomplishments that unquestionably establish His profound impact on global endeavors. He possesses omniscience and omnipotence, permeating every particle of the cosmos. Despite conducting His endeavors within the region of Bharat and dissolving his physical embodiment of Krishna-Avatar approximately 5100 years ago, his consciousness persists and shall continue to permeate Bharat as well as the world.

The Supreme soul Krishna is eternal and transcends all boundaries. His promise to reincarnate Himself from time to time, remains forever. His following revelation in the Gita is true not only for Bharat, the field of His activities (Leela, pastimes), but for whole of the world.

Whenever there is a decline of righteousness (Dharma), and expansion of unrighteousness (Adharma), then I manifest Myself. (Krishna: Gita Ch. 4: 7- yada yada hi..... aham.).

For the protection of the pious ones, for the destruction of the wicked ones, and for the establishment of righteousness, I am born (arise) at every age. (Krishna: Gita Ch.4: 8 - paritranay........ yuge.).

The consciousness of Shri Krishna is pervasive throughout the universe, transcending geographical boundaries. He manifests Himself in the consciousness of those who have steadfast belief in His divine presence. His incarnations, spanning numerous avatars, are dispersed across the globe, adapted to diverse local circumstances.

His eminent purpose lies in safeguarding the righteous, virtuous people and eradicating the evil, malevolent forces that threaten humanity.

Part-3, Chapter 18: Krishna for the Future World

Cosmic Time Waves

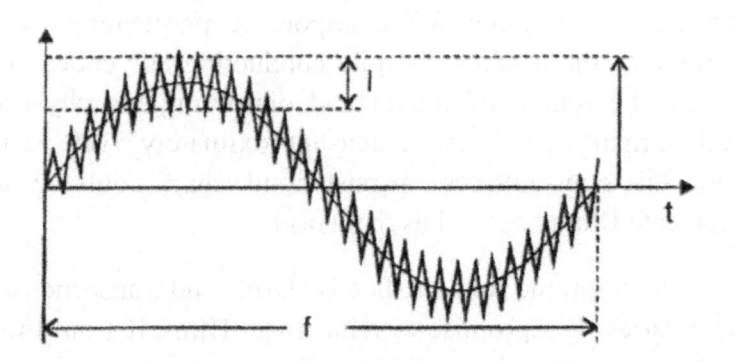

Fig. 48: Sinusoidal waves (1000-2000 years), Ripple waves (50-100 years)

For quick reference, I am reproducing here this topic and the graph from Chapter 6, looking at its relevance for tomorrow (the future) too. As shown in figure 48, we can understand the concept of cosmic time waves. During approximately 1000-2000 years (f), we observe distinct phases in which the Dharma, or righteousness, experiences a major rise (crest) followed by a major decline (trough). These fluctuations are accompanied by smaller ripple waves occurring over periods of roughly 50-100 years, indicating minor rises and declines of Dharma.

At the lowest point of the trough, a significant event takes place: Krishna (Vishnu), the supreme deity, manifests as a Major Avatar to rejuvenate the flow of Dharma. Additionally, during the troughs of the ripple waves, Krishna appears in the form of minor Avatars or partial-Avatars to address the fluctuations in Dharma's intensity (represented by 'l'). Notably, these fluctuations are non-uniform and vary across different time periods.

This recurring phenomenon has already occurred in the past (yesterday), exists in the present (today), and will persist into the future (tomorrow), following the precise and concealed plans of the Creator (Krishna). It signifies that even tomorrow, each individual century (or approximately 50-100 years) and millennium (or approximately 1000-2000), we shall witness periodic fluctuations in the state of righteousness, commonly known as Dharma. These fluctuations, encompassing both moderate and significant fluctuations, as well as the corresponding appearances of various divine incarnations (Avatars - minor and major), are intrinsic elements of Krishna's grand cosmic blueprint.

Krishna Inspired Wisdom Globally

The bewildered spirit soul, under the influence of the three modes of material nature, thinks himself/herself to be the doer of activities, which are in fact conducted by nature.
(Krishna: Gita Ch. 3: 27 - prakrteh………… iti manyate).
Deluded by the three modes (goodness, passion, and ignorance), the entire world does not know Me who is above the modes and inexhaustible.
(Krishna: Gita Ch. 7: 13 -   tribhir guna……….. avyayam).
This divine energy of Mine, consisting of the three modes of material nature, is difficult to overcome. But those who have surrendered unto Me can easily cross beyond it.
(Krishna: Gita Ch. 7: 14 - daivi hy……… taranti te).

The world is the environment for the game of opposites. The world can be seen as a complex framework of contrasting elements, a vast interplay of opposing forces. Throughout existence, we witness the ebb and flow, the rise and fall, the crest and trough of life's rhythmic waves. It is

Part-3, Chapter 18: Krishna for the Future World

in the delicate fusion of positive and negative aspects that energy, light, movement, and vibrations come to fruition. One could assert that the Creator's grand masterpiece lies in the art of harmonizing these opposing forces.

Within the tapestry of our globe, we find the presence of righteous individuals as well as those who embrace wickedness. Intriguingly, both classes of individuals are integral components of Lord Krishna's creation and the divine Leela, representing the divine play. It is essential to recognize that the intertwining balance of good and evil exists purposefully, oscillating in different epochs and serving diverse objectives. This intricate interplay ensures the equilibrium of the cosmic order, reaffirming that even darkness contributes to the unfolding of the grand cosmic scheme.

Pic. 49: The Creator maintains equilibrium of Positive & Negative Forces

Individuals of distinct educational backgrounds, varying levels of perception, diverse understandings, and contrasting actions exhibit diverse characteristics. At times, virtuous individuals might prevail while malign individuals remain restrained. Conversely, situations may arise where evil dominates while the righteous are dormant. Occasionally, a state of equilibrium occurs, with both factions possessing partial dominance and partial dormant (inactive). Importantly, such occurrences are not haphazard; rather, they are deliberate manifestations orchestrated by the omniscient Creator, Shri Krishna.

It is important to understand that both virtuous and evil thoughts originate from the Creator's desire to expand Himself. These thoughts serve as a balance, guiding and motivating each other in diverse ways, while simultaneously acting as limitations within the Creator's expansion process. The existence of positive and negative forces, as well as the coexistence of positivity and negativity, are essential in maintaining this balance and facilitating the Creator's expansion.

This dynamic is an inherent part of the world, consistently occurring and perpetuating itself in accordance with the natural laws established by the Creator. The three qualities of Nature - Sat (truth), Raj (passion), and Tam (ignorance) - govern these processes. Additionally, it is worth noting that periodic fluctuations in righteousness, known as Dharma, are intricately connected to this balance.

Minor shifts in Dharma occur approximately every 50-100 years, while major shifts occur within the span of around a thousand years (millennium). Krishna's minor and major Avatars are also as per His cosmic plans and happen around the trough periods of the cosmic waves, to boost up the rise of the Dharma, as needed.

Thus, the incarnations of Krishna, whether minor or major, align with these periods of flux to strengthen and uplift righteousness as required by the cosmic plan. Furthermore, the expansion of wisdom has always been a fundamental aspect of the Creator's grand design since the inception of creation.

Global spread of Vedic Wisdom

With Krishna's inspiration, tomorrow (during and after a century), righteous knowledge will spread globally. Yoga will become a part of everyday life of people globally. A significant shift towards incorporating yoga, both as a goal and as a path towards perfection, will be witnessed in societies worldwide. This includes the integration of yoga-meditation practices into everyday life, as well as their adoption as foundational elements within educational systems of peace-loving communities.

As part of this transformative movement, the concepts and sutras originating from the Vedas will be embraced as indispensable subjects of study and exploration in various academic institutions globally. Esteemed universities will be investing in advanced research to deepen the understanding of these timeless principles.

By recognizing the inherent connection between yoga-meditation and the profound wisdom of Vedic philosophy, these institutions will seek to unlock further insights for the benefit of humanity.

The expansion of wisdom also recognizes the dynamic nature of our existence. Just as the Creator manifested various forms of life from a single entity, the world thrives on diversity and multiplicity. Monotonousness brings boredom, while diversity brings vibrancy and inspiration, akin to a garden adorned with a myriad of colorful blossoms.

The vibrant and captivating sight of a garden blooming with an array of multicolored flowers can teach us a valuable lesson. Much like this natural phenomenon, our society thrives when it embraces and nurtures diversity, which brings forth increased allure, excitement, and inspiration.

However, it is crucial to exercise discernment, maintain order, and ensure manageability within this diversity. Comprehensive education rooted in the Vedic teachings will be adopted universally thus facilitating synthesizing various aspects of life and seamlessly integrating them into the daily lives of individuals around the world.

Human upliftment in Veda-based research & advancements

Veda based education system will be effective all around. As the goal of Vedas is realization or visualization (Sakshatkaar) of Absolute or Ultimate Truth (Paramatma, God), the Veda-based education system will ascertain that students or aspirants are progressing in the right direction. Vedic wisdom emphasizes the importance of human progress in one's intellectual, societal, and spiritual development. Vedic teachings indicate that the goal is to attain a profound understanding of the Absolute Truth or the

Divine. To ensure that individuals are on the right path, a Veda-based education system is designed to guide students towards this realization.

Such an education system will also promote the practice of Yoga, which serves as a means of self-discipline and connection to the transcendental. Among the various paths of Yoga, the Ashtanga Yoga, formulated by Maharshi Patanjali, is regarded as the most comprehensive and scientifically structured approach.

The Ashtanga Yoga comprises eight interconnected limbs, each contributing to the holistic development of an individual. These limbs include ethical principles (Yamas) and virtuous habits (Niyamas), as well as physical postures (Asanas), breath control (Pranayama), sense withdrawal (Pratyahara), concentration (Dharana), meditation (Dhyana), and finally, the state of transcendence (Samadhi).

1. **Yamas** encompass moral precepts originating from the ancient Vedic scriptures and literature, representing guiding ethical principles and injunctions.
2. **Niyamas** entail virtuous practices and observances derived from profound wisdom found within Vedic scriptures and literature.
3. **Aasan** denotes a contemplative posture that can be maintained over a prolonged duration, characterized by a state of tranquility, stability, ease, and stillness.
4. **Pranayama** is the control or regulation of the breath.
5. **Pratyahara** is a process of retracting the sensory experience from external objects. It is consciously closing one's mind processes to the sensory world.

6. **Dharana** means concentration, introspective focus, and one-pointedness of mind onto a particular inner state, subject or topic.
7. **Dhyana** means contemplating, meditating on whatever Dharana has focused upon. Dharana is a state of mind, Dhyana the process of mind.
8. **Samadhi** means putting together, joining, union, trance. In samadhi, when meditating on an object, only the object of awareness is present.

Yama and Niyama are further clarified as follows:

- **Yamas are five:** Ahimsa (nonviolence), Satya (truthfulness), Asteya (non-stealing), Brahmacharya (celibacy, to remain in divine mode) and Aparigraha (non-possessiveness, no-greed). These Yamas are essential for interaction with people.
- **Niyamas are five:** Shaucha (purity), Santosha (contentment), Tapas (self-discipline, senses-management), Svadhyaya (self-study, inner exploration) and Ishvara Pranidhana (surrender to the Creator). These five Niyamas are essential for inner smooth journey of a person to the Innermost-self.

These five Yamas and five Niyamas together form moral codes of conduct and ascertain advancement of human dignity. These form a strong spiritual foundation needed for exploring the ocean of knowledge, truth and access to the infinite energy ever existing at our core, the Innermost-self.

The explorers, researchers, inventors, or scientists armed with Yama and Niyama, when diving deep in search of the truth in any field of their interest, they get precious knowledge and wisdom extremely useful for benefiting humanity. The followers of Yama and Niyama get detached from the enticement of worldly benefits and pleasures (Vasanas) automatically. This makes their inward journey toward the Innermost-self much easier, smooth, and prompt.

The Innermost-self, own core, is the treasure of the ultimate Truth, unpolluted innovative ideas, and infinite energy. Diving deep into one's own core, the aspirant (student, Sadhak, researcher) brings out unique facts, inventions, truths, and solutions which will help humanity.

The Vedic scriptures hold immense wisdom and knowledge that has been accumulated by ancient scholars, known as Rishis, in Bharat (India) over thousands of years. These scriptures, such as the Vedas and Upanishads, contain numerous concise verses and formulas (Sutras) that are yet to be fully comprehended and deciphered.

As Krishna consciousness and the eternal energy of Sanatan (timeless) principles continues to spread globally, the future will witness the establishment of numerous research centers, colleges, institutions, and universities dedicated to studying and understanding the Vedas. This will lead to groundbreaking discoveries, research, and inventions that will greatly benefit humanity.

These Vedic centers will not only enhance our understanding of various aspects of life but also contribute to better wellness, physical and mental health, nutrition, lifestyle, prosperity, and overall happiness for people worldwide. Furthermore, these endeavors will address concerns related to the well-being of humans, animals, plants, and the environment, thereby fostering a comprehensive approach towards a sustainable and harmonious existence.

Global Advancement of All Sciences Tomorrow

Krishna's personality and His Vedic wisdom is multi-dimensional. His created Vedas pervade all the fields of knowledge. This Vedic wisdom will shape the future of humanity. Krishna is embodiment of Vedic wisdom. He encompasses the essence of knowledge in its entirety.

As the creator and the expert in all knowledge and sciences, He has been and shall continue motivating students and researchers to explore the depths of all sciences, as part of His expansion process. With His inspiration all conscientious students and researchers will come up with excellent research results and inventions beneficial to humanity.

Being the Creator of all and the omniscient, these inventions are nothing new for Him, while these findings may seem novel to humans. Only during select moments and at the most opportune times does He choose to unveil a fraction of Himself through these discoveries and inventions, further expanding our understanding.

Though the fields of science and technology have been compartmentalized into various branches, such as physics, chemistry, biology, and many others, for Krishna all these are unified within His cosmic existence. His omniscience allows Him to have a comprehensive comprehension of all these branches simultaneously. His omnipresence ensures that His wisdom can be found in every corner of the universe.

Krishna has been progressively disclosing His wisdom, His divine essence, going back each yesterday, throughout the past fourteen billion years, till the start of the momentous event known as the Big Bang. His ongoing revelation continues, irrespective of our awareness or recognition thereof, as He gradually unveils parts of His enigmatic nature each moment each day.

As we move into the future, Krishna's sacred wisdom shall continue to manifest itself in various fields of scientific knowledge, transcending borders and manifesting through His chosen vehicles at the most opportune moments.

Every scientific discovery or innovation merely represents a fraction of the vast treasure trove of His revelations. There exists no limit to His mysteries, nor the way they will continue to unfold before us. Each scientific breakthrough and innovation represent a mere fragment of the vast reservoir of knowledge bestowed upon humanity by the divine wisdom of Lord Krishna. He keeps on revealing certain truths at appropriate time periods. Those truths help in His sustenance and expansion projects already preplanned. His celestial revelations continue to transcend our comprehension, and the boundless depths of His mysteries shall remain inexhaustible.

Global research on Yoga basics & practices tomorrow

Tomorrow, With the spread of Krishna consciousness (Sanatan-energy), there will be a significant focus on global research regarding the fundamental principles and practices of Yoga. This research will be conducted in various prestigious institutions and universities, aiming to delve deeper into the science of Yoga and its meditation practices.

Moving beyond the physical aspect of Yoga, researchers will explore diverse facets such as different forms of breathing exercises (Pranayams), the understanding of energy centers (Chakras), concentration techniques (Dharana), meditation (Dhyan), and the attainment of ultimate meditative states (Samadhi) – Yoga or merger with the Creator, Ultimate Truth.

The practical applications stemming from these yogic research endeavors will prove instrumental in ensuring optimal physical, mental, and spiritual well-being for individuals. Additionally, these practices will have the potential to revolutionize healthcare by providing drug-free remedies for numerous complicated diseases. Furthermore, they will help enhance personal and marital relationships, contributing to happier and more successful lives.

This holistic approach to life will extend its benefits to diverse fields including professionals, businesspersons, politicians, bureaucrats, military, and security personnel, as well as ordinary workers and households, enabling them to lead stress-free, peaceful, joyful, and blissful lives. Globally, the Yoga way of life will become a daily routine for everybody.

Moreover, we can discern that adopting a holistic lifestyle centered around the principles of Ashtanga Yoga (including Yama and Niyama) holds the potential to address a myriad of intricate behavioral, political, societal, environmental, economic, and industrial challenges. Furthermore, this will help in maintaining world peace and wider global cooperation in solving many complex international and humanitarian issues.

More explorations in planetary and interstellar systems

Krishna is inspiring scientists to take advantage of enormous Vedic knowledge in further exploring the interplanetary and interstellar systems, both within and beyond our solar influence. In various astronomical and other Vedic scriptures, a lot of information is available on planetary systems related to our sun, and interstellar systems beyond our sun's influence. By tapping into this vast repository of information, scientists can greatly enhance their efforts in delving deeper into interplanetary travel and even establishing human settlements on other planets and their moons.

Furthermore, the scriptures also shed light on the existence of alien life forms inhabiting different planets within the universe, all of which are definitely creations of the Creator. With the guidance and inspiration of Krishna, scientists of tomorrow will unlock the ability to not only discover these extraterrestrial beings but also establish contacts, meaningful interactions, communication, and collaborations, leading us towards a shared quest for truth and a blissful coexistence. All creations and existences follow certain rules, norms and codes pre-established by Him.

Krishna Will Inspire & Ensure Bharat's Global Dominance

The dissemination of Krishna consciousness on a global scale will persist as a manifestation of Krishna's minor or partial-Avatar. Even in this limited incarnation, the essence of positivity, brilliance, and celestial vigor permeates the souls dedicated to Krishna consciousness or those who adhere to the eternal principles of Sanatan. Krishna symbolizes liberation, potency, dynamism, abundance, divinity, affection, beauty, righteousness, illumination, fairness, sagacity, harmony, joy, and triumph.

Bharat's Ascendency in Asia, Global South & Worldwide

As Bharat is Krishna's own land of activity and birthplace, all Krishna-conscious/Sanatani souls from around the world remain connected with Bharat and transmit their spiritual energy, workforce, and material support to Bharat, as a service to Lord Krishna. They get many times of these in return at appropriate time. Powered with these and with Bharat's own Krishna-consciousness/Sanatan-energy, tomorrow, Bharat will progress exponentially and emerge as a fully developed nation. Bharat will extend its support to friendly neighboring nations while simultaneously ensuring appropriate consequences for nations that engage in disruptive behavior.

Asserting its power, Bharat will ascend to become the most influential nation in Asia, forging diplomatic, financial, cultural, business, trade, and military alliances with like-minded nations to strengthen its standing. The entire Asian continent will view Bharat as a reliable and steadfast ally. China will become fragmented and much weaker, and Tibet region will reunite with Bharat.

Expanding its influence beyond Asia, Bharat is poised to assert global dominance, extending its reach into the

Middle East, Eastern Europe, Africa, and across the entirety of the Global South. Nations like Mongolia, Russia, and various former-Soviet Union states will find themselves under Bharat's sway and forming alliances with it.

Some neighboring countries, placing a premium on security and prosperity, may opt for permanent mergers or alliances with Bharat. Concurrently, other nations will forge lasting agreements aimed at enhancing security and military cooperation, with Bharat also taking charge of addressing their foreign policy interests.

Bharat's Eastern & Western Alliances Based on Vedic Wisdom

Tomorrow, Bharat (India) will establish diverse alliances with both developed and underdeveloped nations, spanning various sectors such as business, trade, military, culture, education, technology, research & development, space exploration, oceanic endeavors, and defense, among others. These alliances will be guided by the principles of the Vasudhaiv Kutumb (the world as a family) and peaceful coexistence, prominent in Vedic wisdom.

Bharat will become the most trusted and influential nation, fostering friendly relationships based on mutual respect and integrity. In the spirit of harmony, any disagreements that may arise will be resolved through diplomatic cordial discussions and negotiations, prioritizing peaceful solutions over armed conflict.

The alliances with Bharat will be rooted in trust and comprehensive understanding, as well as a commitment to respect the sovereignty and territorial integrity of all nations involved.

Understanding the importance of noninterference in each other's internal affairs, Bharat's friendly nations will prioritize mutual interests and refrain from meddling in the

Pic 50: Krishna-empowered Peace-loving-alliance: punishing rogue-nations

internal affairs of their allied nations. In exceptional cases where a nation demonstrates a lack of understanding or adherence to principles of justice and peace, resorting to military action or punishment should be a last resort, as Krishna applied in Kaurav-Pandava dispute during His era. Instead, firstly, utilizing economic sanctions and diplomatic strategies shall be tried implementing effectively.

Krishna inspired Asian Cultural Alliance

For the one who sees Me everywhere and sees everything in Me, I am never lost, nor is he ever lost to Me. (Gita Ch. 6:30- yo mam ....pranashyati)

I am in everyone's heart as the Super-soul. As soon as one desires to worship the demigods, I make his faith steady so that he can devote

himself to some particular deity. *(Gita Ch. 7: 21 - yo yo yam....*
....vidadhamyaham.)

Asian culture is the Oriental culture, based on Oriental religions. These religions include the religions of Bharatiya origin: Hinduism, Buddhism, Sikhism and Jainism (mostly included in Sanatan Dharma). Furthermore, this rich heritage extends beyond geographical boundaries to encompass East Asian religions like Shintoism, Taoism, and Confucianism, as well as numerous smaller groups representing diverse religious and tribal traditions.

Despite their unique characteristics, these diverse cultures share significant virtues, such as tolerance, patience, generosity, meditation, and strong moral and ethical principles.

Over the course of millennia, the intermingling of these cultures has fostered an environment of mutual respect and harmony. Followers of these traditions seamlessly navigate their similarities and differences, engaging in cultural exchanges, and experiencing a sense of oneness that transcends individual religious boundaries. They adjust and accommodate mutually, participate in each other's cultural activities, and generally feel as one, friendly and complimenting family-like coexistence.

Asian culture is a bit different from the Occidental culture or Western culture, which is mostly based on Abrahamic religions: Christianity, Judaism, and Islam. Asian culture mostly has its base in peace, nonviolence and meditation, the basics of Sanatan Dharma too. Occidental cultures are slightly different, though also have certain common elements with the Oriental culture.

Shri Krishna, as the Creator, treats all beings equally universally. He encourages individuals to support and grow with one another, respecting each other's faiths and traditions. For Krishna, the Avatar, as His field of activities has been Asia, He inspires Asians to unite and collaborate, drawing upon the shared lessons found within their diverse religions and cultures.

These common elements serve as a foundation for fostering unity among all Asian nations. Krishna also serves as a source of inspiration and empowerment for His homeland, Bharat, to play a leading role in uniting all Asians. This involves establishing cultural alliances that are rooted in mutual understanding and aiding aimed at enhancing the quality of life and prosperity for across Asian nations.

Tomorrow, Bharat will contribute to fostering unity among Asian nations, actively engaging in cultural and religious exchanges that uphold the dignity of humanity. Through this harmonious exchange, each nation will mutually elevate one another, embracing the principle of religious unity and equality. Additionally, they will strengthen bonds with individuals from Western cultures, fostering a spirit of love, cooperation, and shared aspirations to witness the realization of Vasudhaiv Kutumbakam - the global family.

Numerous interfaith prayer centers will emerge worldwide, serving as inclusive spaces where individuals from diverse faiths can converge and offer their respective prayers. Here, humanity will be the universal faith, while differing prayer practices coexist. Ethics, morality, and humanity will serve as the common ground uniting people across the globe.

Krishna for protection of Nature and Environment

Krishna created Nature. He protected it yesterday. He has been protecting it today. He shall continue protecting it tomorrow. He will always protect it. Krishna's divine influence will inspire individuals and groups to take necessary measures to protect the environment.

This includes ensuring the cleanliness and purity of water sources, fostering a pollution-free atmosphere, preserving the integrity of air quality, and safeguarding trees, plants, vegetation, the natural habitat, and diverse species that inhabit it. Thus Krishna, as the creator and preserver of Nature, assumes the responsibility of safeguarding it.

Furthermore, Krishna will inspire people to adopt appropriate waste management practices, ensuring the prevention of pollution resulting from domestic, industrial, and processing waste. Additionally, Krishna will also inspire diligent water processing techniques to prevent the contamination of rivers, lakes, and ponds. The planting of trees on a global scale is also inspired, as it guarantees an ample supply of fresh oxygen, a pristine atmosphere, and improved overall health for humanity.

Krishna-conscious/Sanatani people are Krishna's own extensions. They are considered manifestations of the divine. The worldwide spread of Krishna-consciousness will be concentrated in a few powerful and determined individuals globally, as His mini or partial-Avatars. He will perform various essential and crucial activities through them, to benefit humanity.

The propagation of Krishna-consciousness on a global scale often relies on the dedicated efforts of a select few individuals who possess immense determination and influence, akin to partial embodiments or mini-Avatars of Krishna himself. These chosen individuals will conduct various vital and indispensable endeavors under the guidance of Krishna, all aimed at benefiting humanity at large.

This select group or individuals chosen by Krishna may not necessarily be consciously aware of His presence in the consciousness as "Krishna by name." But they will feel divinely inspired and energized in their Innermost-self, their Inner Core, the abode of the Creator; and they will not rest till they achieve the objective set by the Creator (Krishna).

Krishna inspiring Bharat for key role in world peace

Thus, always keeping the mind balanced, the Yogi, with the mind controlled, attains the peace abiding in Me, which culminates in liberation.
(Krishna: Gita Ch. 6: 15 – yunjannevam sadatma......adhi gachchhati).
The man who is full of faith, who is devoted to it, and who has subdued all thesenses, obtains (this) knowledge; and, having obtained the knowledge, he goes at once to the supreme peace.
(Krishna: Gita Ch. 4: 39 – Shraddhavan labhate .... adhi gachchhati.)

Krishna's guidance is instrumental in inspiring Bharat (India) to play a significant role in achieving global peace. Attaining world peace is contingent upon fostering friendship and unity among strong nations, while effectively addressing and restraining disruptive or rogue elements and nations that deviate from societal norms.

Krishna emphasizes the essential ingredients for peace, which are equally applicable at both the individual and global levels. These encompass a balanced mindset, control over one's senses, adherence to virtuous principles, uprightness, faith in laws set by the Creator, and cultivation of leadership qualities and knowledge among key individuals.

Unfortunately, leaders of certain rogue nations lack sufficient possession of these qualities. Leadership in rogue and terrorist nations often facilitates, encourages, and supports terrorist activities against other nations, as well as peace-loving communities within their own countries. This results in the senseless slaughter of innocent men, women, and children within their borders, as well as in neighboring and other nations. Such actions disrupt the peace of multiple nations and create conditions conducive to genocide within these rogue nations, as well as war with neighboring or other nations.

Persuasive strategies involving incentives will be initially employed to prompt non-compliant nations, gradually followed by imposing restrictions and offering stern warnings to deter their dangerous conduct. If these nations persist in their disobedience or fail to reform, a coalition of peace-loving nations will strive to disempower, denuclearize, and disarm them, particularly if they possess a nuclear arsenal. Every possible means, encompassing military, economic, diplomatic, and clandestine operations, will be utilized to eradicate such rogue entities.

Following their elimination, the Bharat-lead alliance will diligently establish responsible and compassionate leadership to govern these nations, extending comprehensive support to foster stability. Bharat, a mature democracy guided by the principles of Krishna-consciousness, will play a pivotal role in the coalition of all peace-loving nations. The boundless energy of Krishna will effectively manifest through Krishna-conscious Sanatani individuals and leaders, ensuring the accomplishment of His divine plans.

Comprehensive Restructuring of the United Nations

Today, the United Nations UN is like a spineless and toothless tamed lion, with much diluted dignity and capability. Tomorrow, the United Nations will be restructured, re-chartered and reorganized. The new UN charter, guided by the Vedic wisdom, will be more advanced, effective, and powerful, considering many changes and developments in the global equations, global diplomatic and human needs.

Central to this change will be the elevation of Bharat as a dominant force in the decision-making and functioning of the UN. Recognizing the nation's exceptional capabilities and contributions, Bharat will be granted additional powers, including veto power, thereby enabling the country to actively shape the direction and outcomes of the UN.

The philosophy of Vasudhaiva Kutumbakam, or the concept of the whole Earth being one family, will serve as a guiding principle in the UN's operations, promoting increased unity and cooperation among nations. Crucially, Bharat's reputation for mature and impartial judgment will prove invaluable in resolving conflicts and challenges across various countries. The trust and support of numerous influential nations will strengthen Bharat's role and enable the UN to solve various problems in many countries.

There will be a need to address the challenges posed by rogue nations and those who support them in a firm and decisive manner. This will involve measures such as isolation or concerted efforts to encourage their transformation towards more civilized behavior. Additionally, a novel alternative could entail the establishment of an Alliance of Nations, which would take over the governance of these rogue nations, appointing new leaders dedicated to fostering civility, discipline, and the well-being of their citizens.

Mischief and stupidity in the name of religion will end

Whenever there is a decline in religious practice (Dharma), and a predominant rise of irreligion (Adharma) - at that time I incarnate Myself. *(Krishna: Gita Ch.4: 7 - yada yada hi…….. srujami aham)*
To protect the pious and to annihilate the miscreants, as well as to establish the principles of religion (Dharma) – I advent Myself millennium after millennium.
(Krishna: Gita Ch.4: 8 – paritranay sadhunam……yuge yuge).
You must control the senses, then kill this evil thing which obstructs the knowledge and science.
(Krishna: Gita Ch 3: 41 - tasmat………...nashanam)

The senseless and irresponsible actions done in the name of religion will cease. The teachings and practices of various religions bring comfort, peace, and unity to people, fostering a relationship with a loving and merciful Creator. This bond promotes love and support among individuals, contributing to the advancement of communities, nations, and the world as a whole. It is essential to recognize that the Creator is the supreme force that gives life to all living beings. Therefore, all individuals are regarded as the Creator's children, and Mother Nature plays a vital role in nurturing them.

While worldly parents serve as instruments in the process of creation, the Creator treats all beings equally. Numerous religions recognize this truth and transmit it to their followers. Nevertheless, certain negative elements within society reject the notion of peaceful coexistence. They harbor aggressive and expansionist mindsets, driven by egotism and hypocrisy, while pursuing sinister agendas that they perceive as beneficial. These elements can be categorized as rascals, imbued with malicious intentions and affiliations with terror, murder, conflict, and fearmongering.

Such demonic people imagined and created some aggressive dogma or codes of belief, which justifies and authorizes killing those who do not believe their codes and the author of the book of their codes. These codes, disguised as religions, have caused the mass murder of millions who did not adhere to their texts or the so-called self-proclaimed religion. These doctrines are deceptive political ideologies based on terror and violence.

The rapid spread of these terror-based ideologies can be attributed to the aggressive nature of their adherents and the fear instilled in civilized, peace-loving individuals who witness the inherent cruelty and lack of compassion demonstrated by those followers.

The only conditional mercy offered by these individuals is that one must renounce their own faith, way of life, and accept the murderous ideology to save themselves and their families. The more these ideologies proliferate, the more brutal, vicious, and evil they become. Each day, innocent men, women, and children around the world are killed, terrorizing global populations, and evoking triumphant smiles from these individuals, who ironically claim that theirs is a religion of peace. This represents the rise of unrighteousness (Adharma) and the decline of righteousness (Dharma), thus making it an appropriate situation or time for the advent of partial-Avatar of Krishna reflecting the global Krishna-consciousness/Sanatani-energy, to contain these evil elements.

Krishna, observing the ongoing situation, decides to intervene and bring an end to it. According to the teachings found in the Vedic scriptures and literature, described in the *Bhagavad Gita (Chapter 4:6, 7 - yada yada hi......yuge yuge)*, Krishna commences the process of dismantling this destructive ideology. This process began recently and will continue in the future. Its intensity will grow, resulting in the complete eradication of the harmful ideology (now like a ship in turbulent sea) which threatens society.

Hundreds of millions of the wiser and humane ones among them, will be taking shelter in the safer and comfortable ships of other humane faiths (including in the original faiths of their ancestors before their conversion) staffed with kind, loving, broadminded, cultured, decent, humane, and welcoming people. For achieving the higher goal of human dignity and peace on the earth, in this transformation process, hundreds of thousands might lose their lives, in this cosmic plan. Through the widespread acceptance of Krishna-consciousness/Sanatan, Krishna will empower numerous morally upright and determined individuals across nations and communities.

These individuals will function as partial Avatars, imbued with Krishna's eternal energy and wisdom. They will effectively halt the dissemination of this poisonous ideology, eradicating it completely from their respective societies, much faster than its spread. This approach will be implemented on a global scale until the total eradication of this deceptive and harmful belief system is achieved. At the right time, even the source of this ideology will also be destroyed, ensuring its permanent demise from the earth, by the end of this century.

By adhering to Vedic principles, we can dismantle harmful ideologies at a swift pace, fostering a sense of safety, security, peace, happiness, jubilation, and contentment among individuals of diverse backgrounds and across nations. This transformation will be facilitated through the manifestation of numerous partial-Avatars of Krishna.

It is not necessary, and it does not matter that all people will realize that it all happened by mysterious energy, grace, and Leela of Krishna. But Krishna will secretly fulfill His promise of protecting decent people, annihilating evil ones, and establishing the Dharma (righteousness) in the world.

Whenever any other greed and deception-based ideologies will try to misguide and distract the simple people from their original Dharma and degrade the human dignity, Krishna will repeatedly destroy those evil elements and protect the followers of righteous Sanatan Dharma.

Our shared responsibility lies in upholding righteousness (Dharma), as Krishna has pledged to safeguard the virtuous while eliminating those who propagate deceitful and materialistic beliefs. Through this continuous process, we can restore and uphold the principles of Sanatan Dharma, ensuring the preservation of human dignity and the well-being of society as a whole.

Krishna's Divine Universal Love

(Krishna: Gita Ch.12: 13 to 20 - adveshta sarv .... me priyaha):

- One who is not envious but who is a kind friend to all living entities, who does not think himself an owner/proprietor, who is free from false ego and equal both in happiness and distress, who is always satisfied and engaged in devotional service with determination and whose mind and intelligence are in agreement with Me - is very dear to Me.
- He for whom no one is put into difficulty and who is not disturbed by anxiety, who is steady in happiness and distress, is very dear to Me.
- A devotee who is not dependent on the ordinary course of activities, who is pure, skilled/expert, carefree, free from all pains, and who does not strive for some result, is very dear to Me.
- One who neither grasps pleasure or grief, who neither laments nor desires, and who renounces both auspicious and inauspicious things, is very dear to Me.
- One who is equal to friends and enemies, who is equipoise in honor and dishonor, heat and cold, happiness and distress, fame and infamy, who is always free from contamination, always silent and satisfied with anything, who doesn't care for any residence, who is fixed in knowledge and engaged in devotional service, is very dear to Me.
- He who follows this imperishable path of devotional service and who completely engages himself with faith, making Me the supreme goal, is very, very dear to Me.

The emotion of love is deeply intertwined with Krishna, who is revered as the ultimate Creator and Father of the universe. His love encompasses the entirety of His creation, extending from its inception to its culmination – throughout time, past, present, and future, yesterday, today, and tomorrow. While all beings are considered His children due to their creation, Krishna, through His divine play and cosmic illusion, assumes various roles in different situations and time periods.

In addition to His role as the Supreme Creator and Father, Krishna assumes the roles of a son, a brother, a friend, a husband, a student, a teacher, an employee, an employer, a leader, a follower, and many others. In each of these roles, Krishna embodies infinite love, compassion, dignity, and divinity.

Krishna deeply appreciates certain qualities in His creation. He loves a person with all positive qualities, which lead one to spiritual liberation (Moksha). He loves a person without all the negative qualities which bind a person to materialistic pursuits.

The key prerequisite to earn Krishna's love, His divine affection lies in wholehearted devotion to Him without ego. An egoless individual is free, detached, and unburdened by desires or attachments, thereby eliminating anger, greed, envy, and all dualities from their being. Such a person naturally becomes magnetically drawn towards Krishna and becomes rigidly attached to Him, ultimately immersing themselves in His infinite ocean of eternal love.

Through the cosmic phenomenon of the Big Bang, which gave rise to this particular cosmic cycle (Kalp), Krishna manifested Himself in infinite diverse forms, ranging from the grandest to the minutest. Each of these incarnations possessed the same boundless potency as the original embodiment of Krishna.

At the culmination of this cosmic cycle (Kalp), all these infinite manifestations will converge back, will condense into the original, primordial form of Krishna, once again embodying the same original infinite potency.

Pic 51: Person without desires, Envy, Anger, Ego, Greed: Dear to Krishna

This truth is encapsulated in the Vedic Verse:
Om purnamadah .... purnmev avashishyate – meaning:
The entirety is complete, as is. The whole emerges from the whole. Despite the emergence of the whole from the whole, what remains is still the whole.

Krishna loves a person who is free of envy and is friendly to all. He loves an egoless person who is equipoise in happiness and distress, who is ever satisfied and devoted to his Innermost-self. Additionally, the individual is clean, neat, and satisfied with what they have. They remain calm in the face of opposing forces such as heat and cold, fame and disgrace, honors and insults, and pleasures and pains.

They possess a steady wisdom and are devoted to the eternal truth within them.

They strive towards the ultimate goal of realizing the cosmic truth and the divine essence within themselves, which is the Creator Krishna. The love of Krishna brings liberation from the attachments of worldly existence, including the cycle of birth and death. Furthermore, Krishna's love liberates from the bondages of worldly dualities, births, and deaths. Krishna's love elevates a person to divinity beyond a materialistic environment.

Krishna's love for the devoted wise ones

Of these, the wise one who is in full knowledge in union with Me through pure devotional service is the best. For I am very dear to him, and he is dear to Me.
(Krishna: Gita Ch.7:17 - Tesham gyani.....mam priyah).

Krishna holds a special fondness for those who possess profound wisdom and genuine devotion towards Him as attested by the Vedic wisdom. Although some learned individuals may succumb to arrogance due to their knowledge, proclaiming themselves as divine or deities, Krishna remains unattached to such insincere pretenses. In contrast, Krishna deeply cherishes individuals who are not only knowledgeable but also display humility and unwavering devotion towards Him.

The immutable nature of Krishna's love transcends time, remaining consistent across all ages – yesterday, today, and tomorrow – in past, present, and future. Accomplishing Krishna's love represents the ultimate aspiration for individuals. This spiritual state allows one to attain perfection, rendering any further desires, actions, or karmic expectations inconsequential.

The attainment of Krishna's love brings about a profound transformation within an individual, permeating their entire being with a sense of fulfillment, eternal wisdom, boundless energy, enduring tranquility, and everlasting joy. It marks the pinnacle of liberation, granting one Moksha, the liberation from the cycle of birth and death. Getting Krishna's love is liberation, Moksha.

BIBLIOGRAPHY

Bhadwad Gita As It Is - H.D.G. Swami Prabhupada
https://asitis.com/
http://www.dlshq.org/download/bgita.pdf
https://archive.org/details/HindiBookBhagwatPuran/page/n1
Shrimad Bhagwadgita - Gita Press Gorakhpur
Gita for Business Management, Leadership and Performance - Gokul Upadhyay
https://en.wikipedia.org/wiki/Big_Bang
Sangacchadhvam (Isha Basya) from the Rig Veda. X. 191. (Adapted from translation of the Convent Vedanta Society of Northern California and from Nehal Raval's Aradhana).
https://bhaktivinoda.com/4-original-verses-of-srimad-bhagavatam-catur-sloka/

OTHER BOOKS BY SHRI GOKUL UPADHYAY

1. Gita for Business Management, Leadership and Performance
2. Gita's Ten Power-tips for Success and Enlightenment
3. Love and Happiness with the Gita
4. Eternal Superman Hanuman ji Helping Humanity

Above books are available on:
www.kdp.amazon.com
www.amazon.com

5. Adventurous Life with the Yoga of the Gita (Limited prints)
6. Samarpan समर्पण - In Hindi हिन्दी (Limited prints)

Made in the USA
Middletown, DE
04 August 2024